STUDENT ATLAS OF WORLD POLITICS

4th EDITION

John L. Allen
University of Connecticut

Dushkin/McGraw-Hill

A Division of The McGraw-Hill Companies

Book Team

Vice President & Publisher   *Jeffrey L. Hahn*
Production Manager   *Brenda S. Filley*
Designer   *Charles Vitelli*
Typesetting Supervisor   *Juliana Arbo*
Proofreader   *Robin Charney*
Cover design   *Tom Goddard*
Cartography   *Carto-Graphics, Eau Claire, WI*

We would like to thank Digital Wisdom Incorporated for allowing us to use their Mountain High Maps cartography software. This software was used to create maps 63, 64, 65, 66, 67, 68, 69, 70, 71, 72, 73, 74

Dushkin/McGraw-Hill

A Division of The **McGraw·Hill** Companies

The credit section for this book begins on page 169 and is considered an extension of the copyright page.

A Note to the Student

International politics is a drama played out on a world stage. The maps in this atlas serve as the stage settings for the various scenes in this drama; the tables or data sets are the building materials from which the settings are created. Just as the stage setting helps bring to life and give meaning to the actions and words of a play, so can these maps and tables enhance your understanding of the vast and complex drama of global politics. Use this atlas in conjunction with your text on international politics or international affairs. It will help you become more knowledgeable about this international stage as well as the actors.

The maps and data sets in the *Student Atlas of World Politics,* Fourth Edition, are designed to introduce you to the importance of the connections between geography and world politics. The maps are not perfect representations of reality—no maps ever are—but they do represent "models," or approximations of the real world, that should aid in your understanding of the world drama.

A Word about Data Sources

At the very outset of your study of this atlas, you should be aware of some limitations of the maps and data tables. In some instances, a map or a table may have missing data. This may be the result of the failure of a country to report information to a central international body (such as the United Nations or the World Bank). Alternatively, it may reflect shifts in political boundaries, internal conflicts, or changes in responsibility for reporting data that have caused certain countries (such as those that made up the former Yugoslavia) to delay their reports. It is always our wish to be as up-to-date as possible. In the meantime, as events continue to restructure our world, it's an exciting time to be a student of international events!

You will find your study of this atlas more productive in relation to your study of international politics if you examine the maps on the following pages in the context of five distinct analytical themes:

1. *Location: Where Is It?* This involves a focus on the precise location of places in both *absolute* terms (the latitude and longitude of a place) and in *relative* terms (the location of a place in relation to the location of other places). When you think of location, you should automatically think of both forms. Knowing something about absolute location will help you to understand a variety of features of physical geography, since such key elements are so closely related to their position on the earth. But it is equally important to think of location in relative terms. The location of places in relation to other places is often more important in influencing social, economic, and cultural characteristics than the factors of physical geography.

2. *Place: What Is It Like?* This encompasses the political, economic, cultural, environmental, and other characteristics that give a place its identity. You should seek to understand the similarities and differences of places by exploring their basic characteristics. Why are some places with similar environmental characteristics so very different in economic, cultural, social, and political ways? Why are other places with such different environmental characteristics so seemingly alike in terms of their institutions, their economies, and their cultures?

3. *Human/Environment Interactions: How Is the Landscape Shaped?* This theme focuses on the ways in which people respond to and modify their

environments. On the world stage, humans are not the only part of the action. The environment also plays a role in the drama of international politics. But the characteristics of the environment do not exert a controlling influence over human activities; they only provide a set of alternatives from which different cultures, in different times, make their choices. Observe the relationship between the basic elements of physical geography such as climate and terrain and the host of ways in which humans have used the land surfaces of the world.

4. *Movement: How Do People Stay in Touch?* This examines the transportation and communication systems that link people and places. Movement or "spatial interaction" is the chief mechanism for the spread of ideas and innovations from one place to another. It is spatial interaction that validates the old cliché, "the world is getting smaller." We find McDonald's restaurants in Tokyo and Honda automobiles in New York City because of spatial interaction. Advanced transportation and communication systems have transformed the world into which your parents were born. And the world that greets your children will be very different from your world. None of this would happen without the force of movement or spatial interaction.

5. *Regions: Worlds within a World.* This theme, perhaps the most important for this atlas, helps to organize knowledge about the land and its people. The world consists of a mosaic of "regions" or areas that are somehow different and distinctive from other areas. The region of Anglo-America (the United States and Canada) is, for example, different enough from the region of Western Europe that geographers clearly identify them as two unique and separate areas. Yet despite their differences, Anglo-Americans and Europeans share a number of similarities: common cultural backgrounds, comparable economic patterns, shared religious traditions, and even some shared physical environmental characteristics. Conversely, although the regions of Anglo-America and East Asia are also easily distinguished as distinctive units of the earth's surface, they have a greater number of shared physical environmental characteristics. But those who live in Anglo-America and East Asia have fewer similarities and more differences between them than is the case with Anglo-America and Western Europe: different cultural traditions, different institutions, different linguistic and religious patterns. An understanding of both the differences and similarities between regions like Anglo-America and Europe on the one hand, or Anglo-America and East Asia on the other, will help you to understand much that has happened in the human past or that is currently transpiring in the world around you. At the very least, an understanding of regional similarities and differences will help you to interpret what you read on the front page of your daily newspaper or view on the evening news report on your television set.

Not all of these themes will be immediately apparent on each of the 74 maps and 15 tables in this atlas. But if you study the contents of the *Student Atlas of World Politics,* Fourth Edition, along with the reading of your text and think about the five themes, the maps and tables and the text will complement one another and improve your understanding of global politics. As Shakespeare said, "All the world's a stage." Your challenge is now to understand both the stage and the drama being played on it.

John L. Allen

What's New in This Edition?

The fourth edition of *The Student Atlas of World Politics,* with its 74 maps and 15 tables, represents the most significant change from previous editions since the book's evolution from a small, 16-map add-on to a popular text to the 120 pages of the Third Edition, with its 47 maps and 15 tables. Virtually everything that students and professors liked about previous editions has been retained in the Fourth Edition. But we have added many new maps, significantly revised some older maps, brought nearly all the quantitative maps up-to-date with the latest economic, political, demographic, social, and environmental information, and reorganized the sequence of maps and data tables. Completely new to the Fourth Edition are 27 maps: 15 of these are thematic maps focusing on historical, political, and economic information *(Migrations since 1500; European Boundaries, 1914–1948; An Age of Bipolarity: The Cold War ca. 1970; Europe: Political and Economic Changes in the 1990s; Linguistic Diversity; International Conflicts in the Post–World War II World; Flashpoints, Year 2000; Political Boundary Types; International Trade Organizations; International Flows of Capital; The Indebtedness of States; Illiteracy Rates; Unemployment and Labor Migration; Energy Dependency; Flows of Oil.);* 12 of the new maps are regional reference maps. Each of the world's major regions—North America, South America, Europe, Africa, Asia, and Australasia—is portrayed by 2 maps, one of physical geographic features and one of political units and urban places. These 12 reference maps are accompanied by a locator index or "gazeteer" that will enable you to locate places easily. In addition to these completely new maps, maps from earlier editions *(Global Distribution of Minority Groups, World Refugee Population; Post–Cold War International Alliances; Nations with Nuclear Weapons; Military Expenditures as Percent of Gross National Product;* and *Deforestation and Desertification)* have been redrawn with new and revised base information. Most of the remaining economic, social, and demographic maps have also been revised with updated quantitative information from the latest available sources *(Rich and Poor Countries: Gross National Product; Gross National Product Per Capita; Relative Wealth of Nations: Purchasing Power Parity; Economic Output Per Sector; Population Growth Rate; Infant Mortality; Average Life Expectancy at Birth; Urban Population; Population by Age Group; Total Labor Force; Index of Agricultural Production Per Capita; Energy Production Per Capita; Energy Requirements Per Capita).* Only the thematic maps of the first section, and some of the political, economic, social, and environmental maps of the second through the sixth sections, remain as they were in the third edition—either there was no need to change these maps (the pattern of global population density, after all, has not really changed substantially in the last year, nor has the pattern of worldwide soil erosion), or data more recent than that used in the third edition was not yet available. There is one final major change in *Student Atlas of World Politics,* Fourth Edition: all the tables have been consolidated into one section at the end of the volume. We think this will make the tables easier to use and, by having all the quantitative information gathered together in one section of the book, will make cross-country or inter-regional comparisons easier.

About the Author

John L. Allen is Professor of Geography at the University of Connecticut where he has taught since 1967. He is a native of Wyoming and received his bachelor's degree in 1963 and his M.A. in 1964 from the University of Wyoming, and in 1969 he received his Ph.D. from Clark University. His special areas of interest are perceptions of the environment and the impact of human societies on environmental systems. Dr. Allen is the author and editor of many books and articles as well as several other student atlases, including the best-selling *Student Atlas of World Geography*.

Acknowledgments

The author wishes to recognize with gratitude the advice, suggestions, and general assistance of the following reviewers:

Robert Bednarz
Texas A & M University

Gerald E. Beller
West Virginia State College

Kenneth L. Conca
University of Maryland

Paul B. Frederic
University of Maine at Farmington

James F. Fryman
University of Northern Iowa

Lloyd E. Hudman
Brigham Young University

Edward L. Jackiewicz
Miami University of Ohio

Artimus Keiffer
*Indiana University–Purdue University
 at Indianapolis*

Richard L. Krol
Kean College of New Jersey

Robert Larson
Indiana State University

Elizabeth J. Leppman
St. Cloud State University

Mark Lowry II
*United States Military Academy
 at West Point*

Max Lu
Kansas State University

Taylor E. Mack
Mississippi State University

Kenneth C. Martis
West Virginia University

Calvin O. Masilela
West Virginia University

Patrick McGreevy
Clarion University

Tyrel G. Moore
*University of North Carolina
 at Charlotte*

David J. Nemeth
The University of Toledo

Emmett Panzella
Point Park College

Jefferson S. Rogers
University of Tennessee at Martin

Barbara J. Rusnak
United States Air Force Academy

Mark Simpson
University of Tennessee at Martin

Jutta Weldes
Kent State University

Table of Contents

To the Student   iii

Part I. The Contemporary World   1

Map 1 Current World Political Boundaries   2
Map 2 World Climate Regions   4
Map 3 World Topography   6
Map 4 World Ecological Regions   8
Map 5 World Natural Hazards   10
Map 6 Land Use Patterns of the World   12
Map 7 World Population Density   14
Map 8 World Religions   16
Map 9 World Languages   18
Map 10 World External Migrations in Modern Times   20

Part II. States: Alliances and Conflicts   21

Map 11 Sovereign States: Duration of Independence   23
Map 12 European Boundaries, 1914-1948   24
Map 13 Age of Bipolarity: The Cold War ca. 1970   26
Map 14 Europe: Political Changes in the 1990s   27
Map 15 The Middle East: Territorial Changes,
    1918-Present   28
Map 16 Africa: Colonialism to Independence, 1910-1997   29
Map 17 Asia: Colonialism to Independence, 1930-1997   30
Map 18 Global Distribution of Minority Groups   31
Map 19 Linguistic Diversity   32
Map 20 World Refugee Population   33
Map 21 International Conflicts in the Post-World War II
    World   34
Map 22 Post-Cold War International Alliances   36
Map 23 Flashpoints, Year 2000   37
Map 24 Nations with Nuclear Weapons   40
Map 25 Military Expenditures as Percent of Gross National
    Product   41
Map 26 Size of Armed Forces   42
Map 27 Political Boundary Types   44
Map 28 Political Systems   46

Part III. The Global Economy   47

Map 29 International Trade Organizations   48
Map 30 Rich and Poor Countries: Gross National Product   49
Map 31 Gross National Product Per Capita   50
Map 32 Relative Wealth of Nations: Purchasing Power Parity
    51
Map 33 International Flows of Capital   52
Map 34 Economic Output Per Sector   53

Map 35 Employment by Economic Activity   54
Map 36 Central Governmental Expenditures Per Capita   55
Map 37 The Indebtedness of States   56
Map 38 Exports of Primary Products   57
Map 39 Dependence on Trade   58

Part IV. Population and Human Development   **59**

Map 40 Population Growth Rate   60
Map 41 Infant Mortality Rate   61
Map 42 Average Life Expectancy at Birth   62
Map 43 Population by Age Group   63
Map 44 Total Labor Force   64
Map 45 Urban Population   65
Map 46 Illiteracy Rates   66
Map 47 Unemployment and Labor Migration   67
Map 48 The Gender Gap: Inequalities in Education and Employment   68
Map 49 The Index of Human Development   69

Part V. Food, Energy, and Materials   **71**

Map 50 Production of Staples—Cereals, Roots, Tubers   72
Map 51 Agricultural Production Per Capita   73
Map 52 Calories Available as a Percentage of Need   74
Map 53 Energy Production Per Capita   75
Map 54 Energy Requirements Per Capita   76
Map 55 Energy Dependency   77
Map 56 Flows of Oil   78
Map 57 Production of Crucial Materials   79
Map 58 Consumption of Crucial Materials   80

Part VI. Environmental Conditions   **81**

Map 59 Deforestation and Desertification   82
Map 60 Soil Degradation   83
Map 61 Air and Water Quality   84
Map 62 Per Capita CO_2 Emissions   85

Part VII. World Regional Maps   **87**

Map 63 North America: Physical Map   88
Map 64 North America: Political Map   89
Map 65 South America: Physical Map   90
Map 66 South America: Political Map   91
Map 67 Europe: Physical Map   92
Map 68 Europe: Political Map   93
Map 69 Asia: Physical Map   94
Map 70 Asia: Political Map   95
Map 71 Africa: Physical Map   96
Map 72 Africa: Political Map   97
Map 73 Australia and Oceania: Physical Map   98
Map 74 Australia and Oceania: Political Map   99

Part VIII. World Countries: Data Tables 101

Table A World Countries: Area, Population and Population Density, 1998 102

Table B World Countries: Form of Government, Capital City, Major Languages 105

Table C Defense Expenditures, Armed Forces, Refugees, and the Arms Trade 108

Table D Armed Conflict in the 1990s 111

Table E World Countries: Basic Economic Indicators 1997 114

Table F World Countries: Population Growth, 1950-2050 118

Table G World Countries: Basic Demographic Data, 1975-2000 122

Table H World Countries: Mortality, Health, and Nutrition, 1997 126

Table I World Countries: Education and Literacy, 1995-1997 130

Table J World Countries: Agricultural Operations, 1994-1997 134

Table K Land Use and Deforestation, 1980-1996 138

Table L World Countries: Energy Production and Use, 1980-1996 142

Table M World Countries: Water Resources 145

Table N World Countries: Energy Efficiency and Emissions, 1980-1996 151

Part IX. Geographic Index 155

Sources 169

Part I

The Contemporary World

Map 1 Current World Political Boundaries
Map 2 World Climate Regions
Map 3 World Topography
Map 4 World Ecological Regions
Map 5 World Natural Hazards
Map 6 Land Use Patterns of the World
Map 7 World Population Density
Map 8 World Religions
Map 9 World Languages
Map 10 World External Migrations in Modern Times

Map 1 Current World Political Boundaries

The international system includes states (countries) as the most important component. The boundaries of countries are the primary source of political division in the world, and for most people nationalism is the strongest source of political identification.

Scale: 1 to 125,000,000

Note: All world maps are Robinson projection.

Map 2 World Climate Regions

Climates of the World

Tropical Moist Climates
- Rain Forest
- Monsoon
- Savanna

Dry Climates
- Warm Desert
- Warm Steppe
- Cool Desert
- Cool Steppe

Midlatitude Climates
- Summer Dry or Mediterranean
- Moist Subtropical
- Marine West Coast
- Cool Forest
- Subarctic

Polar Climates
- Tundra
- Ice Cap

Azonal Climates
- Undifferentiated Highlands

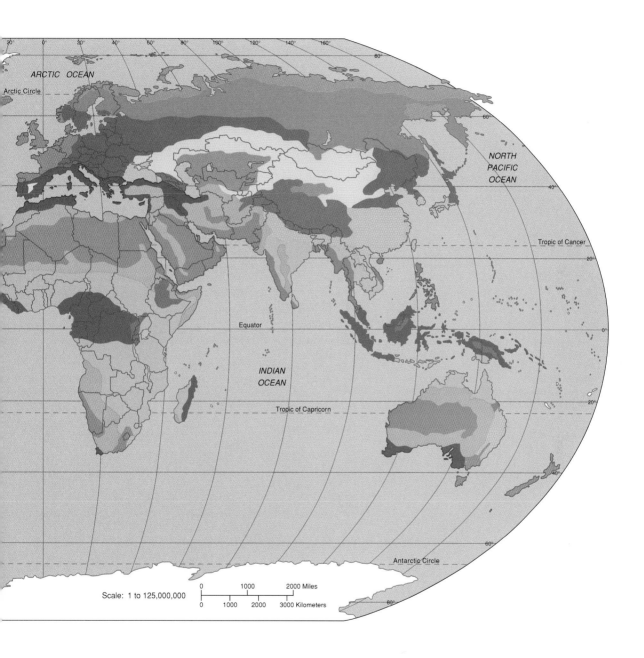

Of the world's many physical geographic features, climate (the long-term average of such weather conditions as temperature and precipitation) is the most important. It is climate that conditions the types of natural vegetation patterns and the types of soil that will exist in an area. It is also climate that determines the availability of our most precious resource: water. From an economic standpoint, the world's most important activity is agriculture; no other element of physical geography is more important for agriculture than climate.

Map 3 World Topography

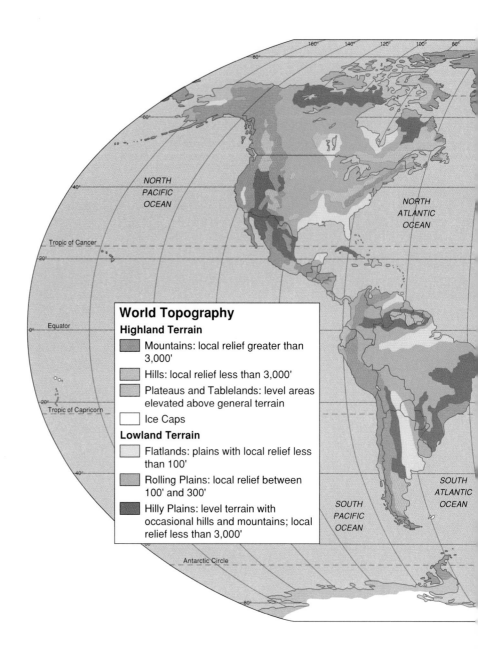

World Topography

Highland Terrain

Mountains: local relief greater than 3,000'

Hills: local relief less than 3,000'

Plateaus and Tablelands: level areas elevated above general terrain

Ice Caps

Lowland Terrain

Flatlands: plains with local relief less than 100'

Rolling Plains: local relief between 100' and 300'

Hilly Plains: level terrain with occasional hills and mountains; local relief less than 3,000'

Second only to climate as a conditioner of human activity—particularly in agriculture and also in the location of cities and industry—is topography or terrain. It is what we often call "landforms." A comparison of this map with the map of land use (Map 6) will show that most of the world's productive agricultural zones are located in lowland regions. Where large regions of agricultural productivity are found, we also tend to find urban concentrations and, with cities, we find industry. There is also a good spatial correlation between the map of landforms and the map showing the distribution and density of the human population (Map 7). Normally, the world's landforms shown on

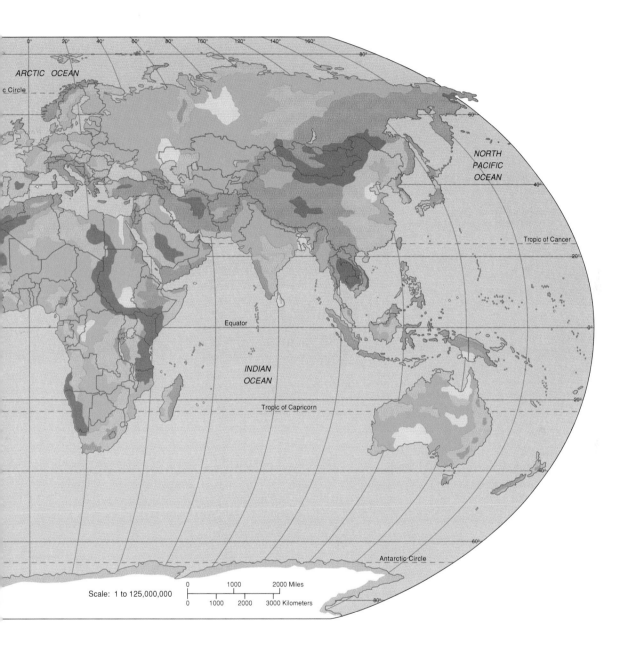

this map are the result of extremely gradual primary geologic activity such as the long-term movement of crustal plates (sometimes called continental drift). This activity occurs over hundreds of millions of years. Also important is the more rapid (but still slow by human standards) geomorphological or erosional activity of water, wind, glacial ice, and waves, tides, and currents. Some landforms may be produced by abrupt or "cataclysmic" events such as a major volcanic eruption or a meteor strike, but these are relatively rare and their effects are usually too minor to show up on a map of this scale.

Map 4 World Ecological Regions

World Ecological Regions

Arctic and Subarctic Zone

- Ice Cap
- Tundra Province: moss-grass and moss-lichen tundra
- Tundra Altitudinal Zone: polar desert (no vegetation)
- Subarctic Province: evergreen forest, needleleaf taiga; mixed coniferous and small-leafed forest
- Subarctic Altitudinal Zone: open woodland; wooded tundra

Humid Temperate Zone

- Moderate Continental Province: mixed coniferous and broadleaf forest
- Moderate Continental Altitudinal Zone: coastal and alpine forest; open woodland
- Warm Continental Province: broadleaf deciduous forest
- Warm Continental Altitudinal Zone: upland broadleaf and alpine needleleaf forest
- Marine Province: lowland, west-coastal humid forest
- Marine Altitudinal Zone: humid coastal and alpine coniferous forest
- Humid Subtropical Province: broadleaf evergreen and broadleaf deciduous forest
- Humid Subtropical Altitudinal Zone: upland, subtropical broadleaf forest
- Prairie Province: tallgrass and mixed prairie
- Prairie Altitudinal Zone: upland mixed prairie and woodland
- Mediterranean Province: sclerophyll woodland, shrub, and steppe grass
- Mediterranean Altitudinal Zone: upland shrub and steppe

Humid Tropical Zone

- Savanna Province: seasonally dry forest; open woodland; tallgrass savanna
- Savanna Altitudinal Zone: open woodland steppe
- Rain Forest Province: constantly humid, broadleaf evergreen forest
- Rain Forest Altitudinal Zone: broadleaf evergreen and subtropical deciduous forest

Arid and Semiarid Zone

- Tropical/Subtropical Steppe Province: dry steppe (short grass), desert shrub, semidesert savanna
- Tropical/Subtropical Steppe Altitudinal Zone: upland steppe (short grass) and desert shrub
- Tropical/Subtropical Desert Province: hot, lowland desert in subtropical and coastal locations; xerophytic vegetation
- Tropical/Subtropical Desert Altitudinal Zone: desert shrub
- Temperate Steppe Province: medium to shortgrass prairie
- Temperate Steppe Altitudinal Zone: alpine meadow and coniferous woodland
- Temperate Desert Province: midlatitude rainshadow desert; desert shrub
- Temperate Desert Altitudinal Zone: extreme continental desert steppe; desert shrub, xerophytic vegetation, shortgrass steppe

NORTH PACIFIC OCEAN

NORTH ATLANTIC OCEAN

Tropic of Cancer

Equator

Tropic of Capricorn

SOUTH PACIFIC OCEAN

SOUTH ATLANTIC OCEAN

Antarctic Circle

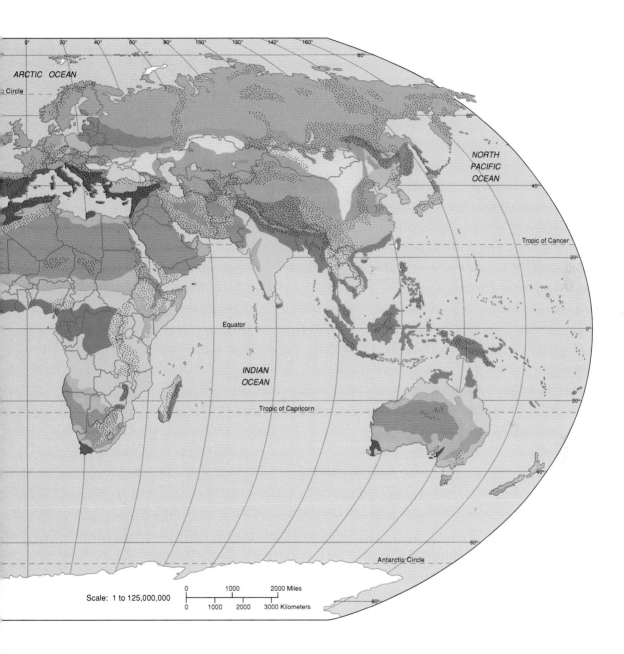

Scale: 1 to 125,000,000

Ecology is the study of the relationships between living organisms and their environmental surroundings. Ecological regions are distinctive areas within which unique sets
of organisms and environments are found. Within each ecological region, a particular
combination of vegetation, wildlife, soil, water, climate, and terrain defines that region's
"habitability," or ability to support life, including human life. Like climate and landforms,
ecological relationships are crucial to the existence of agriculture, the most basic of
our economic activities, and important for many other kinds of economic activity as
well.

Map [5] World Natural Hazards

Natural Hazards

- Temporary (seasonal) pack ice: open water during summer months
- Permanent pack ice: some open water leads during summer months
- Permanent ice sheet
- Severe sea fog: common enough to restrict navigation
- Desert region: agriculture limited to irrigation
- Area subject to desertification: soil and hydrology changes by humans
- Tornado region: high risk of damaging storms
- Tornado region: moderate risk of damaging storms
- Tropical storm tracks (hurricanes, cyclones, typhoons); less than five per year
- Tropical storm tracks (hurricanes, cyclones, typhoons); more than five per year
- Selected rivers subject to severe flooding
- Major flood disasters in the 20th century
- Southern limit of continuous permafrost (permanently frozen subsoil)
- Equatorward limit of large iceberg drift
- Major earthquakes (in the 20th century)
- Major volcanic activity (in the 20th century)
- Coastal areas subject to tsunamis: "tidal" waves produced by submarine volcanic/earthquake activity

Unlike other elements of physical geography, natural hazards are unpredictable. However, there are certain regions where the *probability* of the occurrence of a particular natural hazard is high. This map shows regions affected by major natural hazards at rates that are higher than the global norm. Persistent natural hazards may undermine the utility of an area for economic purposes. Some scholars also suggest that regions of environmental instability may be regions of political instability as well.

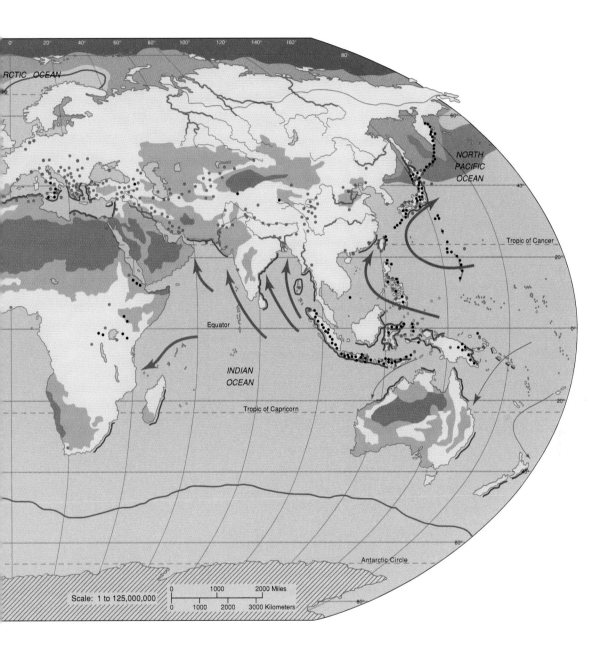

Map 6 Land Use Patterns of the World

World Land Use

Predominant activities by region

- Manufacturing and Commerce
- Commercial Crop and Livestock Agriculture
- Intensive Subsistence Crop and Livestock Agriculture, including Plantations
- Tropical Shifting Subsistence Agriculture
- Livestock Ranching
- Dryland Nomadic Livestock Herding
- Forestry, Fishing, Hunting and Gathering, Recreation and Tourism (Commercial)
- Nomadic Herding, Forestry, Fishing, Hunting (Primarily Subsistence)
- Fishing Grounds (Commercial and Subsistence)
- No Major Economic Activity

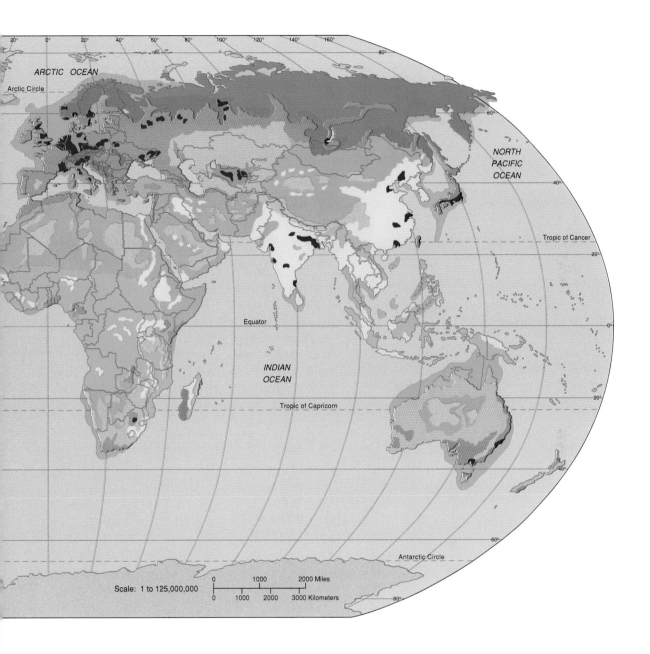

Many of the major land use patterns of the world (such as urbanization, industry, and transportation) are relatively small in area and are not easily seen on maps, but the most important uses people make of the earth's surface have more far-reaching effects. This map illustrates, in particular, the variations in primary land uses (such as agriculture) for the entire world. Note the differences between land use patterns in the more developed countries of the temperate zones and the less developed countries of the tropics.

Map 7 World Population Density

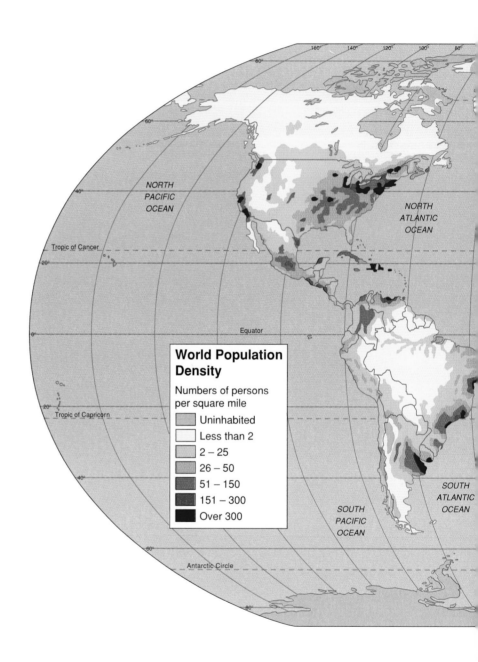

World Population Density

Numbers of persons per square mile

- Uninhabited
- Less than 2
- 2 – 25
- 26 – 50
- 51 – 150
- 151 – 300
- Over 300

No feature of human activity is more reflective of environmental conditions than where people live. In the areas of densest populations, a mixture of natural and human factors has combined to allow maximum food production, maximum urbanization, and maximum centralization of economic activities. Three great concentrations of human population appear on the map—East Asia, South Asia, and Europe—with a fourth, lesser concentration in eastern North America (the "Megalopolis" region of the United States and Canada). One of these great population clusters—South Asia—is still growing rapidly and can be expected to become even more densely populated by the beginning

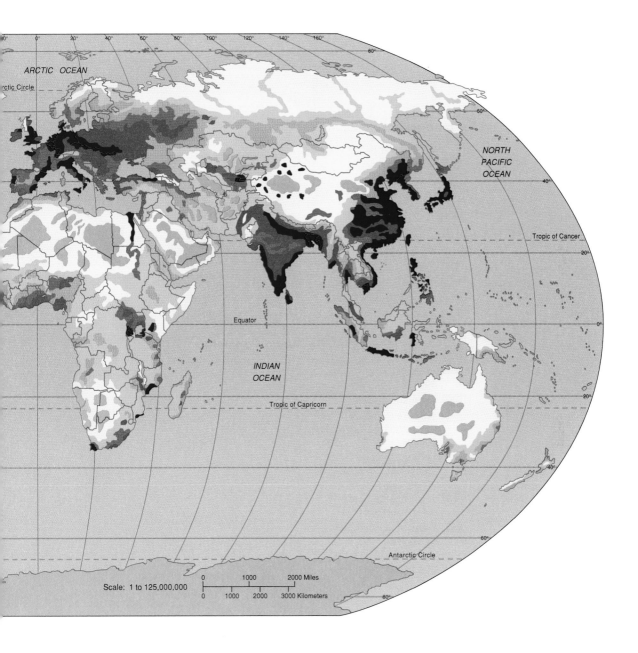

of the twenty-first century. The other concentrations are likely to remain about as they now appear. In Europe and North America, this is the result of economic development that has caused population growth to level off during the last century. In East Asia, population has also begun to grow more slowly. In the case of Japan and the Koreas, this is the consequence of economic development; in the case of China, it is the consequence of government intervention in the form of strict family planning. The areas of future high density (in addition to those already existing) are likely to be in Middle and South America and Africa, where population growth rates are well above the world average.

Map 8 World Religions

Predominant Religions

Christianity (C)*
- Roman Catholic
- Protestant
- Mormon (LDS)
- Eastern Churches
- Mixed Sects

Islam (M)
- Sunni
- Shi'a

Buddhism (B)
- Hinayanistic
- Lamaistic

Hinduism (H)

Judaism (J)

Sikhism

Animism (Tribal)

Chinese Complex
(Confucianism, Taoism, and Buddhism)

Korean Complex
(Buddhism, Confucianism, Christianity, and Chondogyo)

Japanese Complex
(Shinto and Buddhism)

Vietnamese Complex
(Buddhism, Taoism Confucianism, and Cao Dai)

Unpopulated Regions

* Capital letters indicate the presence of locally important minority adherents of nonpredominant faiths.

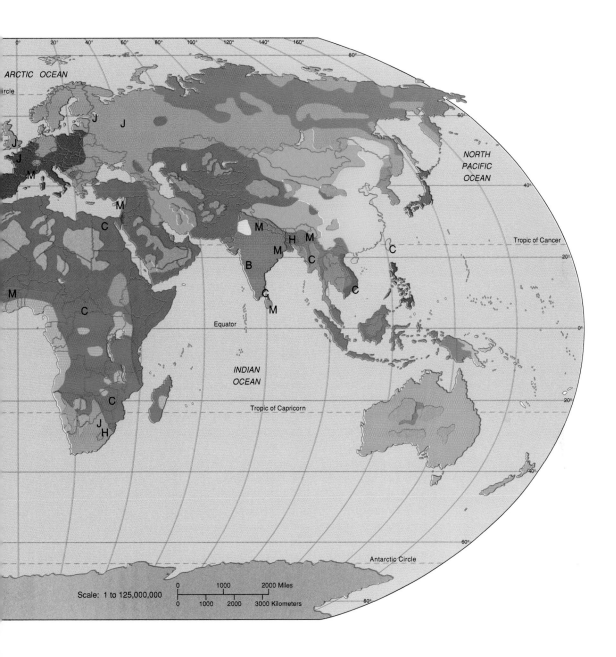

Religious adherence is one of the fundamental defining characteristics of culture. A depiction of the spatial distribution of religions is, therefore, as close as we can come to a map of cultural patterns. More than just a set of behavioral patterns having to do with worship and ceremony, religion is an important conditioner of the ways that people treat one another and the environments that they occupy. In many areas of the world, the ways in which people make a living, the patterns of occupation that they create on the land, and the impacts that they make on ecosystems are the direct consequence of their adherence to a religious faith.

Map ⑨ World Languages

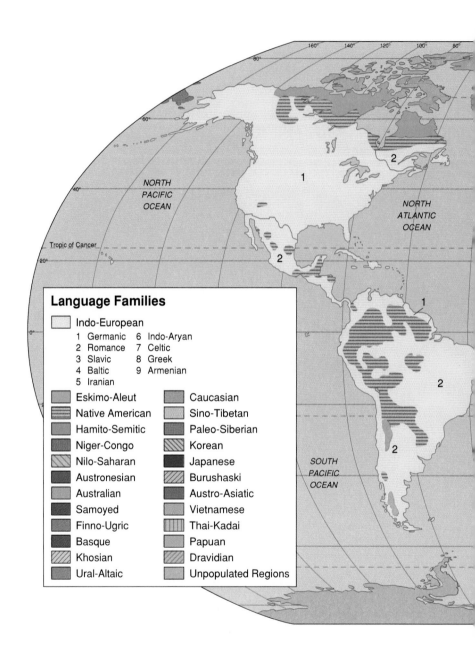

Language Families

☐ Indo-European
1 Germanic 6 Indo-Aryan
2 Romance 7 Celtic
3 Slavic 8 Greek
4 Baltic 9 Armenian
5 Iranian

- Eskimo-Aleut
- Native American
- Hamito-Semitic
- Niger-Congo
- Nilo-Saharan
- Austronesian
- Australian
- Samoyed
- Finno-Ugric
- Basque
- Khosian
- Ural-Altaic

- Caucasian
- Sino-Tibetan
- Paleo-Siberian
- Korean
- Japanese
- Burushaski
- Austro-Asiatic
- Vietnamese
- Thai-Kadai
- Papuan
- Dravidian
- Unpopulated Regions

NORTH PACIFIC OCEAN

NORTH ATLANTIC OCEAN

Tropic of Cancer

SOUTH PACIFIC OCEAN

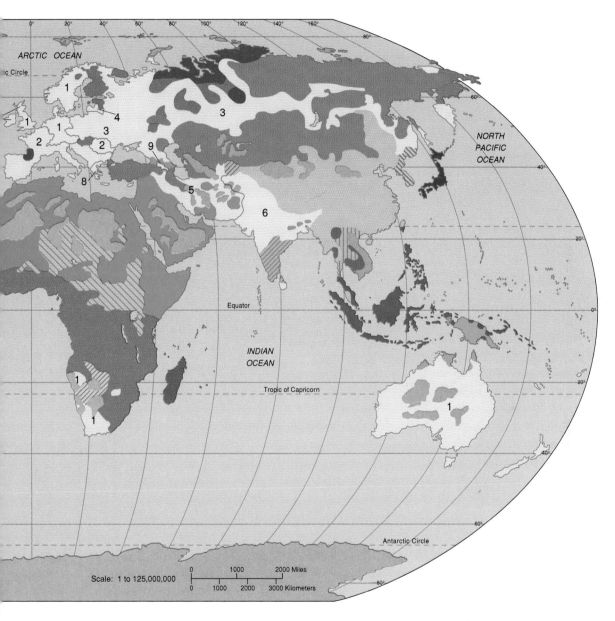

Like religion, language is an important defining characteristic of culture. It is perhaps the most durable of all cultural traits. Even after centuries of exposure to other languages or even of conquest by speakers of other languages, the speakers of a specific tongue will often retain their own linguistic identity. As a geographic element, language helps us to locate areas of potential conflict, particularly in regions where two or more languages overlap. Many, if not most, of the world's conflict zones are also areas of linguistic diversity. Language also provides clues that enable us to chart the course of human migrations, as shown in the distribution of Indo-European languages. And it helps us to understand some of the reasons behind important historical events; linguistic identity differences played an important part in the disintegration of the Soviet Union.

Map 10 World External Migrations in Modern Times

World Migrations Since 1500

- Europeans
- Africans
- South Asians
- Chinese
- European Jews
- Americans and Canadians
- Russians
- Mexicans and Central Americans
- Caribbeans (Cubans, Haitians, Puerto Ricans)
- Southeast Asians

Scale: 1 to 180,000,000

0   1000   2000 Miles
0   1000   2000   3000 Kilometers

Migration has had a significant effect on world geography, contributing to cultural change and development, to the diffusion of ideas and innovations, and to the complex mixture of people and cultures found in the world today. *Internal migration* occurs within the boundaries of a country; *external migration* is movement from one country or region to another. Over the last 50 years, the most important migrations in the world have been internal, largely the rural-to-urban migration that has been responsible for the recent rise of global urbanization. Prior to the mid-20th century, 3 types of external migrations were most important: *voluntary*, most often in search of better economic conditions

and opportunities; *involuntary* or *forced*, involving people who have been driven from their homelands by war, political unrest, or environmental disasters, or who have been transported as slaves or prisoners; and *imposed*, not entirely forced but which conditions make highly advisable. Human migrations in recorded history have been responsible for major changes in the patterns of languages, religions, ethnic composition, and economies. Particularly during the last 500 years, migrations of both the voluntary and involuntary or forced type have literally reshaped the human face of the earth.

Part II

States: Alliances and Conflicts

Map 11 Sovereign States: Duration of Independence
Map 12 European Boundaries, 1914–1948
Map 13 An Age of Bipolarity: The Cold War ca. 1970
Map 14 Europe: Political Changes in the 1990s
Map 15 The Middle East: Territorial Changes, 1918–Present
Map 16 Africa: Colonialism to Independence, 1910–1997
Map 17 Asia: Colonialism to Independence, 1930–1997
Map 18 Global Distribution of Minority Groups
Map 19 Linguistic Diversity
Map 20 World Refugee Population
Map 21 International Conflicts in the Post–World War II World
Map 22 Post–Cold War International Alliances
Map 23 Flashpoints, Year 2000
Map 24 Nations with Nuclear Weapons
Map 25 Military Expenditures as Percentage of Gross Domestic Product
Map 26 Size of Armed Forces
Map 27 Political Boundary Types
Map 28 Political Systems

Map 11 Sovereign States: Duration of Independence

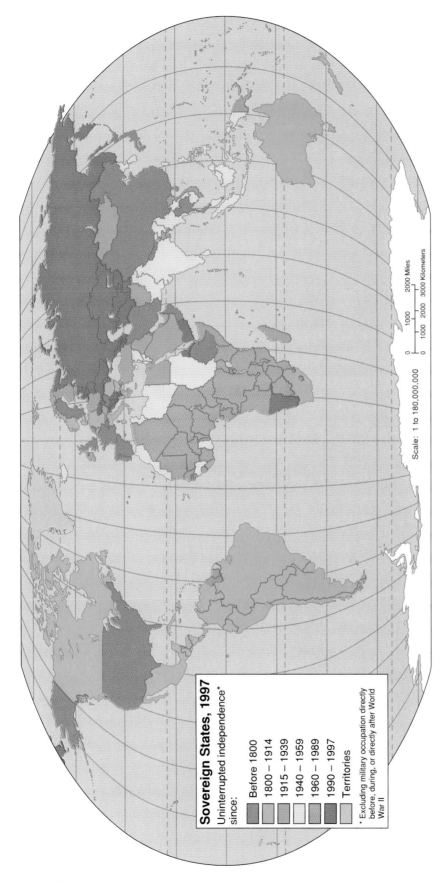

Sovereign States, 1997

Uninterrupted independence* since:

- Before 1800
- 1800 – 1914
- 1915 – 1939
- 1940 – 1959
- 1960 – 1989
- 1990 – 1997
- Territories

* Excluding military occupation directly before, during, or directly after World War II

Scale: 1 to 180,000,000

0   1000   2000 Miles

0   1000   2000   3000 Kilometers

Most countries of the modern world, including such major states as Germany and Italy, became independent after the beginning of the nineteenth century. Of the world's current countries, only 27 were independent in 1800. (Ten of the 27 were in Europe; the others were Afghanistan, China, Colombia, Ethiopia, Haiti, Iran, Japan, Mexico, Nepal, Oman, Paraguay, Russia, Taiwan, Thailand, Turkey, the United States, and Venezuela.) Following 1800, there have been four great periods of national independence. During the first of these (1800–1914), most of the mainland countries of the Americas achieved independence. During the second period (1915–1939), the countries of Eastern Europe emerged as independent entities. The third period (1940–1959) includes World War II and the years that followed, when independence for African and Asian nations that had been under control of colonial powers first began to occur. During the fourth period (1960–1989), independence came to the remainder of the colonial African and Asian nations, as well as to former colonies in the Caribbean and the South Pacific. More than half of the world's countries came into being as independent political entities during this period. Finally, in the last few years (1990–1997), the breakup of the existing states of the Soviet Union, Yugoslavia, and Czechoslovakia created 22 countries where only 3 had existed before.

Map [12] European Boundaries, 1914–1948

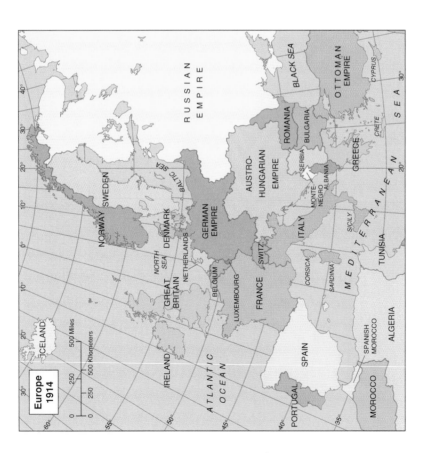

In 1914, on the eve of the First World War, Europe was dominated by the United Kingdom and France in the west, the German Empire and the Austro-Hungarian Empire in Central Europe, and the Russian Empire in the east. Battle lines for the conflict that began in 1914 were drawn when the United Kingdom, France, and the Russian Empire joined together as the Triple Entente. In the view of the Germans, this coalition was designed to encircle Germany and its Austrian ally, which, along with Italy, made up the Triple Alliance. The German and Austrian fears were heightened in 1912–14 when a Russian-sponsored "Balkan League" pushed the Ottoman Turkish Empire from Europe, leaving behind the weak and mutually antagonistic Balkan states Serbia and Montenegro. In August 1914, Germany and Austria-Hungary attacked in several directions and World War I began. Four years later, after massive loss of life and destruction, the Central European empires were defeated. The victorious French, English, and Americans (who had entered the war in 1917) restructured the map of Europe in 1919, carving nine new states out of the remains of the German and Austro-Hungarian empires and the westernmost portions of the Russian Empire which, by the end of the war, was deep in the Revolution that deposed the Czar and brought the Communists to power in a new Union of Soviet Socialist Republics.

Europe 1948

‖ NATO states
⋯ Warsaw Pact states

500 Miles
500 Kilometers

Europe 1943

Axis powers
Under German rule
Axis military occupation
Greater German Reich

Axis satellites
Allied territory
Allied occupied
Neutral powers

500 Miles
500 Kilometers

When the victorious Allies redrew the map of central and eastern Europe in 1919, they caused as many problems as they were trying to solve. The interval between the First and Second World Wars was really just a lull in a long war that halted temporarily in 1918 and erupted once again in 1939. Defeated Germany, resentful of the terms of the 1918 armistice and 1919 Treaty of Versailles and beset by massive inflation and unemployment at home, overthrew the Weimar republican government in 1933 and installed the National Socialist (Nazi) party led by Adolph Hitler in Berlin. Hitler quickly began making good on his promises to create a "thousand year realm" of German influence by annexing Austria and the Czech region of Czechoslovakia and allying Germany with a fellow fascist state in Mussolini's Italy. In September 1939 Germany launched the lightning-quick combined infantry, artillery, and armor attack known as "der Blitzkrieg" and took Poland to the east and, in quick succession, the Netherlands, Belgium, and France to the west. By 1943, the greater German Reich extended from the Russian Plain to the Atlantic and from the Black Sea to the Baltic. But the Axis powers of Germany and Italy could not withstand the greater resources and manpower of the combined United Kingdom–United States–USSR led Allies and, in 1945, Allied armies occupied Germany. Once again, the lines of the central and eastern European map were redrawn. This time, a strengthened Soviet Union took back most of the territory the Russian Empire had lost at the end of the First World War. Germany was partitioned into four occupied sectors (English, French, American, and Russian) and later into two independent countries, the Federal Republic of Germany (West Germany) and the German Democratic Republic (East Germany). Although the Soviet Union's territory stopped at the Polish, Hungarian, Czechoslovakian, and Romanian borders, the eastern European countries (Poland, East Germany, Czechoslovakia, Hungary, Romania, Yugoslavia, Albania, and Bulgaria) became Communist between 1945 and 1948 and were separated by the Iron Curtain from the West.

Map 13 An Age of Bipolarity: The Cold War ca. 1970

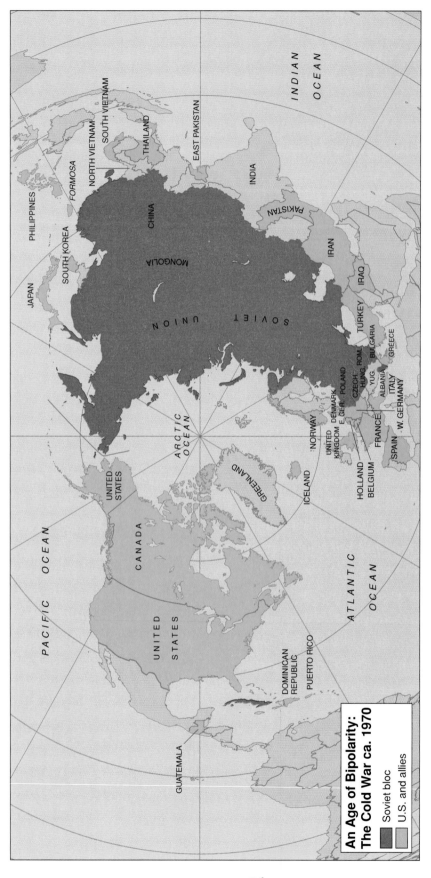

An Age of Bipolarity: The Cold War ca. 1970

- Soviet bloc
- U.S. and allies

Following the Second World War, the world was divided into two armed camps led by the United States and the Soviet Union. The Soviet Union and its allies, the Warsaw Pact countries, feared a U.S.-led takeover of the eastern European countries that became Soviet satellites after the war and the replacing of a socialist political and economic system with a liberal one. The United States and its allies, the NATO (North Atlantic Treaty Organization) countries, equally feared that the USSR would overrun western Europe. Both sides sought to defend themselves by building up massive military arsenals. The United States, adopting an international geopolitical strategy of "containment," sought to ring the Soviet Union with a string of allied countries and military bases that would prevent Soviet expansion in any direction. The levels of spending on military hardware contributed to the devolution of the Soviet Union and the obsolescence of alliances and military bases in an age of advanced guidance and delivery systems made the U.S. military containment less necessary. Following a peak in the early 1960s, the cold war gradually became less significant and the age of bipolar international power essentially ended with the dissolution of the USSR.

Map 14 Europe: Political Changes in the 1990s

Europe: Political Changes in the 1990s

1989

- Union of Soviet Socialist Republics
- Warsaw Pact Countries (excluding the USSR)
- North Atlantic Treaty Organization Countries
- European Community (formerly the EEC)

1999

- Former Republics of the USSR, now independent countries
- Russian Federation
- New European Countries resulting from reunification
- New European Countries resulting from partition
- NATO Countries, 1999
- Associated with NATO / Petitioned for entry
- European Union (formerly the EC)
- 2000 Year of projected entry into the European Union

During the last decade of the twentieth century, one of the most remarkable series of political geographic changes of the last 500 years took place. The bipolar "East-West" structure that had characterized Europe's political geography since the end of the Second World War altered in the space of a very few years. In the mid-1980s, as Soviet influence over eastern and central Europe weakened, those countries began to turn to the capitalist West. Between 1989, when the country of Hungary was the first Soviet satellite to open its borders to travel, and 1991, when the Soviet Union dissolved into 15 independent countries, abrupt change in political systems occurred. The result is a new map of Europe that includes a number of countries not present on the map of 1989. These countries have emerged as the result of reunification, separation, or independence from the old Soviet Union. The new political structure has been accompanied by growing economic cooperation.

Map 15 The Middle East: Territorial Changes, 1918-Present

TERRITORIAL CHANGES IN THE MIDDLE EAST, WORLD WAR I TO PRESENT

- Ottoman Empire to World War I
- British control
- French control
- Kurdish homelands
- International boundaries in 1994

The Middle East, encompassing the northeastern part of Africa and southwestern Asia, has experienced a turbulent history. In the last century alone, many of the region's countries have gone from being ruled by the Turkish Ottoman Empire, to being dependencies of Great Britain or France, to being independent. Having experienced the Crusades and colonial domination by European powers, the region's predominantly Islamic countries are now resentful of interference in the region's affairs by countries with a European and/or Christian heritage. The tension between Israel (settled largely in the late nineteenth and twentieth centuries by Jews of predominantly European background) and its neighbors is a matter of European–Middle Eastern cultural stress as well as a religious conflict between Islamic Arab culture and Judaism.

Map 16 Africa: Colonialism to Independence, 1910–1997

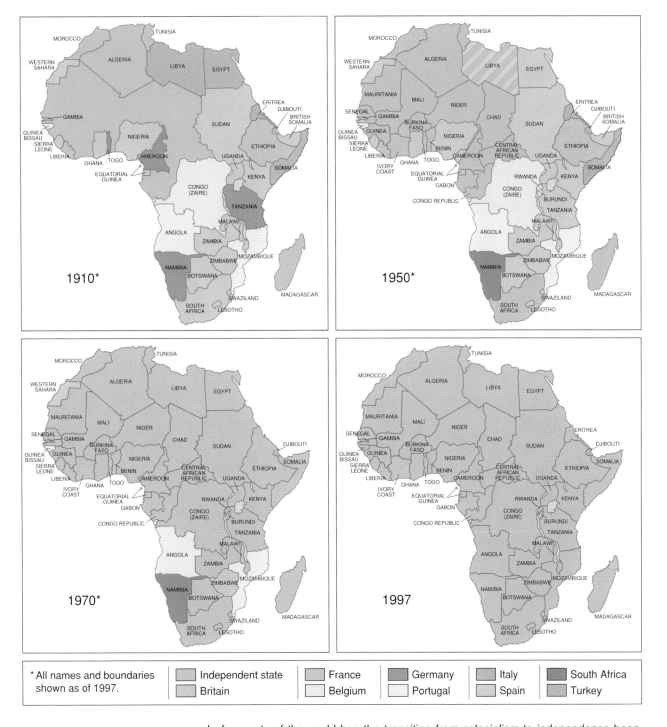

1910*

1950*

1970*

1997

* All names and boundaries shown as of 1997.

Independent state — Britain — France — Belgium — Germany — Portugal — Italy — Spain — South Africa — Turkey

In few parts of the world has the transition from colonialism to independence been as abrupt as on the African continent. Unlike the states of Middle and South America, which generally achieved independence from their colonial masters in the early nineteenth century, most African states did not become independent until the twentieth century, often not until after World War II. In part because they retain borders that are legacies of their former colonial status, many of these recently created African states are beset by internal problems related to tribal and ethnic conflicts.

Map 17 Asia: Colonialism to Independence, 1930–1997

Asian countries, like those in Africa, have recently emerged from a colonial past. With the exception of China, Japan, and Thailand, virtually all Asian nations were until not long ago under the colonial control of Great Britain, France, Spain, the Netherlands, or the United States. For a short period of time between 1930 and 1945, Japan itself was a colonial power with considerable territories on the Asian mainland. The unraveling of colonial control in Asia, particularly in South and Southeast Asia, has precipitated internal conflicts in the newly independent states that make up a significant part of the political geography of the region. One of the last vestiges of European colonialism in Asia disappeared in 1997 with the cession of Hong Kong to China.

Map 18 Global Distribution of Minority Groups

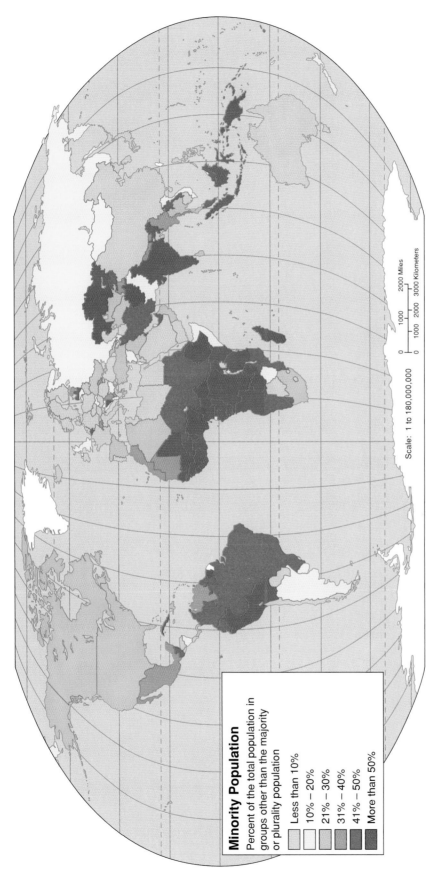

Minority Population

Percent of the total population in groups other than the majority or plurality population

- Less than 10%
- 10% – 20%
- 21% – 30%
- 31% – 40%
- 41% – 50%
- More than 50%

Scale: 1 to 180,000,000

0   1000   2000 Miles

0 1000 2000 3000 Kilometers

The presence of minority ethnic, national, or racial groups within a country's population can add a vibrant and dynamic mix to the whole. Plural societies with a high degree of cultural and ethnic diversity should, according to some social theorists, be among the world's most healthy. Unfortunately, the reality of the situation is quite different from theory or expectation. The presence of significant minority populations played an important role in the disintegration of the Soviet Union; the continuing existence of minority populations within the new states formed from former Soviet republics threatens the viability and stability of those young political units. In Africa, national boundaries were drawn by colonial powers without regard for the geographical distribution of ethnic groups, and the continuing tribal conflicts that have resulted hamper both economic and political development. Even in the most highly developed regions of the world, the presence of minority ethnic populations poses significant problems: witness the separatist movement in Canada, driven by the desire of some French-Canadians to be independent of the English majority, and the continuing ethnic conflict between Flemish-speaking and Walloon-speaking Belgians. This map, by arraying states on a scale of homogeneity to heterogeneity, indicates areas of existing and potential social and political strife.

Map 19 Linguistic Diversity

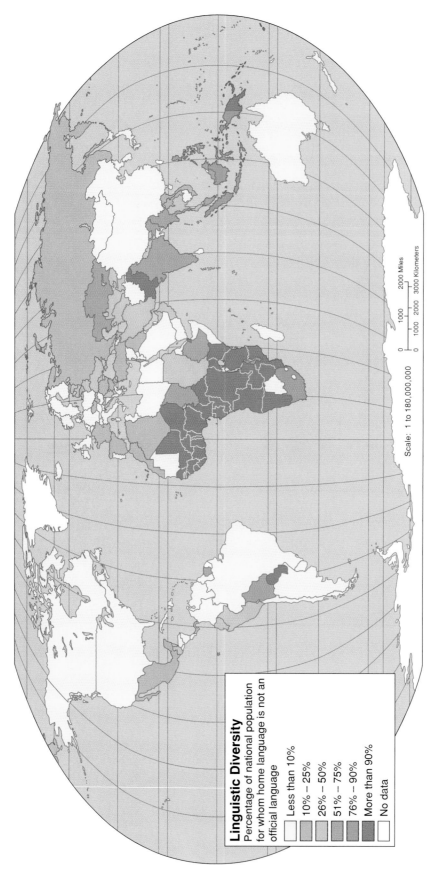

Linguistic Diversity
Percentage of national population for whom home language is not an official language

- Less than 10%
- 10% – 25%
- 26% – 50%
- 51% – 75%
- 76% – 90%
- More than 90%
- No data

Scale: 1 to 180,000,000

0   1000   2000 Miles
0   1000   2000   3000 Kilometers

Of the world's approximately 5,300 languages, less than 100 are "official languages;" those designated by a country as the language of government, commerce, education, and information. This means that for much of the world's population the language that is spoken in the home is different from the official language of the country of residence. The world's former colonial areas in Middle and South America, Africa, and South and Southeast Asia stand out on the map as regions in which there is significant disparity between home languages and official languages. To complicate matters further, for most of the world's population, the primary international languages of trade and tourism (French and English) are neither home nor official languages.

Map 20 World Refugee Population

World Refugee Population

Numbers of international refugees harbored in host country

- Less than 1,000
- 1,000 – 5,000
- 5,001 – 50,000
- 50,001 – 500,000
- More than 500,000
- No data

Number of international refugees by country of origin

Scale: 1 to 180,000,000

0 1000 2000 3000 Kilometers

0 1000 2000 Miles

Regions: CENTRAL AMERICA, SOUTH AMERICA, EUROPE, AFRICA, ASIA, OCEANIA

Country of origin figures:

CUBA 500
EL SALVADOR 5,750
GUATEMALA 30,000
HAITI 6,000
NICARAGUA 18,900
COLOMBIA 3,000

BOSNIA AND HERZOGOVINA 561,143
CROATIA 294,590
RUSSIAN FEDERATION 323,400
YUGOSLAVIA (SERBA-MONTENEGRO) 57,900

ANGOLA 223,000
BURUNDI 248,000
CAMEROON 1,000
CHAD 12,000
CONGO 40,000
DJIBOUTI 5,000
ERITREA 322,500
ETHIOPIA 48,300
GHANA 12,000
KENYA 8,000
LIBERIA 485,000
MALI 33,000
MAURITANIA 55,000
MOROCCO(WESTERN SAHARA) 85,000
NIGER 10,000
NIGERIA 1,000
RWANDA 43,000
SENEGAL 48,000
SIERRA LEONE 297,000
SOMALIA 475,000
SUDAN 193,000
TOGO 6,000
UGANDA 10,000
DEMOCRATIC REPUBLIC OF THE CONGO 119,000

AFGHANISTAN 3,619,500
ARMENIA 188,000
AZERBAIJAN 218,000
BANGLADESH 40,000
BHUTAN 103,000
CAMBODIA 77,000
CHINA (TIBET) 128,000
GEORGIA 11,000
INDIA 13,000
INDONESIA 8,200
IRAN 31,000
IRAQ 524,000
ISRAEL 3,743,000
LAOS 13,800
MYANMAR (BURMA) 215,000
SRI LANKA 100,000
TAJIKISTAN 32,400
TURKEY 10,800
UZBEKISTAN 46,000
VIET NAM 281,000

PAPUA NEW GUINEA 800

Refugees are persons who have been driven from their homes, normally by armed conflict, and have sought refuge by relocating. The most numerous refugees have traditionally been international refugees, who have crossed the political boundaries of their homelands into other countries. This refugee population is recognized by international agencies, and the countries of refuge are often rewarded financially by those agencies for their willingness to take in externally displaced persons. In recent years, largely because of an increase in civil wars, there have been growing numbers of internally displaced persons—those who leave their homes but stay within their country of origin. There are no rewards for harboring such internal refugee populations.

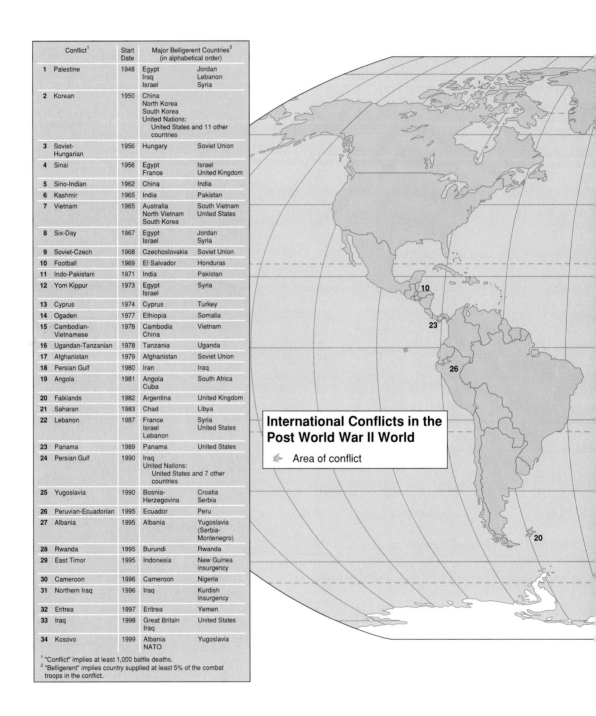

Conflict[1]	Start Date	Major Belligerent Countries[2] (in alphabetical order)	
1 Palestine	1948	Egypt Iraq Israel	Jordan Lebanon Syria

2 Korean	1950	China
		North Korea
		South Korea
		United Nations:
		    United States and 11 other
		    countries	

3 Soviet-Hungarian	1956	Hungary	Soviet Union
4 Sinai	1956	Egypt France	Israel United Kingdom
5 Sino-Indian	1962	China	India
6 Kashmir	1965	India	Pakistan
7 Vietnam	1965	Australia North Vietnam South Korea	South Vietnam United States
8 Six-Day	1967	Egypt Israel	Jordan Syria
9 Soviet-Czech	1968	Czechoslovakia	Soviet Union
10 Football	1969	El Salvador	Honduras
11 Indo-Pakistani	1971	India	Pakistan
12 Yom Kippur	1973	Egypt Israel	Syria
13 Cyprus	1974	Cyprus	Turkey
14 Ogaden	1977	Ethiopia	Somalia
15 Cambodian-Vietnamese	1978	Cambodia China	Vietnam
16 Ugandan-Tanzanian	1978	Tanzania	Uganda
17 Afghanistan	1979	Afghanistan	Soviet Union
18 Persian Gulf	1980	Iran	Iraq
19 Angola	1981	Angola Cuba	South Africa
20 Falklands	1982	Argentina	United Kingdom
21 Saharan	1983	Chad	Libya
22 Lebanon	1987	France Israel Lebanon	Syria United States
23 Panama	1989	Panama	United States

24 Persian Gulf	1990	Iraq
		United Nations:
		    United States and 7 other
		    countries	

25 Yugoslavia	1990	Bosnia-Herzegovina	Croatia Serbia
26 Peruvian-Ecuadorian	1995	Ecuador	Peru
27 Albania	1995	Albania	Yugoslavia (Serbia-Montenegro)
28 Rwanda	1995	Burundi	Rwanda
29 East Timor	1995	Indonesia	New Guinea insurgency
30 Cameroon	1996	Cameroon	Nigeria
31 Northern Iraq	1996	Iraq	Kurdish insurgency
32 Eritrea	1997	Eritrea	Yemen
33 Iraq	1998	Great Britain Iraq	United States
34 Kosovo	1999	Albania NATO	Yugoslavia

[1] "Conflict" implies at least 1,000 battle deaths.
[2] "Belligerent" implies country supplied at least 5% of the combat troops in the conflict.

International Conflicts in the Post World War II World

⚔ Area of conflict

The Korean War and the Vietnam War dominated the post–World War II period in terms of international military conflict. But numerous smaller conflicts have taken place, with fewer numbers of belligerents and with fewer battle and related casualties. These smaller international conflicts have been mostly territorial conflicts, reflecting the continual readjustment of political boundaries and loyalties brought about by the end of colonial empires, and the dissolution of the Soviet Union. Many of

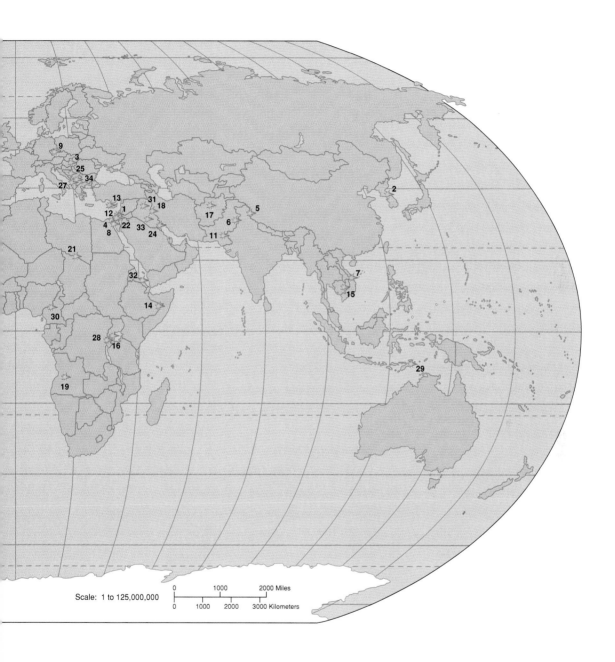

these conflicts were not wars in the more traditional sense, in which two or more countries formally declare war on one another, severing diplomatic ties and devoting their entire national energies to the war effort. Rather, many of these conflicts were and are undeclared wars, sometimes fought between rival groups within the same country with outside support from other countries.

Map 22 Post-Cold War International Alliances

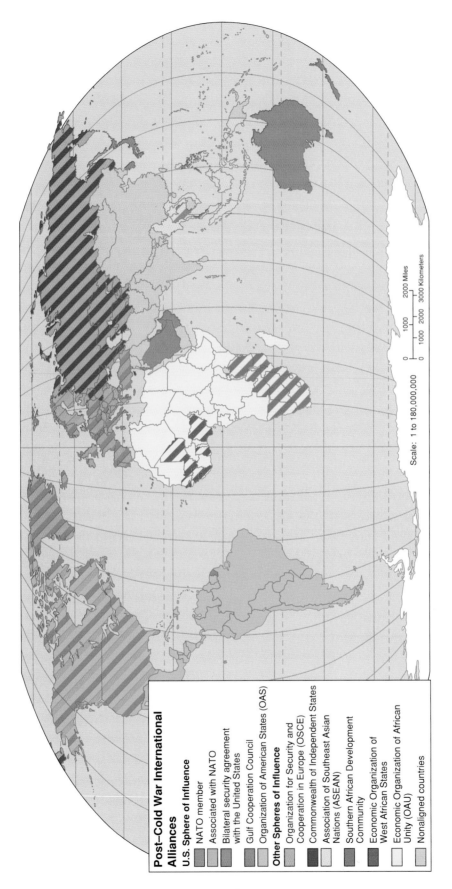

Post-Cold War International Alliances

U.S. Sphere of Influence
- NATO member
- Associated with NATO
- Bilateral security agreement with the United States
- Gulf Cooperation Council
- Organization of American States (OAS)

Other Spheres of Influence
- Organization for Security and Cooperation in Europe (OSCE)
- Commonwealth of Independent States
- Association of Southeast Asian Nations (ASEAN)
- Southern African Development Community
- Economic Organization of West African States
- Economic Organization of African Unity (OAU)
- Nonaligned countries

Scale: 1 to 180,000,000

```
0        1000       2000 Miles
0   1000   2000   3000 Kilometers
```

When the Warsaw Pact dissolved in 1992, the North Atlantic Treaty Organization (NATO) was left as the only major military alliance in the world. Some former Warsaw Pact members (Czech Republic, Hungary, and Poland) have joined NATO and others are petitioning for entry. The bipolar division of the world into two major military alliances is over, at least temporarily, leaving the United States alone as the world's dominant political and military power. But other international alliances such as the Commonwealth of Independent States (including most of the former republics of the Soviet Union) will continue to be important. It may well be that, during the first few decades of the twenty-first century, that economic alliances will begin to overshadow military ones in their relevance for the world's peoples.

Map 23 Flashpoints, Year 2000

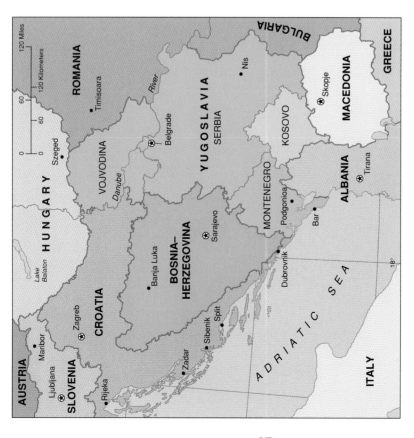

Kosovo: Conflict in this region derives from an ancient enmity between Orthodox Christian Serbs and the majority Kosovo population that is ethnically Albanian and Muslim. Since the fifteenth century and the conquest of much of southeastern Europe by the Turkish Ottoman Empire, religious tension between Christian and Muslim has existed in the region. Prior to 1989, Kosovo was a part of Yugoslavia but was largely independent. After the partitioning of Yugoslavia, the reconstituted state (including the former Yugoslavian territories of Serbia and Montenegro) sought to regain control over the Kosovar Albanian population. This sparked the rise of a nationalist Albanian guerrilla force in Kosovo and fighting between Serbs and Kosovars has brought this region to war.

Israel and Its Neighbors: The modern state of Israel was created out of the former British Protectorate of Palestine, inhabited primarily by Muslim Arabs, after the Second World War. Conflict between Arabs and Israeli Jews has been a constant ever since. Much of the present tension revolves around the West Bank area, not part of the original Israeli state but taken from Jordan, an Arab country, in the Six-Day War of 1967. Many Palestinians had settled this part of Jordan after the creation of Israel and remain as a majority population in the West Bank region today. Israel has established many agricultural settlements within the region since 1967, angering Palestinian Arabs. For Israel, the West Bank is the region of ancient Judea and this region, won in battle, will not be ceded back to Palestinian Arabs without protracted or severe military action.

Jammu and Kashmir: When Britain withdrew from South Asia in 1947, the former States of British India were asked to decide whether they wanted to become part of a new Hindu India or a Muslim Pakistan. In the State of Jammu and Kashmir, the rulers were Hindu and the majority population was Muslim. The majarajah (prince) of Kashmir tried to retain independence from both countries but an uprising of the Muslim majority precipitated a war between India and Pakistan over control of this high mountain region. In 1949 a cease-fire line was established by the UN, leaving most of the territory of Jammu and Kashmir in Indian hands. Since then Pakistan and India have waged intermittent skirmishes over the disputed territory that holds the headwaters of the Indus River, a life-giving stream to desert Pakistan. In 1999 extremist Muslim groups demanding independence escalated the periodic battles into a full-fledged, if small, war between two of Asia's major powers—both possessing nuclear weapons.

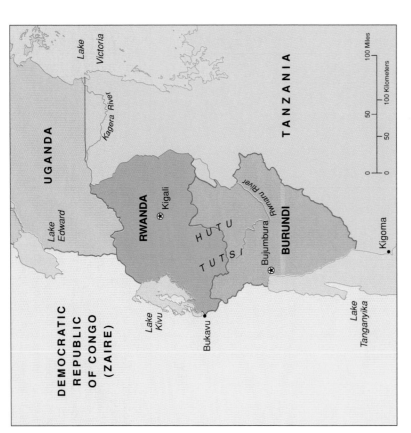

Burundi and Rwanda : Like most sub-Saharan African countries, Burundi and Rwanda were creations of the colonial era of the nineteenth century, first part of German East Africa and, after the First World War, controlled by Belgium. The European colonial powers that divided up Africa did so without regard for existing tribal/cultural/linguistic boundaries. When the European powers withdrew, the countries that were left behind often contained severe tribal factionalism. In the region of Burundi and Rwanda, independence from Belgium meant the onset of conflict between the Tutsi tribe, only about 10% of the population but the historically dominant group, owning most of the land and livestock, and the Hutu majority who were formerly peasants on Tutsi land. The carnage that has resulted is massive even by African standards: over 500,000 deaths from military conflict and over 2 million refugees in adjacent areas of Tanzania.

Sri Lanka: The island state of Sri Lanka, historically known as Ceylon, is potentially one of the most agriculturally productive regions of Asia. Unfortunately, two quite different peoples have occupied the island country: The Buddhist Sinhalese originally from northern India and long the dominant population in Sri Lanka, and the minority Hindu Tamil, a Dravidian people from south India. Since independence from Britain, Sri Lankan governments have sought to "resettle" the Tamil population in south India, actions that finally precipitated an armed rebellion by Tamils against the Sinhalese-dominated government. The Tamils at present are demanding a complete separation of the state into two parts, with a Tamil homeland in the north and along the east coast. At one time viewed as an island paradise, Sri Lanka is now a troubled country with an uncertain future.

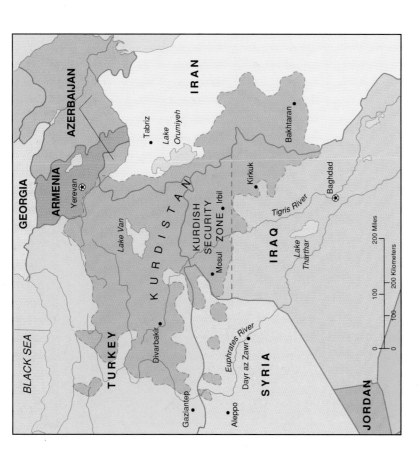

Iraq and Kurdistan: Where Turkey, Iran, and Iraq meet in the high mountain region of the Tauros and Zagros mountains, a nation of 25 million people exists. This nation is the Kurds, the occupants of this area for over 3,000 years but having no state, and receiving considerably less attention than other stateless nations like the Palestinians. Following the 1991 Gulf War between Iraq and a U.S.-led coalition of European and Arabic states, the United Nations demarcated a Kurdish "security zone" in northern Iraq. Continually under attack from Iraq to the south and beset internally by militant extremist groups like the Kurdish Workers party, the security zone is anything but. Unless three powerful states —Turkey, Iran, and Iraq—could be persuaded to give up major portions of their territory for the establishment of an independent Kurdistan, the security zone arrangement may be the closest the Kurds come to their ambition of territorial integrity and independence.

Map 24 Nations with Nuclear Weapons

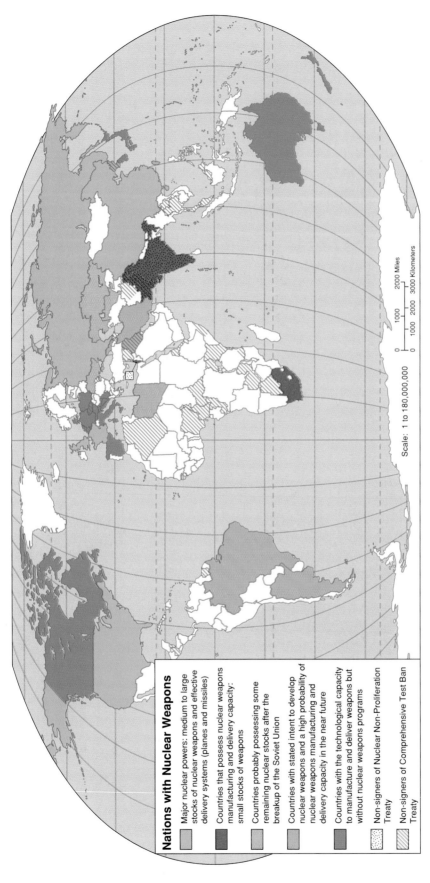

Nations with Nuclear Weapons

Major nuclear powers: medium to large stocks of nuclear weapons and effective delivery systems (planes and missiles)

Countries that possess nuclear weapons manufacturing and delivery capacity: small stocks of weapons

Countries probably possessing some remaining nuclear stocks after the breakup of the Soviet Union

Countries with stated intent to develop nuclear weapons and a high probability of nuclear weapons manufacturing and delivery capacity in the near future

Countries with the technological capacity to manufacture and deliver weapons but without nuclear weapons programs

Non-signers of Nuclear Non-Proliferation Treaty

Non-signers of Comprehensive Test Ban Treaty

Scale: 1 to 180,000,000

0   1000   2000 Miles
0   1000   2000   3000 Kilometers

Since 1980, the number of countries possessing the capacity to manufacture and deliver nuclear weapons has grown dramatically, increasing the chances of accidental nuclear exchanges. In addition to the traditional nuclear powers of the United States, Russia, China, the United Kingdom, and France, some newly independent former Soviet republics (Ukraine, Kazakhstan, Uzbekistan, and Georgia) may retain some of the weapons systems from the old Soviet Union. Also, four other countries are now judged by many authorities to possess nuclear weapons capability: Israel, India, Pakistan, and South Africa. While the stockpile of weapons of these countries is small (ranging from a minimum of 5–10 weapons in Pakistan to a maximum of 50–200 weapons in Israel), the proliferation of countries capable of using nuclear warheads in wartime threatens global security. In addition to countries that already possess the capacity to make and deliver nuclear weapons, seven other countries—Argentina, Brazil, Iran, Iraq, Libya, North Korea, and Taiwan—have or recently have had active nuclear weapons programs and may possess nuclear weapons capacity by the year 2000. Finally, there are countries—virtually all of them in the developed economies of the world—that possess the technological capacity to manufacture nuclear weapons and delivery systems but have chosen not to develop nuclear weapons programs. These countries include, among others, Canada, most western and eastern European countries (other than Britain or France), South Korea, Japan, Australia, and New Zealand.

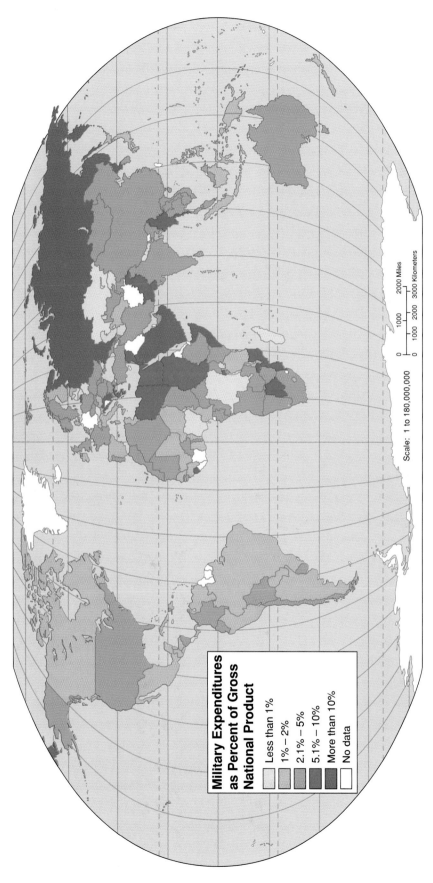

Scale: 1 to 180,000,000

Military Expenditures as Percent of Gross National Product

- Less than 1%
- 1% – 2%
- 2.1% – 5%
- 5.1% – 10%
- More than 10%
- No data

Many countries devote a significant proportion of their total central governmental expenditures to defense: weapons, personnel, and research and development of military hardware. A glance at the map reveals that there are a number of regions in which defense expenditures are particularly high, reflecting the degree of past and present political tension between countries. The clearest example is the Middle East. The steady increase in military expenditures by developing countries is one of the most alarming (and least well known) worldwide defense issues. Where the end of the cold war has meant a substantial reduction of military expenditures for the countries in North America and Europe and for Russia, in many of the world's developing countries military expenditures have risen between 15 percent and 20 percent per year for the past few years, averaging out to 7.5 percent per year for the past quarter century. Even though many developing countries still spend less than 5 percent of their gross national product on defense, these funds could be put to different uses in such human development areas as housing, land reform, health care, and education.

Map 26 Size of Armed Forces

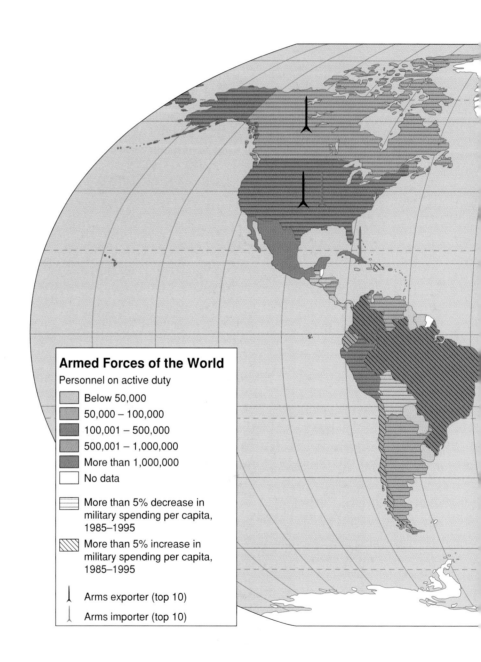

Armed Forces of the World

Personnel on active duty

- Below 50,000
- 50,000 – 100,000
- 100,001 – 500,000
- 500,001 – 1,000,000
- More than 1,000,000
- No data

More than 5% decrease in military spending per capita, 1985–1995

More than 5% increase in military spending per capita, 1985–1995

Arms exporter (top 10)

Arms importer (top 10)

While the size of a country's armed forces is still an indicator of national power on the international scene, it is no longer as important as it once was. The increasing high technology of military hardware allows smaller numbers of military personnel to be more effective. There are some countries, such as China, with massive numbers of military personnel but with relatively limited military power because of a lack of modern weaponry. Additionally, the use of rapid transportation allows personnel to be deployed about the globe or any region of it quickly; this also increases effectiveness of highly trained and well-armed smaller military units. Nevertheless, the world is still a long way from the predicted "push-button warfare" that many

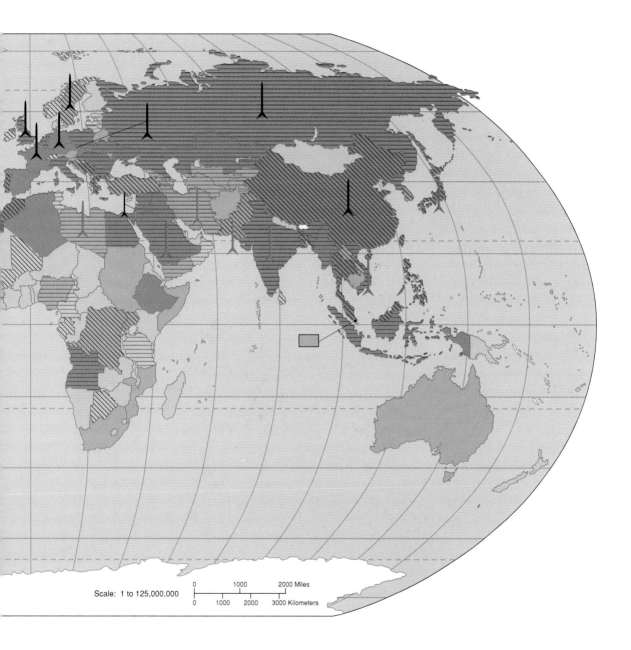

experts have long anticipated. Indeed, the pattern of the last few years has been for most military conflicts to involve ground troops engaged in fairly traditional patterns of operation. Even in the Persian Gulf conflict, with its highly-publicized "smart bombs," the bulk of the military operation that ended the conflict was carried out by infantry and armor operating on the ground and supported by traditional air cover using conventional weaponry. Thus, while the size of a country's armed forces may not be as important as it once was, it is still a major factor in measuring the ability of nations to engage successfully in armed conflict.

Map ‖ 27 ‖ Political Boundary Types

Antecedent: Antecedent boundaries are those that existed as part of the cultural landscape before the establishment of political territories. The boundary between Spain and France is the crest of the Pyrenees Mountains, long a cultural and linguistic barrier and a region of sparse population that appears on population density maps even at the world scale.

Subsequent: Subsequent boundaries are those that develop along with the cultural landscape of a region, part of a continuing evolution of political territory to match cultural region. The border region between Vietnam and China has developed over thousands of years of adjustment of territory between the two different cultural realms. Following the end of the Vietnam War, a lengthy border conflict between Vietnam and China suggests that the process is not yet completed.

Superimposed: Superimposed boundaries are drawn arbitrarily across a uniform or homogenous cultural landscape. These boundaries often result from the occupation of territory by an expansive settlement process (see, for example, many of the boundaries of the western states in the United States) or from the process whereby colonial powers divided territory to suit their own needs rather than those of the indigenous population. The borders of Egypt, Libya, and Sudan meet in the center of a uniform cultural and physical region, artificially dividing what from a natural and human perspective is unified.

Relict: A relict boundary is like a relict landscape. The boundary between the former North and South Vietnam, along the Ben Hai River, is an example of a relict boundary. So too is the dividing line between the former Federal Republic of Germany (West Germany) and the German Democratic Republic (East Germany). Germany has been unified since 1990, with reintegration of the former Communist East into the west economy happening progressively and more rapidly than expected. Nevertheless, there are still significant and visible differences between the urban German west and the rural east, between a progressive and modern economic landscape and a deteriorating one.

Map 28 Political Systems

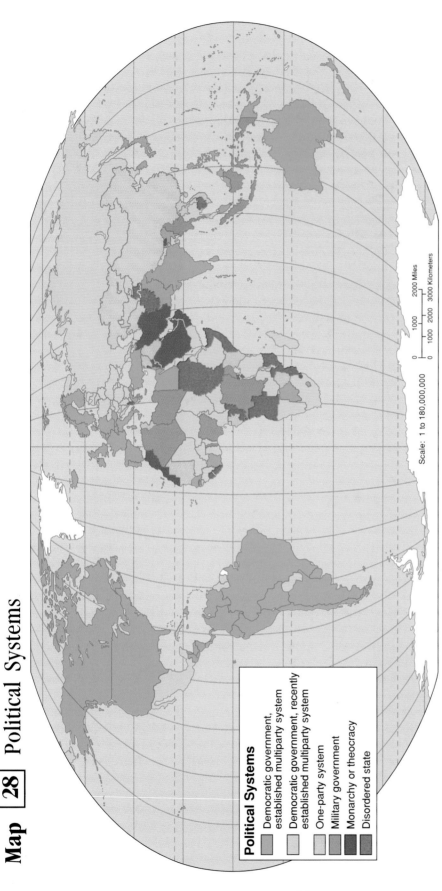

Political Systems

- Democratic government, established multiparty system
- Democratic government, recently established multiparty system
- One-party system
- Military government
- Monarchy or theocracy
- Disordered state

Scale: 1 to 180,000,000

0   1000   2000 Miles

0   1000 2000 3000 Kilometers

World political systems have changed dramatically during the 1990s and may change even more in the future. The categories of political systems shown on the map are subject to some interpretation: established multiparty democracies are those in which elections by secret ballot with adult suffrage are and have been long-term features of the political landscape; recently established multiparty democracies are those in which the characteristic features of multiparty democracies have only recently emerged. The former Soviet satellites of eastern Europe and the republics that formerly constituted the USSR are in this category; so are states in emerging regions that are beginning to throw off the single-party rule that often followed the violent upheavals of the immediate postcolonial governmental transitions. The other categories are more or less obvious. One-party systems are states where single-party rule is constitutionally guaranteed or where a one-party regime is a fact of political

life. Monarchies are countries with heads of state who are members of a royal family; note that a number of countries that have monarchs, such as the U.K. and the Netherlands, do not fall into this category because the monarchs are titular heads of state only. Theocracies are countries in which rule is within the hands of a priestly or clerical class; today, this means primarily fundamentalist Islamic countries such as Iran. Military governments are frequently organized around a junta that has seized control of the government from civil authority; such states are often technically transitional—that is, the military claims that it will return the reins of government to civil authority "when order is restored." Finally, "disordered states" are countries so beset by civil war or widespread ethnic conflict that no organized government can be said to exist within them.

Part III

The Global Economy

Map 29 International Trade Organizations
Map 30 Rich and Poor Countries: Gross National Product
Map 31 Gross National Product Per Capita
Map 32 Relative Wealth of Nations: Purchasing Power Parity
Map 33 International Flows of Capital
Map 34 Economic Output Per Sector
Map 35 Employment by Economic Activity
Map 36 Central Government Expenditures Per Capita
Map 37 The Indebtedness of States
Map 38 Exports of Primary Products
Map 39 Dependence on Trade

Map 29 International Trade Organizations

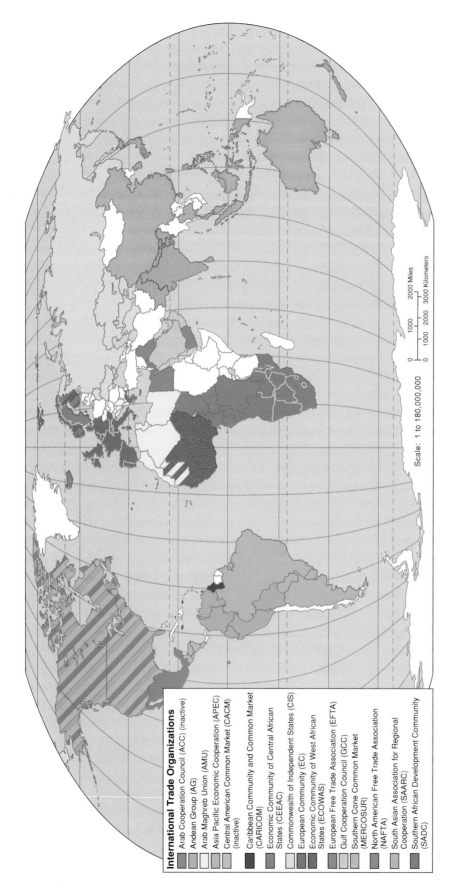

International Trade Organizations

- Arab Cooperation Council (ACC) (inactive)
- Andean Group (AG)
- Arab Maghreb Union (AMU)
- Asia Pacific Economic Cooperation (APEC)
- Central American Common Market (CACM) (inactive)
- Caribbean Community and Common Market (CARICOM)
- Economic Community of Central African States (CEEAC)
- Commonwealth of Independent States (CIS)
- European Community (EC)
- Economic Community of West African States (ECOWAS)
- European Free Trade Association (EFTA)
- Gulf Cooperation Council (GCC)
- Southern Cone Common Market (MERCOSUR)
- North American Free Trade Association (NAFTA)
- South Asian Association for Regional Cooperation (SAARC)
- Southern African Development Community (SADC)

Scale: 1 to 180,000,000

0   1000   2000 Miles

0   1000   2000   3000 Kilometers

One of the most pervasive influences in the global economy over the last half century has been the rapid rise of international trade organizations. Pioneered by the European Economic Community, founded in part to assist in rebuilding the European economy after the Second World War, these organizations have become major players in global movements of goods, services, and labor. Some, like the European Community, are leading to financial and political union. Others, like the Commonwealth of Independent States are attempts to hold on to the remnants of better economic times. Still others, like the Asia Pacific Economic Cooperation, are infant organizations that incorporate vastly different regions, states, and even economic systems, and are attempts to anticipate the direction of future economic growth. The role of the international trade organizations is likely to grow greater in the opening decades of the twenty-first century.

Map 30 Rich and Poor Countries: Gross National Product

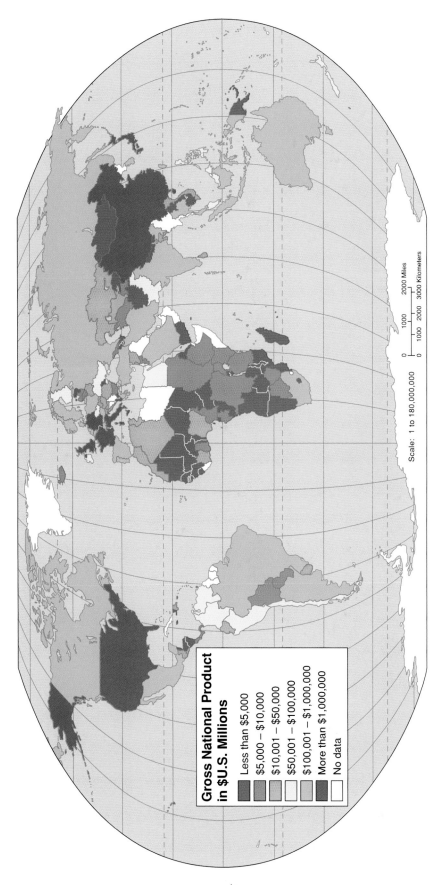

Gross National Product in $U.S. Millions

- Less than $5,000
- $5,000 − $10,000
- $10,001 − $50,000
- $50,001 − $100,000
- $100,001 − $1,000,000
- More than $1,000,000
- No data

Scale: 1 to 180,000,000

0   1000   2000 Miles

0   1000   2000   3000 Kilometers

Gross National Product (GNP) is the value of all the goods and services produced by a country, including its net income from abroad, during a year. Although GNP is commonly used to measure relative levels of economic well-being, it is often misleading and incomplete: it does not, for example, take into account environmental deterioration, the accumulation or degradation of human and social capital, or the value of household work. In spite of its deficiencies, however, GNP is still a reasonable way to illustrate the vast differences in wealth that separate the poorest countries from the richest (as long as you keep in mind that GNP provides no measure of the distribution of wealth within a country). One of the more striking features of the map is the evidence that such a small number of countries possess so much of the world's wealth.

Map [31] Gross National Product Per Capita

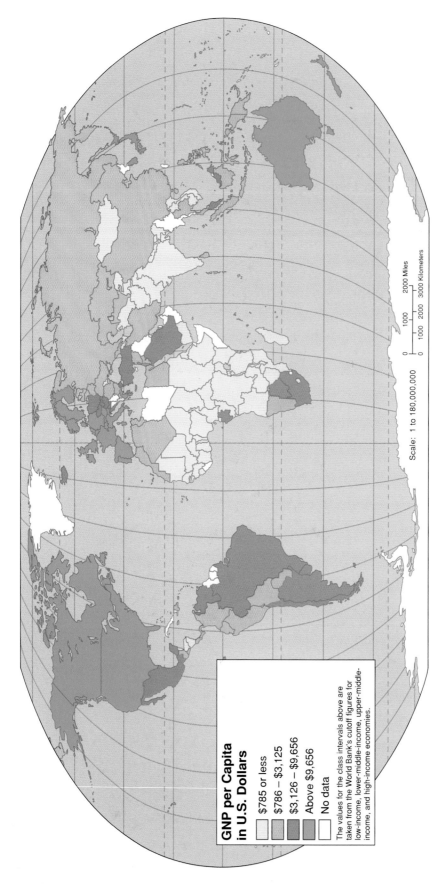

GNP per Capita in U.S. Dollars

- $785 or less
- $786 – $3,125
- $3,126 – $9,656
- Above $9,656
- No data

The values for the class intervals above are taken from the World Bank's cutoff figures for low-income, lower-middle-income, upper-middle-income, and high-income economies.

Scale: 1 to 180,000,000

0   1000   2000 Miles

0   1000   2000   3000 Kilometers

Gross National Product in either absolute or per capita form should be used cautiously as a yardstick of economic strength, because it does not measure the distribution of wealth among a population. There are countries (most notably, the oil-rich countries of the Middle East) where per capita GNP is high but where the bulk of the wealth is concentrated in the hands of a few individuals, leaving the remainder in poverty. Even within countries in which wealth is more evenly distributed (such as those in North America or western Europe), there is a tendency for dollars or pounds sterling or francs or marks to concentrate in the bank accounts of a relatively small percentage of the population. Yet the maldistribution of wealth tends to be greatest in the less developed countries, where the per capita GNP is far lower than in North America and western Europe, and poverty is widespread. In fact, a map of GNP per capita offers a reasonably good picture of comparative economic well-being. It should be noted that a low per capita GNP does not automatically condemn a country to low levels of basic human needs and services. There are a few countries, such as Costa Rica and Sri Lanka, that have relatively low per capita GNP figures but rank comparatively high in other measures of human well-being, such as average life expectancy, access to medical care, and literacy.

Map 32 Relative Wealth of Nations: Purchasing Power Parity

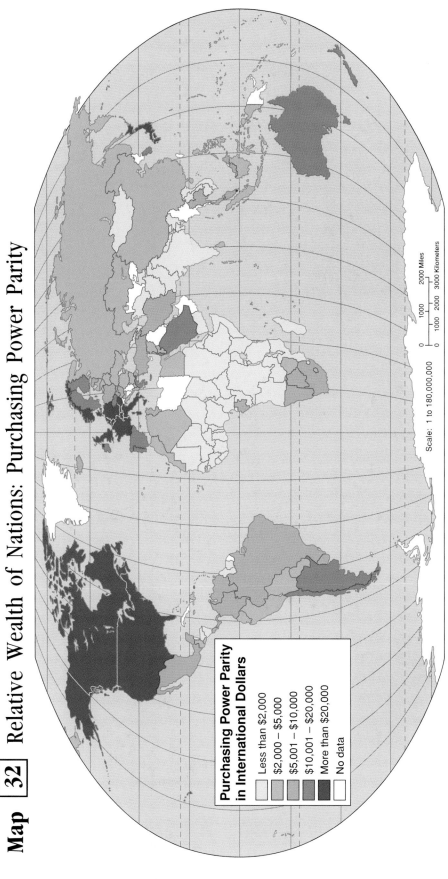

**Purchasing Power Parity
in International Dollars**

- Less than $2,000
- $2,000 – $5,000
- $5,001 – $10,000
- $10,001 – $20,000
- More than $20,000
- No data

Scale: 1 to 180,000,000

```
0        1000        2000 Miles
0   1000  2000  3000 Kilometers
```

Of all the economic measures that separate the "haves" from the "have-nots," perhaps per capita Purchasing Power Parity (PPP) is the most meaningful. While per capita figures can mask significant uneven distributions within a country, they are generally useful for demonstrating important differences between countries. Per capita GNP and GDP (Gross Domestic Product) figures, and even per capita income, have the limitation of seldom reflecting the true purchasing power of a country's currency at home. In order to get around this limitation, international economists seeking to compare national currencies developed the PPP measure, which shows the level of goods and services that holders of a country's money can acquire locally. By converting all currencies to the "international dollar," the World Bank and other organizations using PPP can now show more truly comparative values, since the new currency value shows the number of units of a country's currency required to buy the same quantity of goods and services in the local market as one U.S. dollar would buy in an average country. The use of PPP currency values can alter the perceptions about a country's true comparative position in the world economy. More than per capita income figures, PPP provides a valid measurement of the ability of a country's population to provide for itself the things that people in the developed world take for granted: adequate food, shelter, clothing, education, and access to medical care. A glance at the map shows a clear-cut demarcation between temperate and tropical zones, with most of the countries with a PPP above $5,000 in the midlatitude zones and most of those with lower PPPs in the tropical and equatorial regions. Where exceptions to this pattern occur, they usually stem from a tremendous maldistribution of wealth among a country's population.

Map ‖33‖ International Flows of Capital

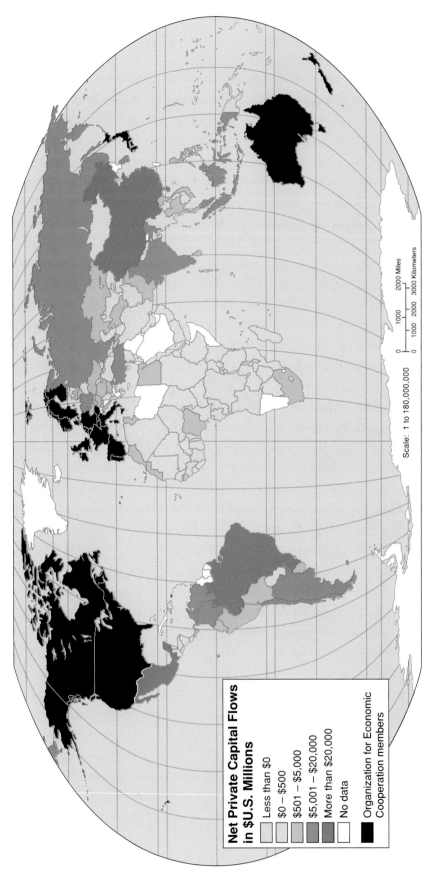

Net Private Capital Flows in $U.S. Millions

- Less than $0
- $0 – $500
- $501 – $5,000
- $5,001 – $20,000
- More than $20,000
- No data
- Organization for Economic Cooperation members

Scale: 1 to 180,000,000

0   1000   2000   2000 Miles
0   1000   2000   3000 Kilometers

International capital flows include private debt and nondebt flows from one country to another, shown on the map as flows into a country. Nearly all of the capital comes from those countries that are members of the Organization for Economic Cooperation and Development (OECD), shown in black on the map. Capital flows include commercial bank lending, bonds, other private credits, foreign direct investment, and portfolio investment. Most of these flows are indicators of the increasing influence developed countries exert over the developing economies. Foreign direct investment or FDI, for example, is a measure of the net inflow of investment monies used to acquire long-term management interest in businesses located somewhere other than in the economy of the investor. Usually this means the acquisition of at least 10% of the stock of a company by a foreign investor and is, then, a measure of what might be termed "economic colonialism": control of a region's economy by foreign investors that could, in the world of the future, be as significant as colonial political control was in the past. International capital flows have increased greatly in the last decade as the result of the increasing liberalization of developing countries, the strong economic growth exhibited by many developing countries, and the falling costs and increased efficiency of communication and transportation services.

Map 34 Economic Output Per Sector

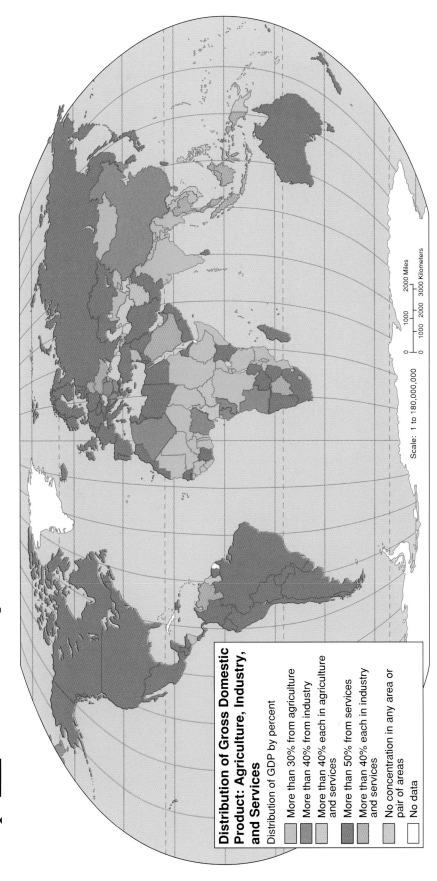

Distribution of Gross Domestic Product: Agriculture, Industry, and Services

Distribution of GDP by percent

- More than 30% from agriculture
- More than 40% from industry
- More than 40% each in agriculture and services
- More than 50% from services
- More than 40% each in industry and services
- No concentration in any area or pair of areas
- No data

Scale: 1 to 180,000,000

0   1000   2000 Miles

0   1000   2000   3000 Kilometers

The percentage of the gross domestic product (the final output of goods and services produced by the domestic economy, including net exports of goods and nonfactor—nonlabor, noncapital—services) that is devoted to agricultural, industrial, and service activities is considered a good measure of the level of economic development. In general, countries with more than 40 percent of their GDP derived from agriculture are still in a "colonial dependency" economy—that is, raising agricultural goods primarily for the export market and dependent upon that market (usually the richer countries). Similarly, countries with more than 40 percent of GDP devoted to both agriculture and services often emphasize resource extractive (primarily mining and forestry) activities. These also tend to be "colonial dependency" countries, providing raw materials for foreign markets. Countries with more than 40 percent of their GDP obtained from industry are normally well along the path to economic development. Countries with more than half of their GDP based on service activities fall into two ends of the development spectrum. On the one hand are countries heavily dependent upon both extractive activities and tourism and other low-level service functions. On the other hand are countries that can properly be termed "postindustrial": they have already passed through the industrial stage of their economic development and now rely less on the manufacture of products than on finance, research, communications, education, and other service-oriented activities.

Map 35 Employment by Economic Activity

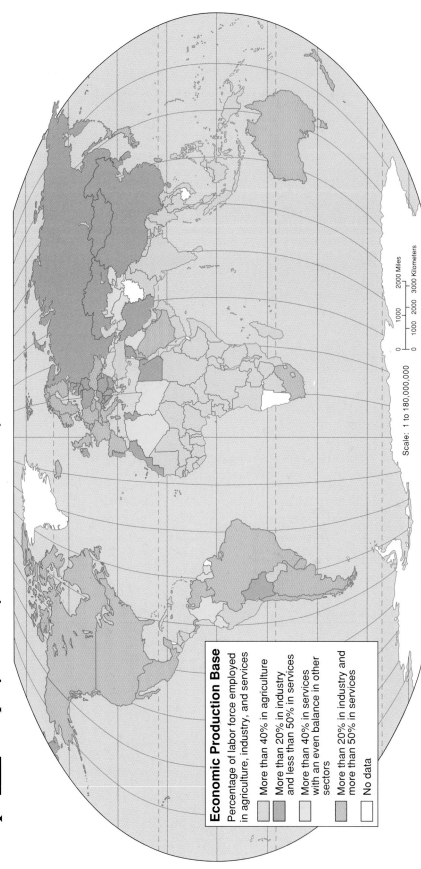

Economic Production Base

Percentage of labor force employed in agriculture, industry, and services

More than 40% in agriculture

More than 20% in industry and less than 50% in services

More than 40% in services with an even balance in other sectors

More than 20% in industry and more than 50% in services

No data

Scale: 1 to 180,000,000

0   1000   2000 Miles

0   1000   2000   3000 Kilometers

The employment structure of a country's population is one of the best indicators of the country's position on the scale of economic development. At one end of the scale are those countries with more than 40 percent of their labor force employed in agriculture. These are almost invariably the least developed, with high population growth rates, poor human services, significant environmental problems, and so on. In the middle of the scale are two types of countries: those with more than 20 percent of their labor force employed in industry and those with a fairly even balance among agricultural, industrial, and service employment but with at least 40 percent of their labor force employed in service activities. Generally, these countries have undergone the industrial revolution fairly recently and are still developing an industrial base while building up their service activities. This category also includes countries with a disproportionate share of their economies in service activities primarily related to resource extraction. On the other end of the scale from the agricultural economies are countries with more than 20 percent of their labor force employed in industry and more than 50 percent in service activities. These countries are, for the most part, those with a highly automated industrial base and a highly mechanized agricultural system (the "postindustrial," developed countries). They also include, particularly in Middle and South America and Africa, industrializing countries that are also heavily engaged in resource extraction as a service activity.

Map 36 Central Government Expenditures Per Capita

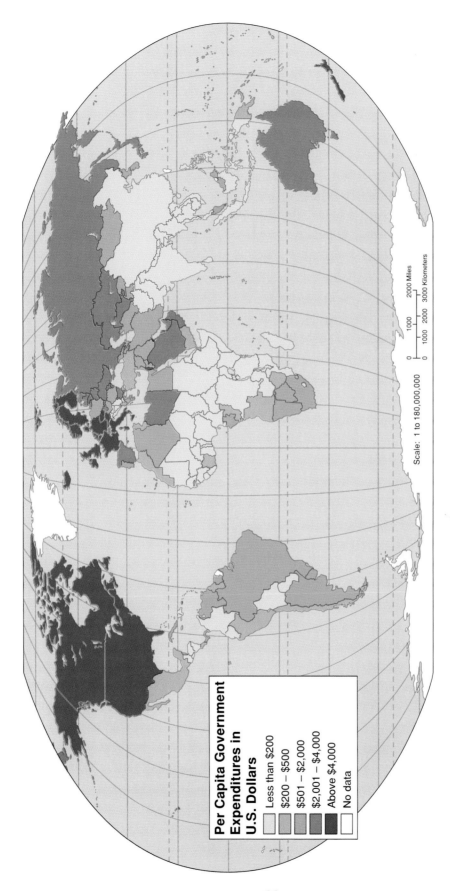

Per Capita Government Expenditures in U.S. Dollars

- Less than $200
- $200 – $500
- $501 – $2,000
- $2,001 – $4,000
- Above $4,000
- No data

Scale: 1 to 180,000,000

0 1000 2000 Miles

0 1000 2000 3000 Kilometers

The amount of money that the central government of a country spends upon a variety of essential governmental functions is a measure of relative economic development, particularly when it is viewed on a per-person basis. These functions include such governmental responsibilities as agriculture, communications, culture, defense, education, fishing and hunting, health, housing, recreation, religion, social security, transportation, and welfare. Generally, the higher the level of economic development, the greater the per capita expenditures on these services. However, the data do mask some internal variations. For example, countries that spend 20 percent or more of their central government expenditures on defense will often show up in the more developed category when, in fact, all that the figures really show is that a disproportionate amount of the money available to the government is devoted to purchasing armaments and maintaining a large standing military force. Thus, the fact that Libya spends $2,937 per capita—more than 10 times the average for Africa—does not suggest that the average Libyan is 10 times better off than the average Tanzanian. Nevertheless, this map—particularly when compared with Map 54, Energy Requirements Per Capita—does provide a reasonable approximation of economic development levels.

– 55 –

Map 37 The Indebtedness of States

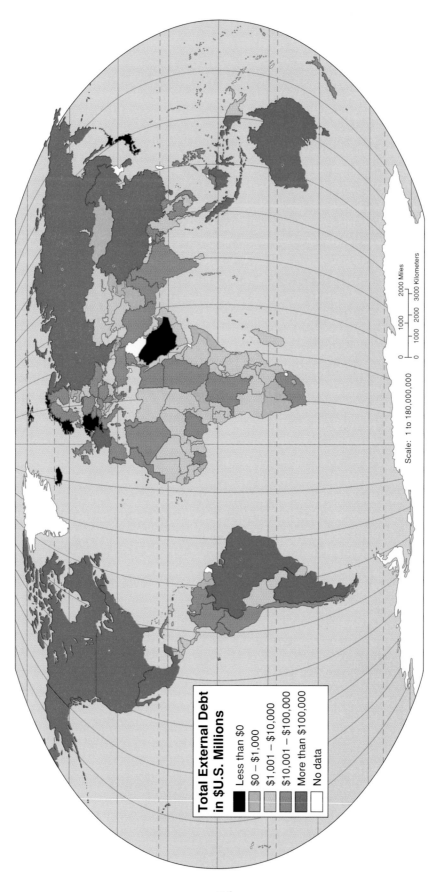

Total External Debt in $U.S. Millions

- Less than $0
- $0 – $1,000
- $1,001 – $10,000
- $10,001 – $100,000
- More than $100,000
- No data

Scale: 1 to 180,000,000

0   1000   2000 Miles

0   1000   2000   3000 Kilometers

Many governments spend more on a wide variety of services and activities than they collect in taxes and other revenues. In order to finance this deficit spending, governments borrow money—often from banks or other investors outside their country. Repayment of these debts, or even meeting interest payments on them, often means expending a country's export income—in other words, exchanging a country's wealth in production or, more often, re-sources, for debt service. Where the debt is external, as it is in most developing countries, governments become more open to outside influence in political as well as economic terms. Even internal debt service or repayment of monies owed to investors within a country gives financial establishments a measure of influence over government decisions. The amounts of debt shown on the map indicate the total external indebtedness of states.

Map 38 Exports of Primary Products

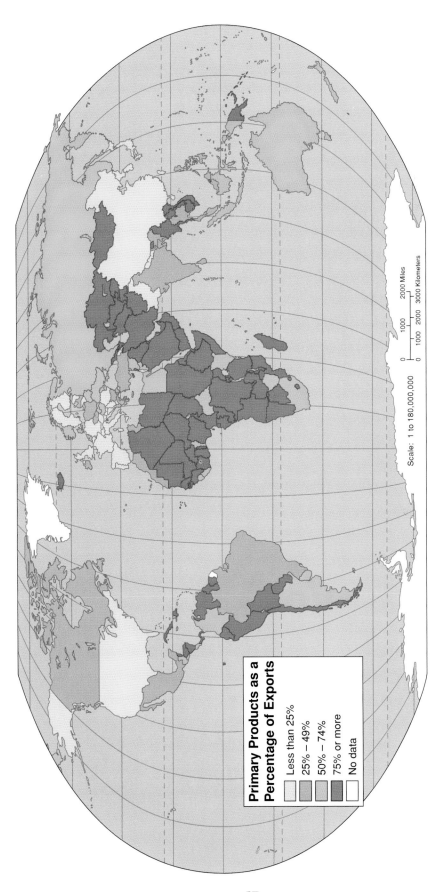

Primary Products as a Percentage of Exports

- Less than 25%
- 25% – 49%
- 50% – 74%
- 75% or more
- No data

Scale: 1 to 180,000,000

0   1000   2000 Miles

0   1000   2000   3000 Kilometers

Primary products are those that require additional processing before they enter the consumer market: metallic ores that must be converted into metals and then into metal products such as automobiles or refrigerators; forest products such as timber that must be converted to lumber before they become suitable for construction purposes; and agricultural products that require further processing before being ready for human consumption. It is an axiom in international economics that the more a country relies on primary products for its export commodities, the more vulnerable its economy is to market fluctuations. Those countries with only primary products to export are hampered in their economic growth. A country dependent on only one or two products for export revenues is unprotected from economic shifts, particularly a changing market demand for its products. Imagine what would happen to the thriving economic status of the oil-exporting states of the Persian Gulf, for example, if an alternate source of cheap energy were found. A glance at this map, together with Map 49, shows that those countries with the lowest levels of economic development tend to be concentrated on primary products and, therefore, have economies that are especially vulnerable to economic instability.

Map 39 Dependence on Trade

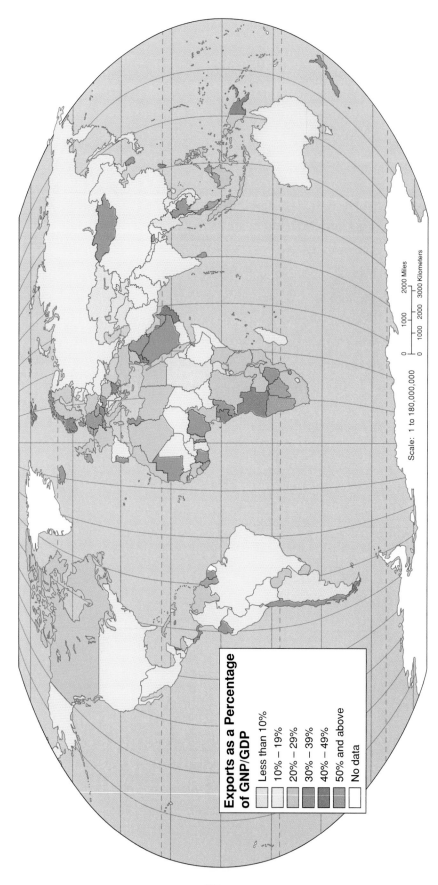

Exports as a Percentage of GNP/GDP

- Less than 10%
- 10% – 19%
- 20% – 29%
- 30% – 39%
- 40% – 49%
- 50% and above
- No data

Scale: 1 to 180,000,000

0   1000   2000 Miles
0   1000   2000   3000 Kilometers

As the global economy becomes more and more a reality, the economic strength of virtually all countries is increasingly dependent upon trade. For many developing nations, with relatively abundant resources and limited industrial capacity, exports provide the primary base upon which their economies rest. Even countries like the United States, Japan, and Germany, with huge and diverse economies, depend on exports to generate a significant percentage of their employment and wealth. Without imports, many products that consumers want would be unavailable or more expensive; without exports, many jobs would be eliminated.

Part IV

Population and Human Development

Map 40 Population Growth Rate
Map 41 Infant Mortality Rate
Map 42 Average Life Expectancy at Birth
Map 43 Population by Age Group
Map 44 Total Labor Force
Map 45 Urban Population
Map 46 Illiteracy Rates
Map 47 Unemployment and Labor Migration
Map 48 The Gender Gap: Inequalities in Education and Employment
Map 49 The Index of Human Development

Map 40 Population Growth Rate

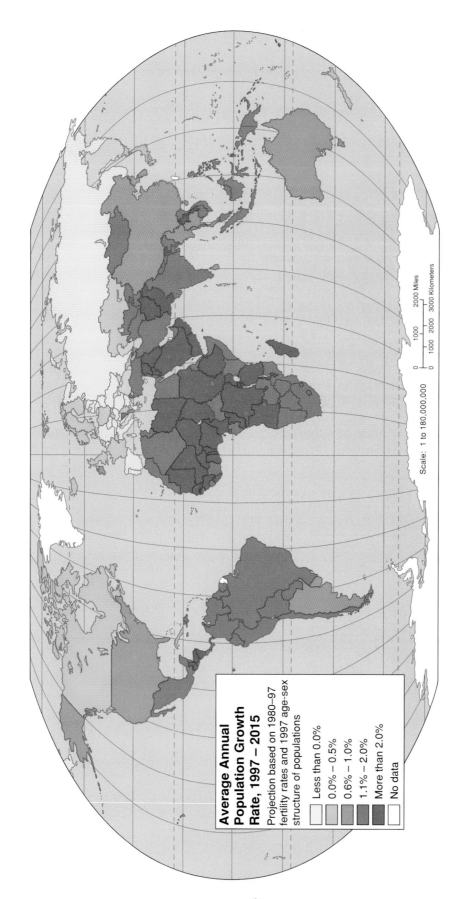

Average Annual Population Growth Rate, 1997 – 2015

Projection based on 1980–97 fertility rates and 1997 age-sex structure of populations

- Less than 0.0%
- 0.0% – 0.5%
- 0.6% – 1.0%
- 1.1% – 2.0%
- More than 2.0%
- No data

Scale: 1 to 180,000,000

0   1000   2000 Miles

0   1000   2000   3000 Kilometers

Of all the statistical measurements of human population, that of the rate of population growth is the most important. The growth rate of a population is a combination of natural change (births and deaths), in-migration, and out-migration; it is obtained by adding the number of births to the number of immigrants during a year and subtracting from that total the sum of deaths and emigrants for the same year. For a specific country, this figure will determine many things about the country's future ability to feed, house, educate, and provide medical services to its citizens. Some of the countries with the largest populations (such as India) also have high growth rates. Since these countries tend to be in developing regions, the combination of high population and high growth rates poses special problems for political stability and continuing economic development; the combination also carries heightened risks for environmental degradation. Many people believe that the rapidly expanding world population is a potential crisis that may cause environmental and human disaster by the middle of the twenty-first century.

Map 41 Infant Mortality Rate

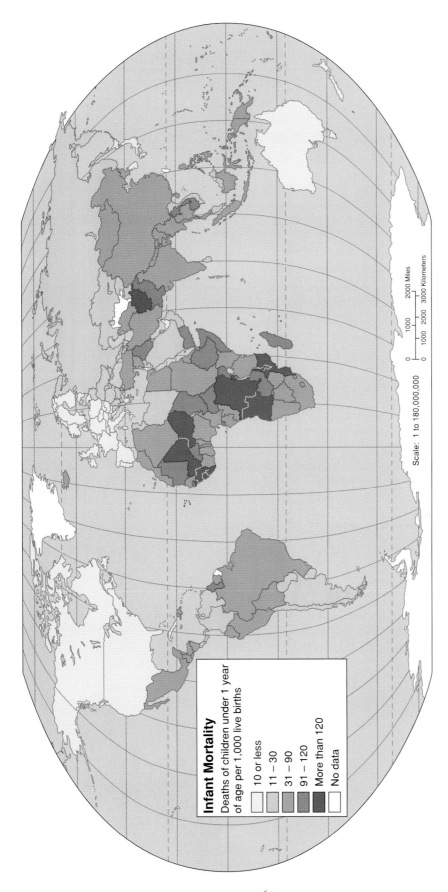

Infant Mortality
Deaths of children under 1 year of age per 1,000 live births

- 10 or less
- 11 – 30
- 31 – 90
- 91 – 120
- More than 120
- No data

Scale: 1 to 180,000,000

0   1000   2000 Miles
0 1000 2000 3000 Kilometers

Infant mortality rates are calculated by dividing the number of children born in a given year who die before their first birthday by the total number of children born that year and then multiplying by 1,000; this shows how many infants have died for every 1,000 births. Infant mortality rates are prime indicators of economic development. In highly developed economies, with advanced medical technologies, sufficient diets, and adequate public sanitation, infant mortality rates tend to be quite low. By contrast, in less developed countries, with the disadvantages of poor diet, limited access to medical technology, and the other problems of poverty, infant mortality rates tend to be

high. Although worldwide infant mortality has decreased significantly during the last 2 decades, many regions of the world still experience infant mortality above the 10 percent level (100 deaths per 1,000 live births). Such infant mortality rates represent not only human tragedy at its most basic level, but also are powerful inhibiting factors for the future of human development. Comparing infant mortality rates in the midlatitudes and the tropics shows that children in most African countries are more than 10 times as likely to die within a year of birth as children in European countries.

Map 42 Average Life Expectancy at Birth

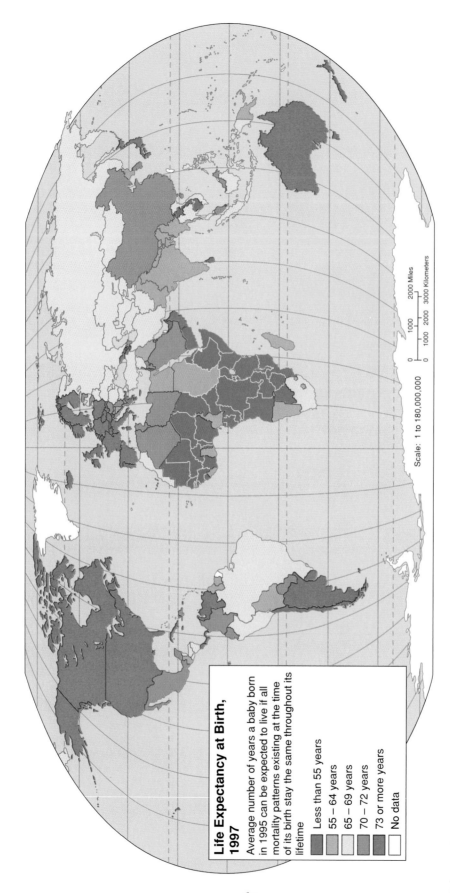

Life Expectancy at Birth, 1997

Average number of years a baby born in 1995 can be expected to live if all mortality patterns existing at the time of its birth stay the same throughout its lifetime

- Less than 55 years
- 55 – 64 years
- 65 – 69 years
- 70 – 72 years
- 73 or more years
- No data

Scale: 1 to 180,000,000

```
0        1000      2000 Miles
0   1000  2000  3000 Kilometers
```

Average life expectancy at birth is a measure of the average longevity of the population of a country. Like all average measures, it is distorted by extremes. For example, a country with a high mortality rate among children will have a low average life expectancy. Thus, an average life expectancy of 45 years does not mean that everyone can be expected to die at the age of 45. More normally, what the figure means is that a substantial number of children die between birth and 5 years of age, thus reducing the average life expectancy for the entire population. In spite of the dangers inherent in misinterpreting the data, average life expectancy (along with infant mortality and several other measures) is a valid way of judging the relative health of a population. It reflects the nature of the health care system, public sanitation and disease control, nutrition, and a number of other key human need indicators. As such, it is a measure of well-being that is significant in indicating economic development and predicting political stability.

– 62 –

Map 43 Population by Age Group

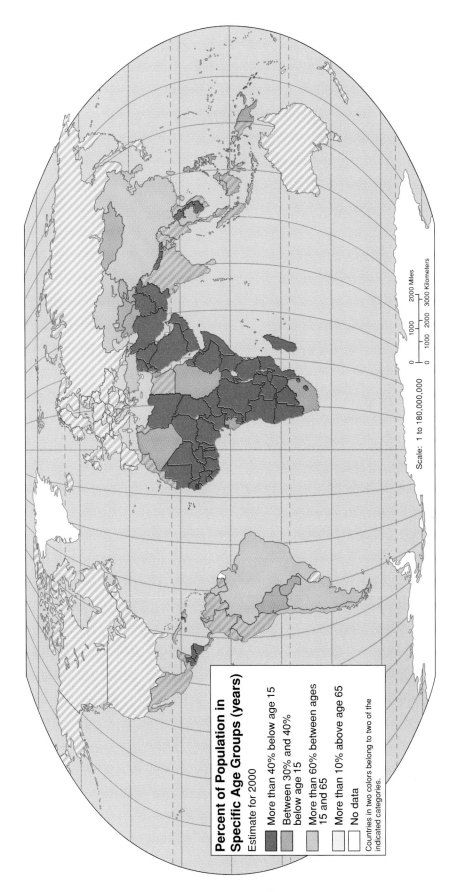

Percent of Population in Specific Age Groups (years)

Estimate for 2000

- More than 40% below age 15
- Between 30% and 40% below age 15
- More than 60% between ages 15 and 65
- More than 10% above age 65
- No data

Countries in two colors belong to two of the indicated categories.

Scale: 1 to 180,000,000

0   1000   2000 Miles

0   1000   2000   3000 Kilometers

Of all the measurements that illustrate the dynamics of a population, age distribution may be the most significant, particularly when viewed in combination with average growth rates. The particular relevance of age distribution is that it tells us what to expect from a population in terms of growth over the next generation. If, for example, approximately 40–50 percent of a population is below the age of 15, that suggests that in the next generation about one-quarter of the total population will be women of childbearing age. When age distribution is combined with fertility rates (the average number of children born per woman in a population), an especially valid measurement of future growth potential may be derived. A simple example: Nigeria, with a 1995 population of 127 million, has 47 percent of its population below the age of 15 and a fertility rate of 6.4; the United States, with a 1995 population of 263 million, has 22 percent of its population below the age of 15 and a fertility rate of 2.1. During the period in which those women presently under the age of 15 are in their childbearing years, Nigeria can be expected to add a total of approximately 197 million persons to its total population. Over the same period, the United States can be expected to add only 61 million.

Map $\boxed{44}$ Total Labor Force

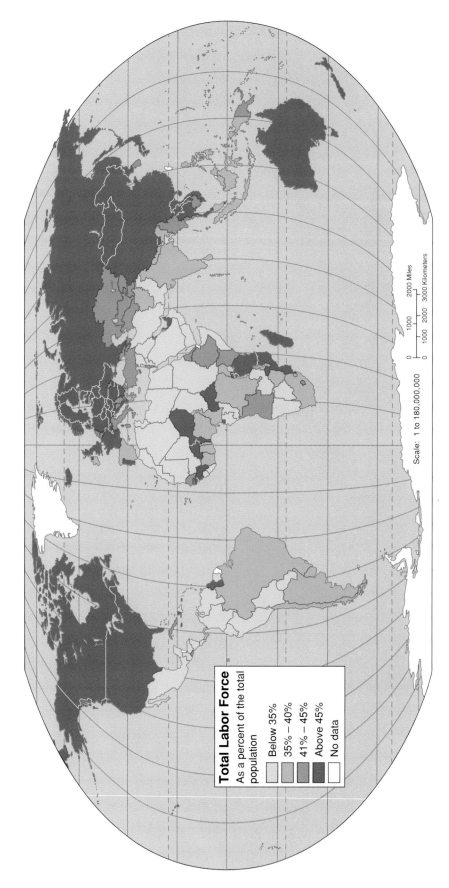

Total Labor Force

As a percent of the total population

- Below 35%
- 35% – 40%
- 41% – 45%
- Above 45%
- No data

Scale: 1 to 180,000,000

0   1000   2000 Miles

0   1000 2000 3000 Kilometers

The term *labor force* refers to the economically active portion of a population, that is, all people who work or are without work but are available for and are seeking work to produce economic goods and services. The total labor force thus includes both the employed and the unemployed (as long as they are actively seeking employment). Labor force is considered a better indicator of economic potential than employment/unemployment figures, since unemployment figures will include experienced workers with considerable potential who are temporarily out of work. Unemployment figures will also incorporate per-sons seeking employment for the first time (many recent college graduates, for example). Generally, countries with higher percentages of total population within the labor force will be countries with higher levels of economic development. This is partly a function of levels of education and training and partly a function of the age distribution of populations. In developing countries, substantial percentages of the total population are too young to be part of the labor force.

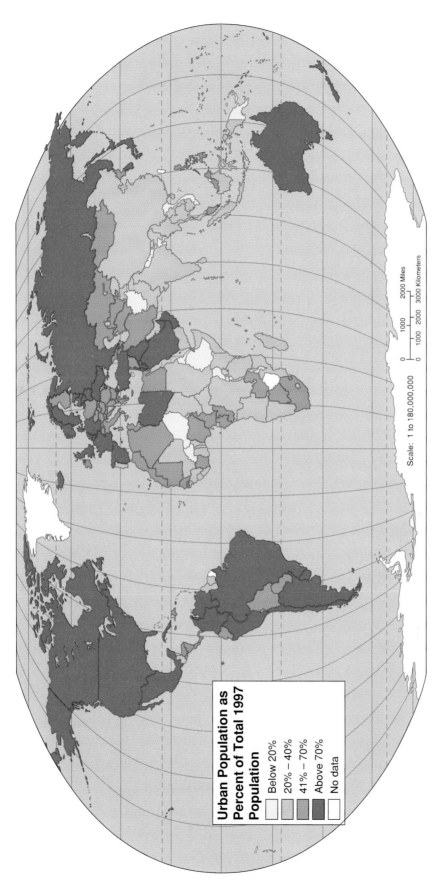

Map 45 Urban Population

Urban Population as Percent of Total 1997 Population

- Below 20%
- 20% – 40%
- 41% – 70%
- Above 70%
- No data

Scale: 1 to 180,000,000

0   1000   2000 Miles
0   1000   2000   3000 Kilometers

The proportion of a country's population that resides in urban areas was formerly considered a measure of relative economic development, with countries possessing a large urban population ranking high on the development scale and countries with a more rural population ranking low. Given the rapid rate of urbanization in developing countries, however, this traditional measure is no longer so valuable. What relative urbanization rates now tell us is something about levels of economic development in a negative sense. Latin American, African, and Asian countries with more than 40 percent of their populations living in urban areas generally suffer from a variety of problems:

rural overpopulation and flight from the land, urban poverty and despair, high unemployment, and poor public services. The rate of urbanization in less developed nations is such that many cities in these nations will outstrip those in North America and Europe by the end of this century. It has been estimated, for example, that Mexico City—now the world's second largest metropolis—may have as many as 27 million inhabitants by the year 2000. Urbanization was once viewed as an indicator of economic health and political maturity. For many countries it is instead a harbinger of potential economic and environmental disaster.

Map 46 Illiteracy Rates

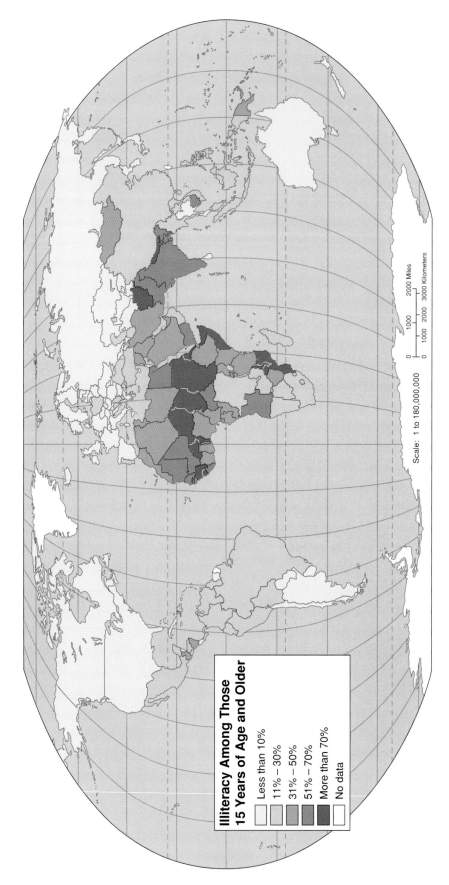

Illiteracy Among Those 15 Years of Age and Older

- Less than 10%
- 11% – 30%
- 31% – 50%
- 51% – 70%
- More than 70%
- No data

Scale: 1 to 180,000,000

0   1000   2000 Miles

0 1000 2000 3000 Kilometers

Illiteracy rates are based on the percentages of people age 15 or above (classed as adults in most countries) who are not able, with understanding, to write and read a brief, simple statement about everyday life in their home or official language. As might be expected illiteracy rates tend to be higher in the lesser-developed states where educational systems are less of a government priority. Rates of literacy or illiteracy also tend to be gender-differen-tiated, with women in many countries experiencing educational neglect or discrimination that makes it more likely they will be illiterate. In many developing countries, between five and ten times as many women will be illiterate as men and the illiteracy rate for women may even exceed 90%. Both male and female illiteracy severely compromise economic development.

– 66 –

Map 47 Unemployment and Labor Migration

Proportion of Labor Force Unemployed 1997

- Less than 5%
- 5% – 10%
- 11% – 15%
- 16% – 20%
- More than 20%
- Labor suppliers
- Labor receivers

Scale: 1 to 180,000,000

0   1000   2000 Miles

0 1000 2000 3000 Kilometers

The percentage of a country's labor force that is classified as "unemployed" include those without work but who are available for work and seeking employment. Countries may define the labor force in different ways, however. In many developing countries, for example, "employability" based on age may be more extensive than in more highly developed economies with stringent child labor laws. Generally, countries with higher percentages of their labor forces employed will be countries with higher levels of economic development. Where unemployment tends to be high, the out-migration of labor also tends to be high as workers unable to find employment at home cross international boundaries in search of work. Again, there tends to be a difference based on levels of economic development with the more developed countries experiencing inflows of labor while the reverse is true in the lesser-developed world.

Map 48 The Gender Gap: Inequalities in Education and Employment

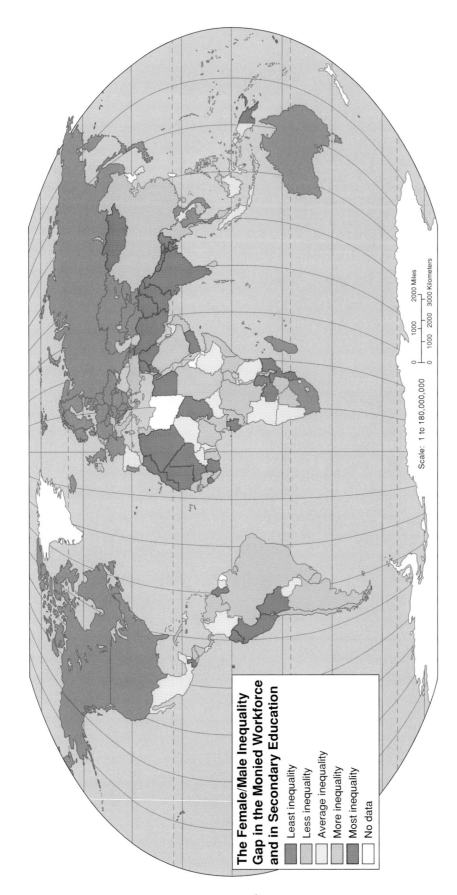

The Female/Male Inequality Gap in the Monied Workforce and in Secondary Education

- Least inequality
- Less inequality
- Average inequality
- More inequality
- Most inequality
- No data

Scale: 1 to 180,000,000

0   1000   2000 Miles

0   1000   2000   3000 Kilometers

While women in developed countries, particularly in North America and Europe, have made significant advances in socioeconomic status in recent years, in most of the world females suffer from significant inequality when compared with their male counterparts. Although women have received the right to vote in most of the world's countries, in over 90 percent of these countries that right has only been granted in the last 50 years. In most regions, literacy rates for women still fall far short of those for men; in Africa and Asia, for example, only about half as many women are as literate as men. Women marry considerably younger than men and attend school for shorter periods of time. Inequalities in education and employment are perhaps the most telling indicators of the unequal status of women in most of the world. Lack of secondary education in comparison with men prevents women from entering the workforce with equally high-paying jobs. Even where women are employed in positions similar to those held by men, they still tend to receive less compensation. The gap between rich and poor involves not only a clear geographic differentiation, but a clear gender differentiation as well.

Map 49 The Index of Human Development

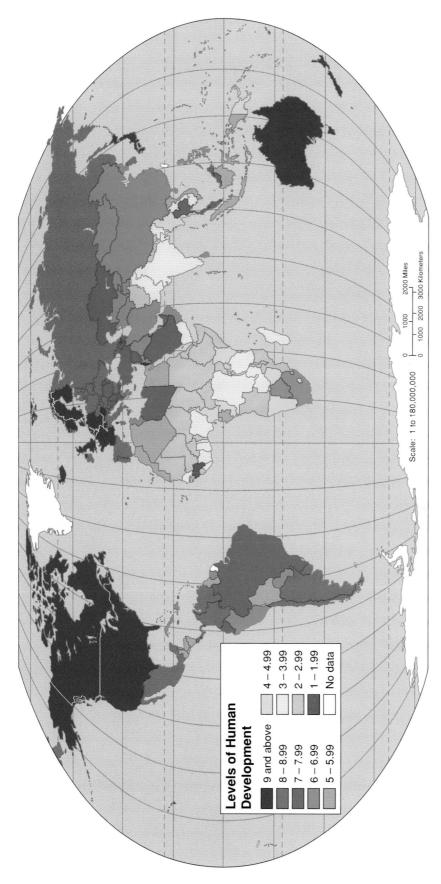

Levels of Human Development

- 9 and above
- 8 – 8.99
- 7 – 7.99
- 6 – 6.99
- 5 – 5.99
- 4 – 4.99
- 3 – 3.99
- 2 – 2.99
- 1 – 1.99
- No data

Scale: 1 to 180,000,000

0   1000   2000 Miles

0   1000 2000 3000 Kilometers

The development index upon which this map is based takes into account a wide variety of demographic, health, and educational data, including population growth, per capita gross domestic product, longevity, literacy, and years of schooling. The map reveals significant improvement in the quality of life in Middle and South America, although it is questionable whether the gains made in those regions can be maintained in the face of the dramatic population increases expected over the next 30 years. More clearly than anything else, the map illustrates the near-desperate situation in Africa and South Asia. In those regions, the unparalleled growth in population threatens to overwhelm all efforts to improve the quality of life. In Africa, for example, the population is increasing by 20 million persons per year. With nearly 45 percent of the continent's population aged 15 years or younger, this growth rate will accelerate as the women reach childbearing age. Africa, along with South Asia, faces the very difficult challenge of providing basic access to health care, education, and jobs for a rapidly increasing population. The map also illustrates the striking difference in quality of life between those who inhabit the world's equatorial and tropical regions and those fortunate enough to live in the temperate zones, where the quality of life is significantly higher.

Part V

Food, Energy, and Materials

Map 50 Production of Staples—Cereals, Roots, Tubers

Map 51 Agricultural Production Per Capita

Map 52 Calories Available as a Percentage of Need

Map 53 Energy Production Per Capita

Map 54 Energy Requirements Per Capita

Map 55 Energy Dependency

Map 56 Flows of Oil

Map 57 Production of Crucial Materials

Map 58 Consumption of Crucial Materials

Map 50 Production of Staples—Cereals, Roots, Tubers

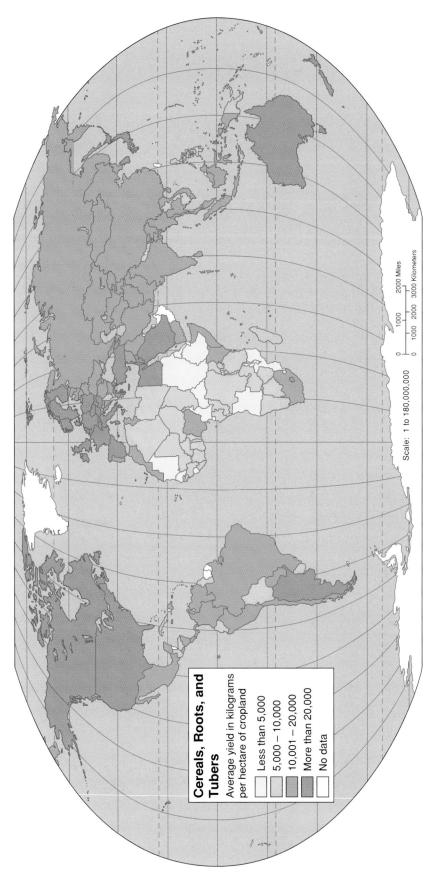

Cereals, Roots, and Tubers

Average yield in kilograms per hectare of cropland

- Less than 5,000
- 5,000 – 10,000
- 10,001 – 20,000
- More than 20,000
- No data

Scale: 1 to 180,000,000

0 · 1000 · 2000 Miles

0 · 1000 · 2000 · 3000 Kilometers

For most of the world's population, food crops (as opposed to livestock foods) provide the bulk of dietary intake. Good agricultural land is simply too scarce to be used for the inefficient process of raising food to feed animals, which, in turn, feed people. Global production of the staple (most important) food crops has increased over the last 10 years—but so has global population. In Africa, for example, despite a 30 percent increase in staple crop production since 1981, per capita food output has dropped more than 5 percent because of population growth that is faster than the growth in agricultural output. The map illustrates considerable regional differences in outputs of food staples per areal unit of cropland. Globally, 1 hectare (2.47 acres) of cropland in 1990 yielded, on average, about 2.6 metric tons (2,600 kilograms or about 5,700

pounds) of cereals or about 11.8 metric tons of roots and tubers. Yet in Africa, 1 hectare yielded only 1.2 metric tons of cereals or 7.9 metric tons of roots and tubers. In Europe, on the other hand, 1 hectare yielded 4.2 tons of cereals or 21.2 metric tons of roots and tubers. Such great differences are explainable primarily in terms of agricultural inputs: different farming methods, varying levels of fertilizers, agricultural chemicals, irrigation, and machinery. The European farmer applies 2.3 times the global average of fertilizer per hectare, the African farmer only one-fifth of the global average. These conditions are not likely to change and the map may be viewed as an indicator not just of present agricultural output but of potential food production as well.

Map 51 Agricultural Production Per Capita

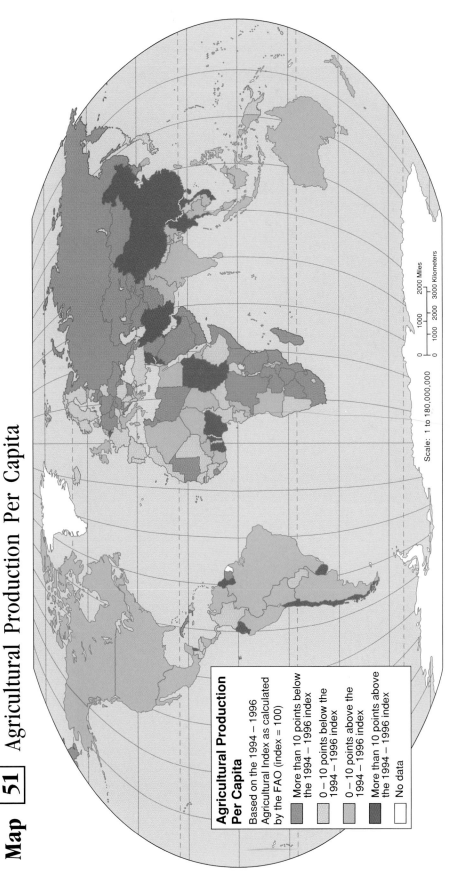

Agricultural Production Per Capita

Based on the 1994 – 1996
Agricultural Index as calculated
by the FAO (index = 100)

- More than 10 points below the 1994 – 1996 index
- 0 – 10 points below the 1994 – 1996 index
- 0 – 10 points above the 1994 – 1996 index
- More than 10 points above the 1994 – 1996 index
- No data

Scale: 1 to 180,000,000

0   1000   2000 Miles
0   1000   2000   3000 Kilometers

Agricultural production includes the value of all crop and livestock products originating within a country for the base period of 1994–1996. The index value portrays the disposable output (after deductions for livestock feed and seed for planting) of a country's agriculture in comparison with the base period 1989–1991. Thus, the production values show not only the relative ability of countries to produce food but also show whether or not that ability has in-creased or decreased over an 8-year period. In general, global food production has kept up with or very slightly exceeded population growth. However, there are significant regional variations in the trend of food production keeping up with or surpassing population growth. For example, agricultural production in Africa and in Middle America has fallen, while production in South America, Asia, and Europe has risen. In the case of Africa, the drop in production

reflects a population growing more rapidly than agricultural productivity. Where rapid increases in food production per capita exist (as in certain countries in South America, Asia, and Europe), most often the reason is the development of new agricultural technologies that have allowed food production to grow faster than population. In much of Asia, for example, the so-called Green Revolution of new, highly productive strains of wheat and rice made positive index values possible. Also in Asia, the cessation of major warfare allowed some countries (Cambodia, Laos, and Vietnam) to show substantial increases over the 1982–1984 index. In some cases, a drop in production per capita reflects government decisions to limit production in order to maintain higher prices for agricultural products. The United States and Japan fall into this category.

Map 52 Calories Available as a Percentage of Need

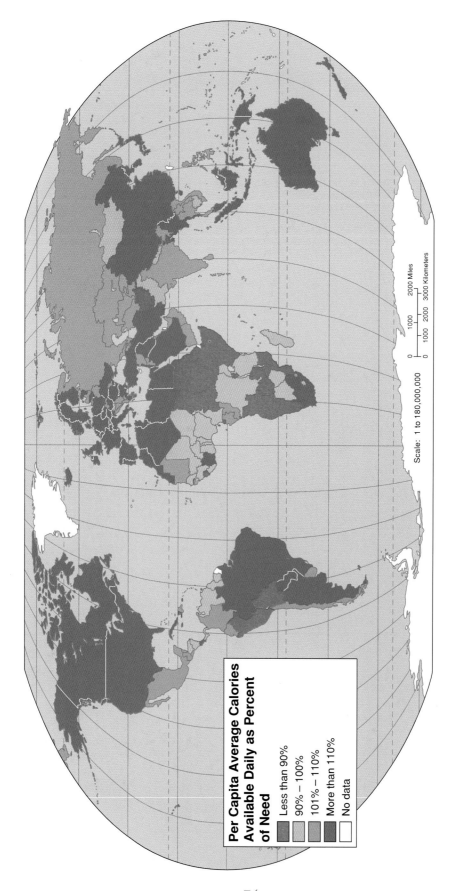

Per Capita Average Calories Available Daily as Percent of Need

- Less than 90%
- 90% – 100%
- 101% – 110%
- More than 110%
- No data

Scale: 1 to 180,000,000

0   1000   2000 Miles

0 1000 2000 3000 Kilometers

The data shown on this map, which indicate the presence or absence of critical food shortages, do not necessarily indicate the presence of starvation or famine. But they certainly do indicate potential problem areas for the next decade. The measurements are in calories from *all* food sources: domestic production, international trade, drawdown on stocks or food reserves, and direct foreign contributions or aid. The quantity of calories available is that amount, estimated by the UN's Food and Agriculture Organization (FAO), that reaches consumers. The calories actually consumed may be lower than the figures shown, depending on how much is lost in a variety of ways: in home storage (to pests such as rats and mice), in preparation and cooking, through consumption by pets and domestic animals, and as discarded foods, for example. The estimate of need is not a global uniform value but is calculated for each country on the basis of the age and sex distribution of the population and the estimated level of activity of the population. Compare this map with Map 51 for a good measure of potential problem areas for food shortages within the next decade.

Map 53 Energy Production Per Capita

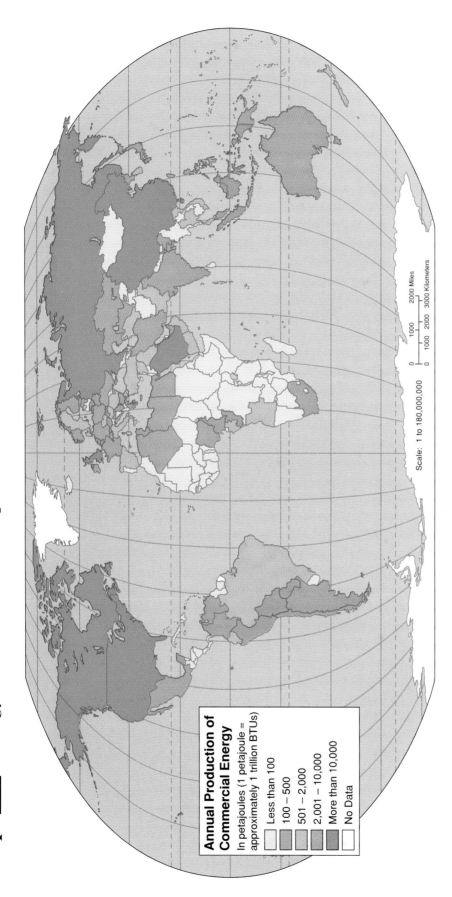

Annual Production of Commercial Energy

In petajoules (1 petajoule = approximately 1 trillion BTUs)

- Less than 100
- 100 – 500
- 501 – 2,000
- 2,001 – 10,000
- More than 10,000
- No Data

Scale: 1 to 180,000,000

0   1000   2000 Miles
0   1000   2000   3000 Kilometers

The production of commercial energy in all its forms—solid fuels (primarily coal), liquid fuels (primarily petroleum), natural gas, geothermal, wind, solar, hydroelectric, and nuclear—is a good measure of a country's ability to produce sufficient quantities of energy to meet domestic demands or to provide a healthy export commodity—or, in some instances, both. Commercial energy production is also a measure of the level of economic development, although a fairly subjective one. With exceptions, wealthier countries produce more energy from all sources than do poorer countries. Countries such as Japan and many European states rank among the world's wealthiest, but are energy-poor and produce relatively little of their own energy. They have the ability, however, to pay for it. On the other hand, countries such as those of the Persian Gulf or the oil-producing states of Middle and South America may rank relatively low on the scale of economic development but rank high as producers of energy. The map does not show the enormous amounts of energy from noncommercial sources (traditional fuels like firewood and animal dung) used by the world's poor, particularly in Middle and South America, Africa, South Asia, and East Asia. In these regions, firewood and animal dung may account for more actual energy production than coal or oil. Indeed, for many in the developing world, the real energy crisis is a shortage of wood for cooking and heating.

– 75 –

Map **54** Energy Requirements Per Capita

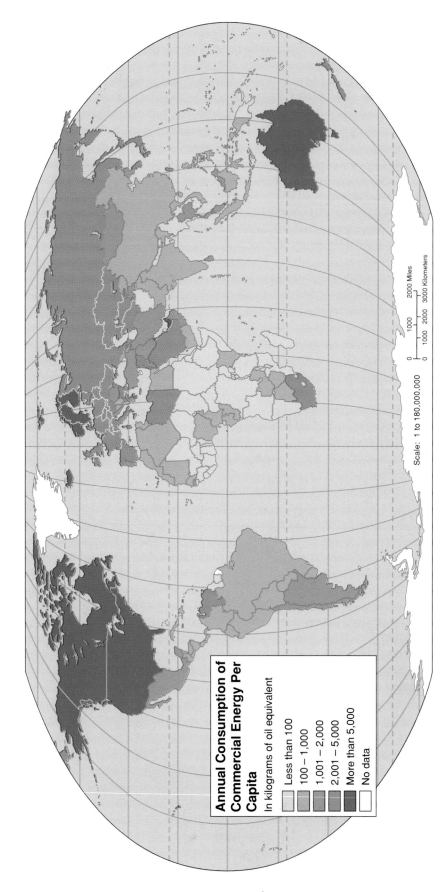

Annual Consumption of Commercial Energy Per Capita

In kilograms of oil equivalent

- Less than 100
- 100 – 1,000
- 1,001 – 2,000
- 2,001 – 5,000
- More than 5,000
- No data

Scale: 1 to 180,000,000

0	1000	2000 Miles
0	1000	2000	3000 Kilometers

Of all the quantitative measures of economic well-being, energy consumption per capita may be the most expressive. All of the countries defined by the World Bank as having high incomes consume at least 100 gigajoules of commercial energy (the equivalent of about 3.5 metric tons of coal) per person per year, with some, such as the United States and Canada, having consumption rates in the 300 gigajoule range (the equivalent of more than 10 metric tons of coal per person per year). With the exception of the oil-rich Persian Gulf states, where consumption figures include the costly "burning off" of excess energy in the form of natural gas flares at wellheads, most of the highest-consuming countries are in the Northern Hemisphere, concentrated in North America and Western Europe. At the other end of the scale are low-income countries, whose consumption rates are often less than 1 percent of those of the United States and other high consumers. These figures do not, of course, include the consumption of noncommercial energy—the traditional fuels of firewood, animal dung, and other organic matter—widely used in the less developed parts of the world.

Map 55 Energy Dependency

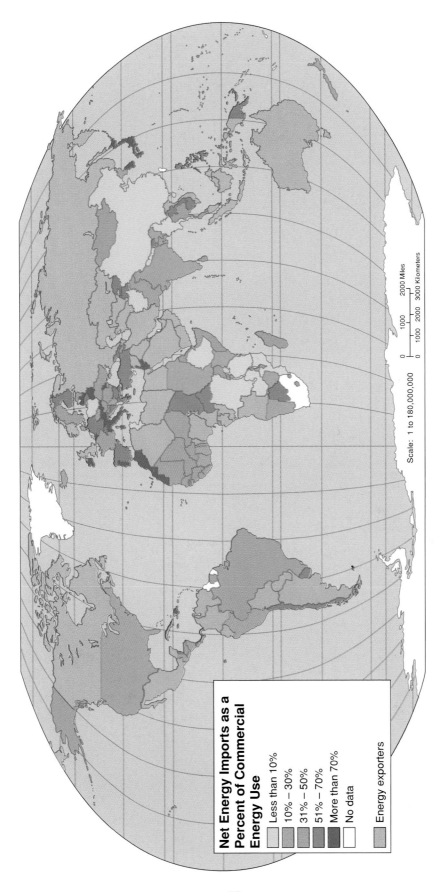

Scale: 1 to 180,000,000

Net Energy Imports as a Percent of Commercial Energy Use

- Less than 10%
- 10% – 30%
- 31% – 50%
- 51% – 70%
- More than 70%
- No data

- Energy exporters

The patterns on the map show dependence on commercial energy before transformation to other end-use fuels such as electricity or refined petroleum products; energy from traditional sources such as fuelwood or dried animal dung is not included. Energy dependency is the difference between domestic consumption and domestic production of commercial energy and is most often expressed as a net energy import or export. Less than 20% of the world's countries are net exporters of energy: most are importers. The growth in global commercial energy use over the last decade indicates growth in the modern sectors of the economy—industry, transportation, and urbanization—particularly in the lesser developed countries. Still, the primary consumers of energy—and those having the greatest dependence on foreign sources of energy—are the more highly developed countries of Europe, North America, and Japan.

Map 56 Flows of Oil

Flows of Oil in Millions of Tons per Year
Lines are approximate proportional width.

Scale: 1 to 180,000,000

0   1000   2000 Miles

0   1000   2000   3000 Kilometers

The pattern of oil movements from producing region to consuming region is one of the dominant facts of contemporary international maritime trade. Supertankers carrying a million tons of crude oil at rates in excess of $0.10 per ton per mile make the transportation of oil not only a necessity for the world's energy-hungry countries but also an enormously profitable proposition. One of the major negatives of these massive oil flows is the damage done to the oceanic ecosystems—not just from the well-publicized and dramatic events like the wrecking of the *Exxon Valdez* but from the incalculable amounts of oil from leakage, scrubbings, purgings, etc. that are a part of the oil transport technology. It is clear from the map that the primary recipients of these oil flows are the world's most highly developed economies.

Map 57 Production of Crucial Materials

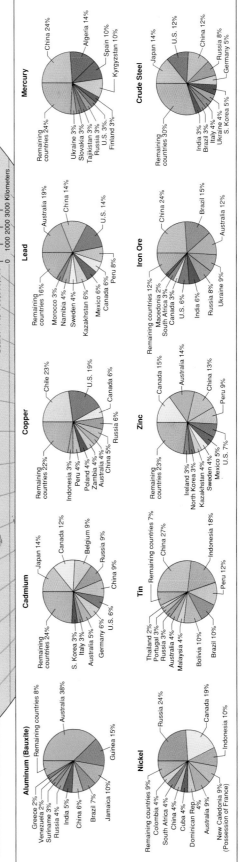

Production of Crucial Materials

- No significant production of crucial materials
- One crucial material
- Two crucial materials
- Three crucial materials
- Four crucial materials
- Five or more crucial materials

Scale: 1 to 190,000,000

0   1000 2000 3000 Kilometers

0   1000   2000 Miles

Aluminum (Bauxite)
- Remaining countries 8%
- Australia 38%
- Greece 2%
- Venezuela 2%
- Suriname 3%
- Russia 4%
- India 5%
- China 6%
- Brazil 7%
- Jamaica 10%
- Guinea 15%

Nickel
- Remaining countries 9%
- Russia 24%
- Canada 19%
- Indonesia 10%
- Colombia 4%
- South Africa 4%
- China 4%
- Cuba 4%
- Dominican Rep. 4%
- Australia 9%
- New Caledonia 9% (Possession of France)

Cadmium
- Remaining countries 24%
- Japan 14%
- Canada 12%
- Belgium 9%
- Russia 9%
- China 9%
- U.S. 6%
- Germany 6%
- Australia 5%
- Italy 3%
- S. Korea 3%

Tin
- Remaining countries 7%
- China 27%
- Indonesia 18%
- Peru 12%
- Brazil 10%
- Bolivia 10%
- Malaysia 4%
- Australia 4%
- Russia 3%
- Portugal 3%
- Thailand 2%

Copper
- Remaining countries 22%
- Chile 23%
- U.S. 19%
- Canada 6%
- Russia 6%
- China 5%
- Australia 4%
- Zambia 4%
- Poland 4%
- Peru 4%
- Indonesia 3%

Zinc
- Remaining countries 23%
- China 13%
- Canada 15%
- Australia 14%
- Peru 9%
- U.S. 7%
- Mexico 5%
- Sweden 4%
- Kazakhstan 4%
- North Korea 3%
- Ireland 3%

Lead
- Remaining countries 16%
- Australia 19%
- China 14%
- U.S. 14%
- Peru 8%
- Canada 6%
- Mexico 6%
- Kazakhstan 6%
- Sweden 4%
- Namibia 4%
- Morocco 3%

Iron Ore
- Remaining countries 12%
- China 24%
- Brazil 15%
- Australia 12%
- Ukraine 9%
- Russia 8%
- India 6%
- U.S. 6%
- Canada 3%
- South Africa 3%
- Macedonia 2%

Mercury
- Remaining countries 24%
- China 24%
- Algeria 14%
- Spain 10%
- Kyrgyzstan 10%
- Finland 3%
- U.S. 3%
- Russia 3%
- Tajikistan 3%
- Slovakia 3%
- Ukraine 3%

Crude Steel
- Remaining countries 30%
- Japan 14%
- U.S. 12%
- China 12%
- Russia 8%
- Germany 5%
- S. Korea 5%
- Ukraine 4%
- Italy 4%
- Brazil 3%
- India 3%

The data on this map portray the production of the world's most important metals for the operation of a modern industrial economy. The sector graphs across the bottom of the map show the percentage of production of crucial materials by the 10 leading countries for each of 10 materials. For copper, lead, mercury, nickel, tin, and zinc, the annual production data reflect the metal content of the ore mined. Aluminum (or bauxite ore) and iron ore production are expressed in gross weight of ore mined. Cadmium production refers to the refined metal, and crude steel production to usable ingots, cast products, and liquid steel. By comparing this map with Map 58, you will discover that some of the world's top producer nations of these critical materials are also among the world's top consumer nations.

– 79 –

Map 58 Consumption of Crucial Materials

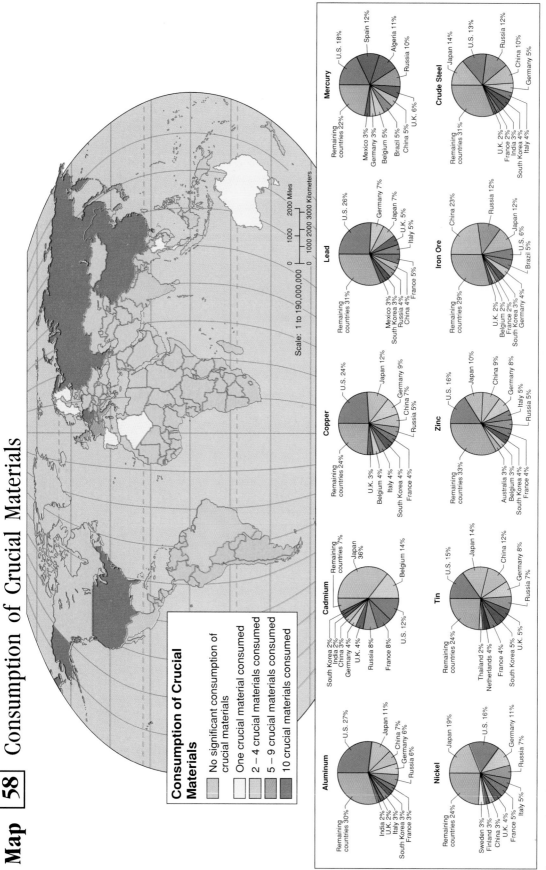

Consumption of Crucial Materials

- No significant consumption of crucial materials
- One crucial material consumed
- 2 – 4 crucial materials consumed
- 5 – 9 crucial materials consumed
- 10 crucial materials consumed

Scale: 1 to 190,000,000

0   1000   2000 Miles
0   1000 2000 3000 Kilometers

Mercury
U.S. 18%
Spain 12%
Algeria 11%
Russia 10%
U.K. 6%
China 5%
Brazil 5%
Belgium 5%
Germany 3%
Mexico 3%
Remaining countries 22%

Crude Steel
U.S. 13%
Russia 12%
China 10%
Germany 5%
Italy 4%
South Korea 4%
India 3%
France 2%
U.K. 2%
Remaining countries 31%
Japan 14%

Lead
U.S. 26%
Germany 7%
Japan 7%
U.K. 5%
Italy 5%
France 5%
China 4%
Russia 4%
South Korea 3%
Mexico 3%
Remaining countries 31%

Iron Ore
China 23%
Russia 12%
Japan 12%
U.S. 6%
Brazil 5%
Germany 4%
South Korea 3%
France 2%
Belgium 2%
U.K. 2%
Remaining countries 29%

Copper
U.S. 24%
Japan 12%
Germany 9%
China 7%
Russia 5%
France 4%
South Korea 4%
Italy 4%
Belgium 4%
U.K. 3%
Remaining countries 24%

Zinc
U.S. 16%
Japan 10%
China 9%
Germany 8%
Italy 5%
Russia 5%
France 4%
South Korea 4%
Belgium 3%
Australia 3%
Remaining countries 33%

Cadmium
Japan 36%
Belgium 14%
U.S. 12%
France 8%
Russia 8%
U.K. 4%
Germany 4%
China 3%
India 2%
South Korea 2%
Remaining countries 7%

Tin
Japan 14%
China 12%
Germany 8%
Russia 7%
U.K. 5%
South Korea 5%
France 4%
Netherlands 4%
Thailand 2%
U.S. 15%
Remaining countries 24%

Aluminum
U.S. 27%
Japan 11%
China 7%
Germany 6%
Russia 6%
France 3%
South Korea 3%
Italy 3%
U.K. 2%
India 2%
Remaining countries 30%

Nickel
Japan 19%
U.S. 16%
Germany 11%
Russia 7%
Italy 5%
France 5%
U.K. 4%
China 3%
Finland 3%
Sweden 3%
Remaining countries 24%

Consumption data refer to the domestic use of refined metals (for example, the tons of steel used in the manufacture of automobiles). Some countries rank among the top in both production and consumption, and those that do are among the most highly developed nations. The United States, for example, ranks in the top 4 consumers for each metal; but the United States also ranks in the top 10 producer countries for 7 of the metals. Many countries that rank high as producers but not as consumers have "colonial dependency" economies, producing raw materials for an export market, often at the mercy of the marketplace. Jamaica and Suriname, for example, depend extremely heavily upon the sale of bauxite ore (crude aluminum). When the United States, Japan, or Russia cuts its use of aluminum, the economies of Jamaica and Suriname crash.

Part VI

Environmental Conditions

Map 59 Deforestation and Desertification
Map 60 Soil Degradation
Map 61 Air and Water Quality
Map 62 Per Capita CO_2 Emissions

Map 59 Deforestation and Desertification

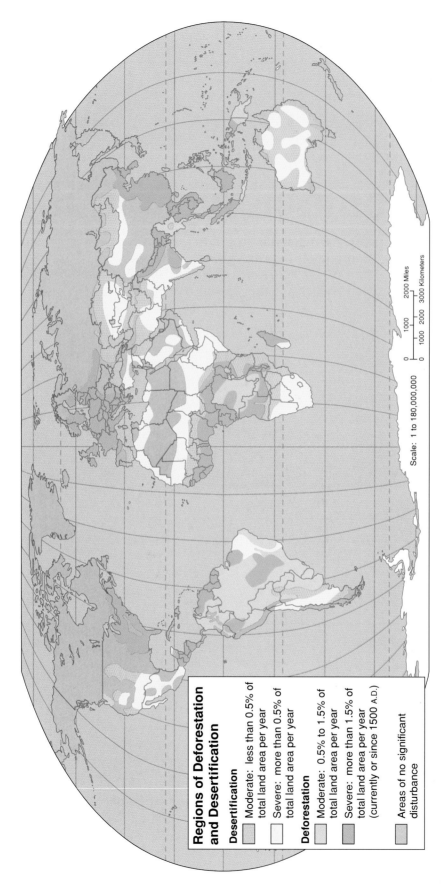

Regions of Deforestation and Desertification

Desertification

Moderate: less than 0.5% of total land area per year

Severe: more than 0.5% of total land area per year

Deforestation

Moderate: 0.5% to 1.5% of total land area per year

Severe: more than 1.5% of total land area per year (currently or since 1500 A.D.)

Areas of no significant disturbance

Scale: 1 to 180,000,000

0   1000   2000 Miles

0   1000   2000   3000 Kilometers

While those of us in the developed countries of the world tend to think of environmental deterioration as the consequence of our heavily industrialized economies, in fact the worst examples of current environmental degradation are found within the world's less developed regions. There, high population growth rates and economies limited primarily to farming have forced the increasing use of more marginal (less suited to cultivation) land. In the world's grassland and arid environments, which occupy approximately 40 percent of the world's total land area, increasing cultivation pressures are turning vul-

nerable areas into deserts incapable of sustaining agricultural productivity. In the world's forested regions, particularly in the tropical forests of Middle and South America, Africa, and Asia, a similar process is occurring: increasing pressure for more farmland is creating a process of deforestation or forest clearing that destroys the soil, reduces the biological diversity of the forest regions, and—ultimately—may have the capacity to alter the global climate by contributing to an increase in carbon dioxide in the atmosphere. This increases the heat trapped in the atmosphere and enhances the greenhouse effect.

Global Soil Degradation

- Areas of serious concern
- Areas of moderate concern
- Stable or nonvegetated areas
- Areas under stress from acidification

Scale: 1 to 180,000,000

0   1000   2000 Miles

0   1000   2000   3000 Kilometers

Recent research has shown that more than 3 billion acres of the world's surface suffer from serious soil degradation, with more than 22 million acres so severely eroded or poisoned with chemicals that they can no longer support productive crop agriculture. Most of this soil damage has been caused by poor farming practices, overgrazing of domestic livestock, and deforestation. These activities strip away the protective cover of natural vegetation—forests and grasslands—allowing wind and water erosion to remove the topsoil that contains the necessary nutrients and soil microbes for plant growth. But millions of acres of topsoil have been degraded by chemicals as well. In some instances these chemicals are the result of overapplication of fertilizers, herbicides, pesticides, and other agricultural chemicals. In other instances, chemical deposition from industrial and urban wastes and from acid precipitation has poisoned millions of acres of soil. As the map shows, soil erosion and pollution are problems not just in developing countries with high population densities and increasing use of marginal lands but in the more highly developed regions of mechanized, industrial agriculture as well. While many methods for preventing or reducing soil degradation exist, they are seldom used because of ignorance, cost, or perceived economic inefficiency.

Map 61 Air and Water Quality

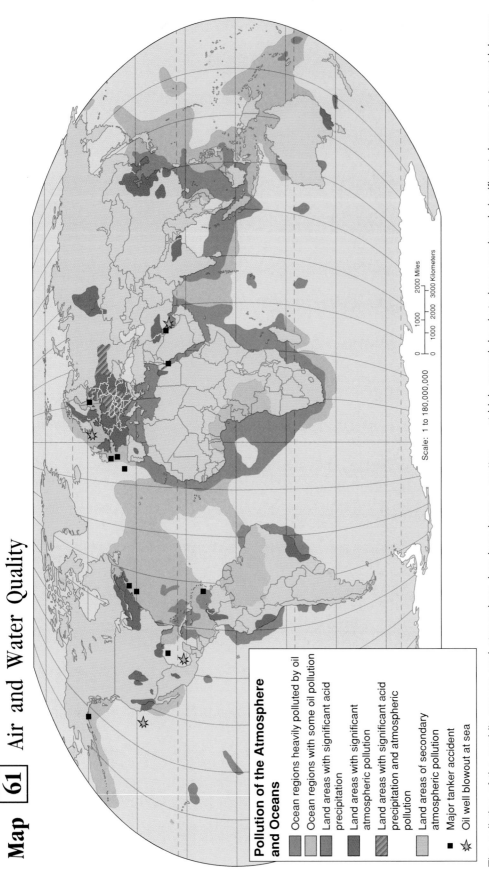

Pollution of the Atmosphere and Oceans

- Ocean regions heavily polluted by oil
- Ocean regions with some oil pollution
- Land areas with significant acid precipitation
- Land areas with significant atmospheric pollution
- Land areas with significant acid precipitation and atmospheric pollution
- Land areas of secondary atmospheric pollution
- ■ Major tanker accident
- ✦ Oil well blowout at sea

Scale: 1 to 180,000,000

0   1000   2000 Miles

0   1000   2000   3000 Kilometers

The pollution of the world's oceans and atmosphere has long been a matter of concern to environmental scientists. The great circulation systems of ocean and air are the controlling factors of the earth's natural environment, and modifications to those systems have unknown consequences. This map is based on what we can measure: (1) areas of oceans where oil pollution has been proven to have inflicted significant damage to ocean ecosystems and lifeforms (including phytoplankton—the oceans' primary food producers, the equivalent of land vegetation); (2) areas of oceans where unusually high concentrations of hydrocarbons from oil spills may have inflicted some damage to the oceans' biota; (3) land areas where the combination of sulphur and nitrogen oxides with atmospheric water vapor has produced acid precipitation at high enough levels to have produced significant damage to terrestrial vegetation systems; (4) land areas where the emissions from industrial, transportation, commercial, residential, and other uses of fossil fuels have produced concentrations of atmospheric pollutants high enough to be damaging to human health; and (5) land areas of secondary air pollution where the primary pollutant is smoke from forest clearance. A glance at the map shows that there are few areas of the world where some form of oceanic or atmospheric pollution is not a part of our environmental system. Scientists are still debating the long-range implications of this pollution, but nearly all agree that the consequences, whatever they may be, will not be good.

Map 62 Per Capita CO₂ Emissions

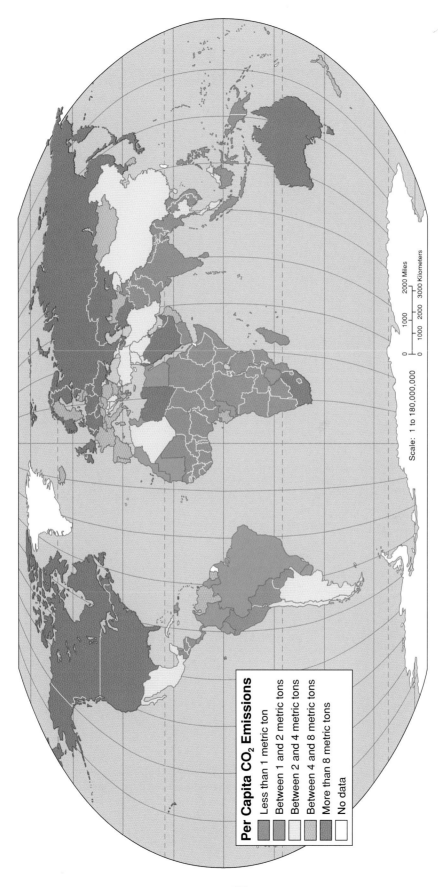

Per Capita CO₂ Emissions

- Less than 1 metric ton
- Between 1 and 2 metric tons
- Between 2 and 4 metric tons
- Between 4 and 8 metric tons
- More than 8 metric tons
- No data

Scale: 1 to 180,000,000

Carbon dioxide emissions are a major indicator of economic development, since they are generated largely by burning of fossil fuels for electrical power generation, for industrial processes, for domestic and commercial heating, and for the internal combustion engines of automobiles, trucks, buses, planes, and trains. Scientists have long known that carbon dioxide in the atmosphere increases the ability of atmosphere to retain heat, a phenomenon known as the greenhouse effect. While the greenhouse effect is a natural process (and life on earth as we know it would not be possible without it), many scientists are concerned that an increase in carbon dioxide in the atmosphere will augment this process, creating a global warming trend and a potential worldwide change of climate patterns. These climatological changes threaten disaster for many regions and their peoples in both the developed and less developed areas of the world. You will note from the map that the countries of the mid-latitude regions generate extremely high levels of carbon dioxide per capita.

Part VII

World Regional Maps

Map 63 North America: Physical Map
Map 64 North America: Political Map
Map 65 South America: Physical Map
Map 66 South America: Political Map
Map 67 Europe: Physical Map
Map 68 Europe: Political Map
Map 69 Asia: Physical Map
Map 70 Asia: Political Map
Map 71 Africa: Physical Map
Map 72 Africa: Political Map
Map 73 Australia and Oceania: Physical Map
Map 74 Australia and Oceania: Political Map

Map 63 North America: Physical Map

Elevation

Feet
3000
1500
300
0 Sea level 0
100
1000 Below sea level

⊛ National capital
• City

Map 64 North America: Political Map

Map 65 South America: Physical Map

Map 66 South America: Political Map

Legend
- ⊛ National capital
- ⊙ State capital
- • City

Map 67 Europe: Physical Map

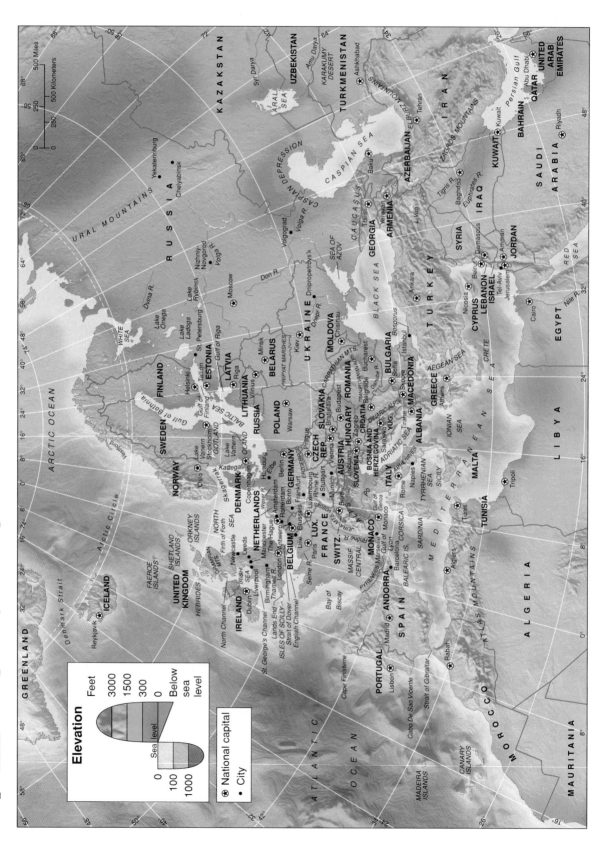

Elevation

Feet
- 3000
- 1500
- 300
- 0
- Below sea level

Sea level
- 0
- 100
- 1000

⊛ National capital
• City

Map 68 Europe: Political Map

National capital ⊛
City •

Map 69 Asia: Physical Map

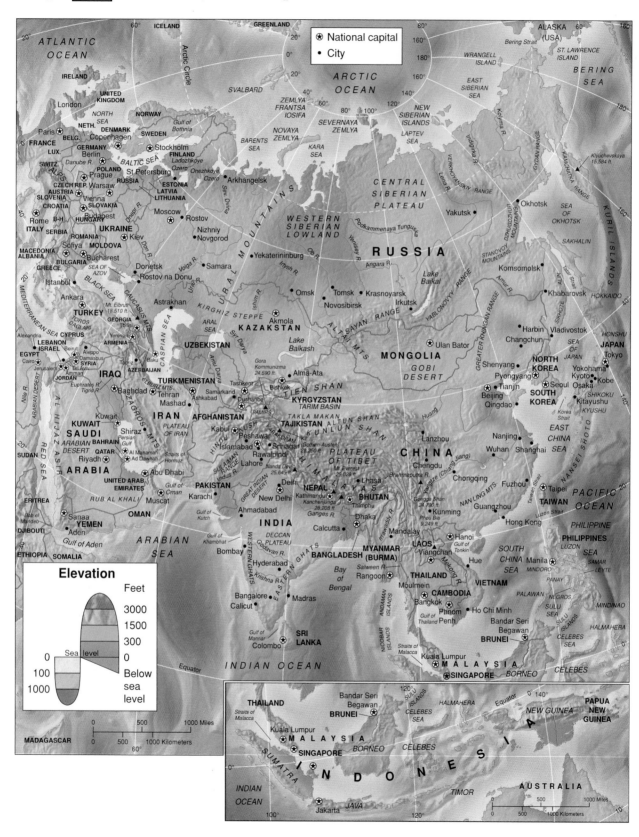

Elevation

Feet
3000
1500
300
0 Sea level 0
100 Below
1000 sea level

National capital
City

Map 70 Asia: Political Map

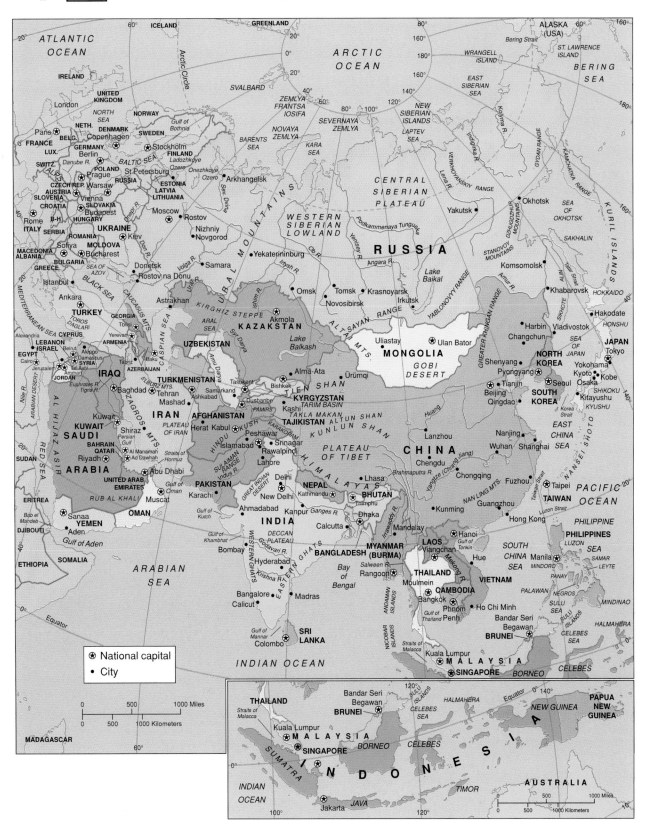

Map [71] Africa: Physical Map

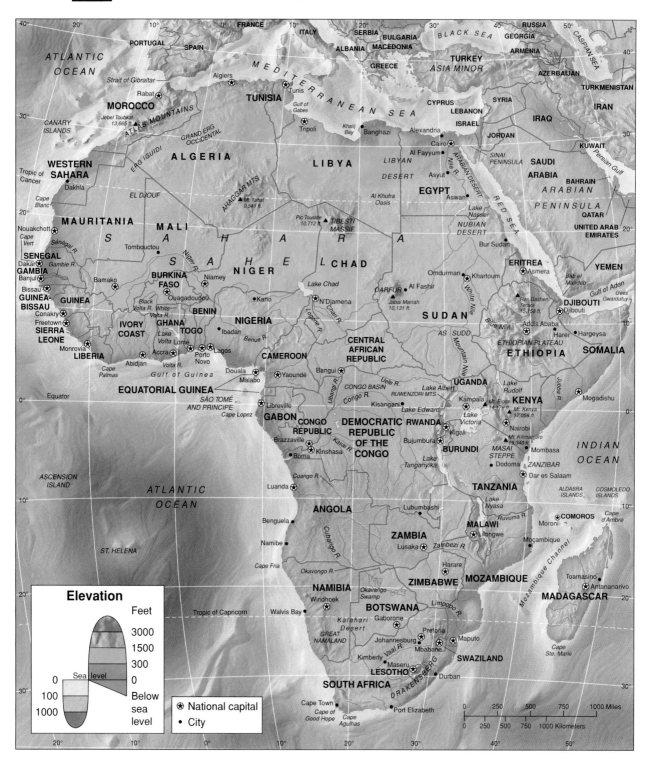

Map 72 Africa: Political Map

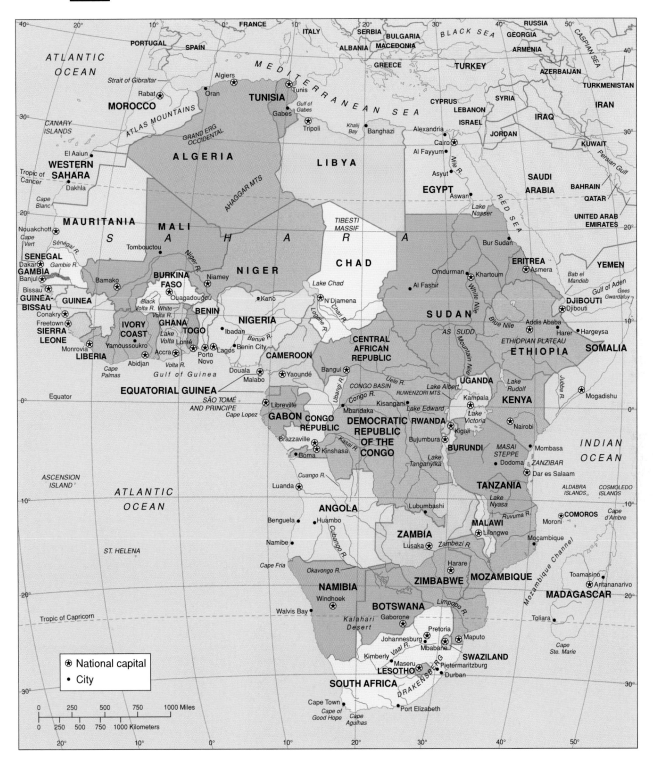

Map 73 Australia and Oceania: Physical Map

PACIFIC OCEAN

Equator

FIJI

VANUATU

SOLOMON ISLANDS

SANTA CRUZ ISLANDS

NEW CALEDONIA

ESPIRITU SANTO

NEW HEBRIDES

MALEKULA

Port Vila

Noumea

Tropic of Capricorn

PACIFIC OCEAN

NEW GEORGIA ISLAND

SAN CRISTOBAL

Honiara

GUADALCANAL

NORTH ISLAND

Auckland

Mt. Ruapehu 9,177 ft.

Lower Hutt

Wellington

Christchurch

Cook Strait

East Cape

North Cape

Cape Farewell

SOUTHERN ALPS

Mt. Cook 12,316 ft.

SOUTH ISLAND

NEW ZEALAND

Dunedin

Southwest Cape

ADMIRALTY ISLANDS

BISMARCK ARCHIPELAGO

NEW HANOVER

NEW IRELAND

NEW BRITAIN

TROBRIAND ISLANDS

WOODLARK ISLAND

D'ENTRECASTEAUX ISLANDS

South Cape

CORAL SEA

PAPUA NEW GUINEA

Mt. Bangeta 13,520 ft.

Mt. Albert Edward 13,090 ft.

Mt. Victoria 13,238 ft.

Repulse Bay

Mt. Dalrymple 5,100 ft.

Rockhampton

TASMAN SEA

PEGUNUNGAN VAN REES

Jayapura

Sepik R.

Mt. Wilhelm 14,793 ft.

BISMARCK RA.

NEW GUINEA

Mt. Giluwe 14,330 ft.

Gulf of Papua

Port Moresby

Owen Stanley Ra.

Puncak Jaya 16,503 ft.

Puncak Tricora 15,584 ft.

PEGUNUNGAN MAOKE

Merauke

Fly R.

Torres Strait

Cape York

GREAT BARRIER REEF

Cape Melville

Cairns

Mt. Bartle Frere 5,322 ft.

Halifax Bay

Townsville

Burdekin R.

Belyando R.

Brisbane

Mt. Roberts 4,495 ft.

Capoompeta 5,100 ft.

The Round Mountain 5,300 ft.

Newcastle

Sydney

Botany Bay

Wollongong

AUSTRALIAN CAPITAL TERRITORY

Canberra

Bass Strait

Mt. Ossa 5,305 ft.

Hobart

TASMANIA

BORNEO

CELEBES

CERAM

BURU

INDONESIA

SUMBAWA

FLORES

JAVA

Surabaya

Ujung Pandang

SUMBA

SUNDA ISLANDS

TIMOR

TIMOR SEA

ARAFURA SEA

Cape Arnhem

Gulf of Carpentaria

ARNHEM LAND

Cape van Diemen

Darwin

Katherine

Daly R.

Roper R.

NORTHERN TERRITORY

Tennant Creek

Alice Springs

MACDONNELL RANGES

Mt. Ziel 4,955 ft.

SIMPSON DESERT

AUSTRALIA

Ayers Rock 2,844 ft.

Mt. Woodroffe 4,724 ft.

MUSGRAVE RANGES

EVERARD RANGES

STUART RANGE

Oodnadatta

Lake Eyre

GREAT DIVIDING RANGE

QUEENSLAND

ARTESIAN BASIN

GREAT DIVIDING RANGE

Darling R.

Namoi R.

Macquarie R.

BLUE MTS.

Mt. Kosciusko 7,310 ft.

SNOWY MTS.

Murrumbidgee R.

Murray R.

Cape Howe

NEW SOUTH WALES

VICTORIA

Melbourne

Geelong

Ballarat

Cape Otway

Adelaide

Victoria R.

Mt. Ham 2,800 ft.

King Leopold Ranges

Wyndham

Derby

Fitzroy R.

Cape Leveque

Roebuck Bay

De Grey R.

Mt. Bruce 4,052 ft.

HAMERSLEY RANGE

Ashburton R.

Gascoyne R.

GREAT SANDY DESERT

GIBSON DESERT

WESTERN AUSTRALIA

GREAT VICTORIA DESERT

Lake Woomera

Lake Everard

Lake Gairdner

Lake Torrens

SOUTH AUSTRALIA

FLINDERS RA.

Port Lincoln

Hughes

NULLARBOR PLAIN

Great Australian Bight

Kalgoorlie-Boulder

Lake

SWANLAND

Swan R.

Perth

DARLING RANGE

Fremantle

Geographe Bay

Cape Naturaliste

West Cape Howe

Albany

Cape Londonderry

Murchison R.

North West Cape

Cape Farquhar

Carnarvon

Steep Point

INDIAN OCEAN

INDIAN OCEAN

Cape Jaffa

Elevation

Feet		Sea level
3000		0
1500		100
300		1000
0		
Below sea level		

⊛ National capital
◉ State capital
• City

500 Miles

500 Kilometers

250

0

– 98 –

Map 74 Australia and Oceania: Political Map

Part VIII

World Countries: Data Tables

TABLE A World Countries: Area, Population and Population Density, 1998

TABLE B World Countries: Form of Government, Capital City, Major Languages

TABLE C Defense Expenditures, Armed Forces, Refugees, and the Arms Trade

TABLE D Armed Conflict in the 1990s

TABLE E World Countries: Basic Economic Indicators 1997

TABLE F World Countries: Population Growth, 1950–2050

TABLE G World Countries: Basic Demographic Data, 1975–2000

TABLE H World Countries: Mortality, Health, and Nutrition, 1997

TABLE I World Countries: Education and Literacy, 1995–1997

TABLE J World Countries: Agricultural Operations, 1994–1997

TABLE K Land Use and Deforestation, 1980–1996

TABLE L World Countries: Energy Production and Use, 1980–1996

TABLE M World Countries: Water Resources

TABLE N World Countries: Energy Efficiency and Emissions, 1980–1996

Table A

World Countries: Area, Population, and Population Density, 1998

COUNTRY	AREA (Mi^2)	AREA (Km^2)	POPULATION (1997)[a]	DENSITY (Pop/Mi^2)	DENSITY (Pop/Km^2)
Afghanistan	251,826	652,229	23,738,085	94	36
Albania	11,100	28,749	3,293,252	297	115
Algeria	919,595	2,381,750	29,830,370	32	13
Andorra	175	453	74,839	428	165
Angola	481,354	1,246,706	10,523,994	22	8
Antigua and Barbuda	171	443	68,175	399	154
Argentina	1,073,400	2,780,104	35,797,536	33	13
Armenia	11,506	29,801	3,465,611	301	116
Australia	2,966,155	7,682,337	18,438,824	6	2
Austria	32,377	83,856	8,054,078	249	96
Azerbaijan	33,436	86,599	7,735,918	231	89
Bahamas	5,382	13,939	262,034	49	19
Bahrain	267	692	603,318	2,260	872
Bangladesh	55,598	143,999	125,340,261	2,254	870
Barbados	166	430	257,731	1,553	599
Belarus	80,155	207,601	10,439,916	130	50
Belgium	11,783	30,518	10,203,563	866	334
Belize	8,866	22,963	224,663	25	10
Benin	43,475	112,600	5,902,178	136	52
Bhutan	18,200	47,138	1,865,191	102	40
Bolivia	424,165	1,098,587	7,669,868	18	7
Bosnia-Herzegovina	19,741	51,129	2,607,734	132	51
Botswana	231,800	600,362	1,500,765	6	2
Brazil	3,286,488	8,511,999	164,611,355	50	19
Brunei Darussalam	2,226	5,765	307,616	138	53
Bulgaria	42,823	110,912	8,652,745	202	78
Burkina Faso	105,869	274,201	10,891,159	103	40
Burundi	10,745	27,830	6,052,614	563	217
Cambodia	69,898	181,036	11,164,861	160	62
Cameroon	183,569	475,443	14,877,510	81	31
Canada	3,849,674	9,970,650	29,123,194	8	3
Cape Verde	1,557	4,033	393,843	253	98
Central African Republic	240,535	622,985	3,342,051	14	5
Chad	495,755	1,284,005	7,166,023	14	6
Chile	292,135	756,629	14,508,168	50	19
China	3,689,631	9,556,139	1,210,004,956	328	127
Colombia	440,831	1,141,752	37,418,290	85	33
Comoros	863	2,235	589,797	683	264
Congo (Zaire)	905,446	2,345,104	47,440,362	52	20
Congo Republic	132,047	342,002	2,583,198	20	8
Costa Rica	19,730	51,101	3,353,174	170	66
Côte d'Ivoire	124,518	322,501	14,966,218	120	46
Croatia	21,829	56,537	5,026,995	230	89
Cuba	42,804	110,862	10,999,041	257	99
Cyprus	3,593	9,306	752,808	210	81
Czech Republic	30,613	79,288	10,318,958	337	130
Denmark	16,638	43,092	5,268,775	317	122
Djibouti	8,958	23,201	434,116	48	19
Dominica	305	790	83,226	273	105
Dominican Republic	18,704	48,443	828,151	44	17
Ecuador	109,484	283,563	11,690,535	107	41
Egypt	386,662	1,001,454	64,791,891	168	65
El Salvador	8,124	21,041	5,661,827	697	269
Equatorial Guinea	10,831	28,052	442,516	41	16
Eritrea	45,300	117,327	3,589,687	79	31
Estonia	17,413	45,100	1,444,721	83	32
Ethiopia	483,123	1,251,288	58,732,577	122	47
Fiji	7,078	18,332	792,441	112	43
Finland	130,559	338,148	5,109,148	39	15
France	211,208	547,028	58,040,230	275	106
Gabon	103,347	267,669	1,190,159	12	4
Gambia	4,127	10,689	1,248,085	302	117
Georgia	26,911	69,699	5,174,642	192	74
Germany	137,882	357,114	84,068,216	610	235
Ghana	92,098	238,534	18,100,703	197	76
Greece	50,962	131,992	10,583,126	208	80

(continued on next page)

COUNTRY	AREA (Mi²)	AREA (Km²)	POPULATION (1997)[a]	DENSITY (Pop/Mi²)	DENSITY (Pop/Km²)
Grenada	133	344	95,537	718	277
Guatemala	42,042	108,889	11,558,407	275	106
Guinea	94,926	245,858	7,405,375	78	30
Guinea-Bissau	13,948	36,125	1,178,584	84	33
Guyana	83,000	214,970	706,116	9	3
Haiti	10,714	27,749	6,611,407	617	238
Honduras	43,277	112,087	5,751,384	133	51
Hungary	35,920	93,033	9,935,774	277	107
Iceland	36,769	95,232	272,550	7	3
India	1,237,062	3,203,989	967,612,804	782	302
Indonesia	742,410	1,922,841	209,774,138	283	109
Iran	632,457	1,638,063	67,540,002	107	41
Iraq	169,235	438,318	22,219,289	131	51
Ireland	27,137	70,285	3,555,500	131	51
Israel[b]	8,019	20,769	5,534,872	690	266
Italy	116,234	301,046	57,534,088	495	191
Jamaica	4,244	10,992	2,615,582	616	238
Japan	145,870	377,803	125,716,637	862	333
Jordan	35,135	91,000	4,324,638	123	48
Kazakhstan	1,049,156	2,717,313	16,895,572	16	6
Kenya	224,961	582,649	28,803,085	128	49
Kiribati	280	725	82,449	294	114
Korea, North	46,540	120,539	24,317,004	522	202
Korea, South	38,230	99,016	45,948,811	1,202	464
Kuwait	6,880	17,819	2,076,805	302	117
Kyrgyzstan	76,641	198,500	4,540,185	59	23
Laos	91,429	236,801	5,116,959	56	22
Latvia	24,595	63,701	2,437,649	99	38
Lebanon	4,015	10,399	3,858,736	961	371
Lesotho	11,720	30,355	2,007,814	171	66
Liberia	38,250	99,067	2,602,068	68	26
Libya	679,362	1,759,547	5,648,359	8	3
Liechtenstein	62	161	31,461	507	196
Lithuania	25,174	65,201	3,635,932	144	56
Luxembourg	998	2,585	422,474	423	163
Macedonia	9,928	25,714	2,113,866	213	82

COUNTRY	AREA (Mi²)	AREA (Km²)	POPULATION (1997)[a]	DENSITY (Pop/Mi²)	DENSITY (Pop/Km²)
Madagascar	226,658	587,044	14,061,627	62	24
Malawi	45,747	118,485	9,609,081	210	81
Malaysia	129,251	334,760	20,376,235	158	61
Maldives	115	298	280,391	2,438	941
Mali	478,767	1,240,006	9,945,383	21	8
Malta	122	316	379,365	3,110	1,201
Marshall Islands	70	181	60,652	866	335
Mauritania	395,956	1,025,525	2,411,317	6	2
Mauritius	788	2,041	1,154,272	1,465	566
Mexico	756,066	1,958,210	97,563,374	129	50
Micronesia	271	702	127,616	471	182
Moldova	13,012	33,701	4,475,232	344	133
Monaco	1	2	31,892	43,688	16,868
Mongolia	604,829	1,566,506	2,538,211	4	2
Morocco	275,114	712,545	30,391,423	110	43
Mozambique	308,642	799,382	18,165,476	59	23
Myanmar (Burma)	261,228	676,580	46,821,943	179	69
Namibia	317,818	823,148	1,727,183	5	2
Nauru	8	21	10,390	1,267	489
Nepal	56,827	147,182	22,641,061	398	154
Netherlands	16,133	41,784	15,653,091	970	375
New Zealand	103,519	268,114	3,358,275	32	13
Nicaragua	50,054	129,640	4,386,399	88	34
Niger	489,191	1,267,004	9,388,859	19	7
Nigeria	356,669	923,772	107,129,469	300	116
Norway	125,050	323,879	4,404,456	35	14
Oman	82,030	212,458	2,264,590	28	11
Pakistan	310,432	804,018	132,185,299	426	164
Palau	177	458	17,240	97	38
Panama	29,157	75,517	2,693,417	92	36
Papua New Guinea	178,704	462,843	4,496,221	25	10
Paraguay	157,048	406,754	5,651,634	36	14
Peru	496,225	1,285,222	24,949,512	50	19
Philippines	115,831	300,002	76,103,564	657	254
Poland	120,728	312,685	38,700,291	321	124
Portugal	35,516	91,986	9,867,654	278	107

(continued on next page)

COUNTRY	AREA (Mi²)	AREA (Km²)	POPULATION (1997)[a]	DENSITY (Pop/Mi²)	DENSITY (Pop/Km²)
Qatar	4,416	11,437	665,485	151	58
Romania	91,699	237,500	21,399,114	233	90
Russian Federation	6,592,849	17,075,469	147,987,101	22	9
Rwanda	10,169	26,338	7,737,537	761	294
St. Kitts and Nevis	104	269	41,803	402	155
St. Lucia	238	616	159,639	671	259
St. Vincent/Grenadines	150	388	119,092	794	307
Samoa	1,093	2,831	219,509	201	78
San Marino	24	62	24,714	1,030	398
São Tomé and Principe	372	963	147,865	397	153
Saudi Arabia	830,000	2,149,699	20,087,965	24	9
Senegal	75,951	196,713	9,403,546	124	48
Seychelles	175	453	78,142	447	172
Sierra Leone	27,925	72,326	4,891,546	175	68
Singapore	246	637	3,461,929	14,073	5,434
Slovak Republic	18,933	49,036	5,393,016	285	110
Slovenia	7,819	20,251	1,945,998	0	0
Solomon Islands	10,954	28,371	426,855	39	15
Somalia	246,201	637,660	9,940,232	40	16
South Africa	433,680	1,123,231	42,327,458	98	38
Spain	194,885	504,752	39,244,195	201	78
Sri Lanka	24,962	64,652	18,762,075	752	290
Sudan	967,500	2,505,824	32,594,128	34	13
Suriname	63,251	163,820	443,446	7	3
Swaziland	6,704	17,363	1,031,600	154	59
Sweden	173,732	449,966	8,946,193	51	20
Switzerland	15,943	41,292	7,248,984	455	176

COUNTRY	AREA (Mi²)	AREA (Km²)	POPULATION (1997)[a]	DENSITY (Pop/Mi²)	DENSITY (Pop/Km²)
Syria	71,498	185,180	16,137,899	226	87
Taiwan	13,900	36,001	21,655,515	1,558	602
Tajikistan	55,251	143,100	6,013,855	109	42
Tanzania	364,900	945,090	29,460,753	81	31
Thailand	198,115	513,118	59,450,818	300	116
Togo	21,925	56,786	4,735,610	216	83
Tonga	290	751	107,335	370	143
Trinidad and Tobago	1,980	5,128	1,273,141	643	248
Tunisia	63,170	163,610	9,183,097	145	56
Turkey	300,948	779,455	63,528,225	211	82
Turkmenistan	188,456	488,101	4,225,351	22	9
Tuvalu	10	26	10,297	1,030	398
Uganda	93,104	241,139	20,604,874	221	85
Ukraine	233,090	603,703	50,684,635	217	84
United Arab Emirates	32,278	83,600	2,262,309	70	27
United Kingdom	94,248	244,102	58,610,182	622	240
United States	3,787,425	9,809,425	267,954,767	71	27
Uruguay	68,500	177,415	3,261,707	48	18
Uzbekistan	172,742	447,402	23,860,452	138	53
Vanatu	4,707	12,191	181,358	39	15
Venezuela	352,145	912,055	22,396,407	64	25
Vietnam	128,066	331,691	75,123,880	587	226
Yemen	205,356	531,872	13,972,477	68	26
Yugoslavia (Serbia-Montenegro)	26,913	69,705	10,655,317	396	153
Zambia	290,586	752,617	9,349,975	32	12
Zimbabwe	150,873	390,761	11,423,175	76	29

[a] Primary source for population figures: United Nations Population Division and International Labour Organisation.

[b] The figures for Israel do not include the West Bank and Gaza. The former has an area of approximately 2,300 square miles, a population of 1.8 million, and a density of about 780 persons per square mile; the latter has an area of 100 square miles, a population of nearly 900,000 persons, and an estimated population density of 8,700 persons per square mile.

Sources: The World Almanac and Book of Facts, 1998 (St. Martin's Press, New York, 1998); *The New York Times 1998 Almanac* (Penguin Putnam, Inc., New York, 1998); U.S. Census Bureau, *World Population Profile* (1998).

Table B

World Countries: Form of Government, Capital City, Major Languages

Notes: Unless indicated otherwise, republics are multi-party. "Theocratic" normally refers to fundamentalist Islamic rule. "Transitional" governments are those still in the process of change from a previous form (eg. single-party communist state to multi-party republic).

COUNTRY	GOVERNMENT	CAPITAL	MAJOR LANGUAGES
Afghanistan	Theocratic republic/transitional	Kabul	Dari, Pashton, Uzbek, Turkmen
Albania	Democratic	Tiranë	Albanian, Greek
Algeria	Military-transitional	Algiers	Arabic, Berber dialects, French
Andorra	Parliamentary democracy	Andorra	Catalán, French, Spanish
Angola	Multi-party democracy	Luanda	Portugese, indigenous
Antigua and Barbuda	Parliamentary democracy	St. John's	English, local dialects
Argentina	Federal republic	Buenos Aires	Spanish, English, Italian, German
Armenia	Republic	Yerevan	Armenian, Azerbaijani, Russian
Australia	Federal parliamentary	Canberra	English, indigenous
Austria	Federal republic	Vienna	German
Azerbaijan	Republic	Baku	Azerbaijani, Russian, Armenian
Bahamas	Independent commonwealth	Nassau	English
Bahrain	Traditional monarchy	Al Manamah	Arabic, English, Farsi, Urdu
Bangladesh	Republic	Dhaka	Bangla, English
Barbados	Parliamentary state	Bridgetown	English
Belarus	Republic	Minsk	Byelorussian, Russian
Belgium	Constitutional monarchy	Brussels	Dutch (Flemish), French, German
Belize	Parliamentary state	Belmopan	English, Spanish, Garifuna, Mayan
Benin	Multi-party republic	Porto-Novo	French, Fon, Adja, indigenous
Bhutan	Monarchy	Thimphu	Dzongha, Tibetan, Nepalese
Bolivia	Republic	La Paz	Spanish, Quechua, Aymara
Bosnia-Herzegovina	Republic/transitional	Sarajevo	Serb, Croat, Albanian
Botswana	Parliamentary republic	Gaborone	English, Tswania
Brazil	Federal republic	Brasilia	Portugese, Spanish, English, French
Brunei	Constitutional monarchy	Bandar	Malay, English, Chinese
Bulgaria	Republic/transitional	Sofia	Bulgarian
Burkina Faso	Provisional military	Ouagadougou	French, indigenous
Burundi	Republic/transitional	Bujumbura	French, Kirundi, Swahili
Cambodia	Transitional UN management	Phnom Penh	Khmer, French
Cameroon	Multi-party republic	Yaoundé	English, French, indigenous
Canada	Federal parliamentary	Ottawa	English, French
Cape Verde	Republic	Praia	Portugese, Crioulu
Central African Republic	Republic	Bangui	French, Sango, Arabic, indigenous
Chad	Republic	N'Djamena	Arabic, French, indigenous
Chile	Republic	Santiago	Spanish
China	Single-party communist state	Beijing	Chinese dialects
Colombia	Republic	Bogotá	Spanish
Comoros	Republic	Moroni	Arabic, French, Shaafi Islam
Congo (Zaire)	Republic	Kinshasa	French, Lingala, Kingwana, Kikongo, Tshuliba
Congo Republic	Multi-party republic	Brazzaville	French, indigenous
Costa Rica	Republic	San José	Spanish
Côte d'Ivoire	Republic	Abidjan	French, indigenous
Croatia	Parliamentary democracy	Zaghreb	Croat, Serb
Cuba	Single-party communist state	Havana	Spanish
Cyprus	Republic	Nicosia	Greek, Turkish, English
Czech Republic	Federal republic	Prague	Czech, Slovak, Hungarian
Denmark	Constitutional monarchy	Copenhagen	Danish
Djibouti	Republic	Djibouti	French, Somali, Afar, Arabic
Dominica	Republic	Rosseau	English, French
Dominican Republic	Republic	Santo Domingo	Spanish
Ecuador	Republic	Quito	Spanish, Quechua, indigenous
Egypt	Republic	Cairo	Arabic
El Salvador	Republic	San Salvador	Spanish, Nahua
Equatorial Guinea	Republic	Malabo	Spanish, indigenous, English
Eritrea	Transitional government	Asmara	Afar, Bilen, Hadareb, Kunuama, Nara
Estonia	Republic	Tallinn	Estonian, Russian
Ethiopia	Republic/transitional	Addis Ababa	Amharic, Tigrinya, Orominga, Arabic
Fiji	Republic	Suva	English, Fijian, Hindustani
Finland	Republic	Helsinki	Finnish, Swedish
France	Republic	Paris	French

(continued on next page)

COUNTRY	GOVERNMENT	CAPITAL	MAJOR LANGUAGES
Gabon	Single-party republic	Libreville	French, Fang, indigenous
Gambia	Republic	Banjul	English, Malinke, Wolof, Fula
Georgia	Republic	Tbilisi	Georgian, Russian, Armenian
Germany	Federal republic	Berlin and Bonn	German
Ghana	Parliamentary democracy	Accra	English, Akan, indigenous
Greece	Parliamentary democracy	Athens	Greek
Grenada	Parliamentary state	St. George's	English, French
Guatemala	Republic	Guatemala	Spanish, indigenous
Guinea	Republic/transitional	Conakry	French, indigenous
Guinea-Bissau	Single-party republic	Bissau	Portugese, Crioulo, indigenous
Guyana	Republic	Georgetown	English, indigenous
Haiti	Republic	Port-au-Prince	Creole, French
Honduras	Republic	Tegucigalpa	Spanish, indigenous
Hungary	Republic	Budapest	Hungarian
Iceland	Republic	Reykjavik	Icelandic
India	Federal republic	New Delhi	English, Hindi, Telugu, Bengali
Indonesia	Republic	Jakarta	Indonesian, Javanese, Sundanese
Iran	Theocratic republic	Tehran	Farsi, Turkish, Kurdish, Arabic, English
Iraq	Single-party republic	Baghdad	Arabic, Kurdish, Assyrian, Armenian
Ireland	Republic	Dublin	English, Irish Gaelic
Israel	Republic	Jerusalem	Hebrew, Arabic, Yiddish
Italy	Republic	Rome	Italian
Jamaica	Parliamentary state	Kingston	English, Creole
Japan	Constitutional monarchy	Tokyo	Japanese
Jordan	Constitutional monarchy	Amman	Arabic
Kazakhstan	Republic/transitional	Alma-Ata	Kazakh, Russian, German, Ukranian
Kenya	Republic	Nairobi	English, Swahili, indigenous
Kiribati	Republic	Tarawa	English, Gilbertese
Korea, North	Single-party communist state	Pyongyang	Korean
Korea, South	Republic	Seoul	Korean
Kuwait	Constitutional monarchy	Kuwait	Arabic, English
Kyrgyzstan	Republic/transitional	Bishkek	Kirghiz, Russian, Uzbek
Laos	Single-party communist state	Viangchan	Lao, French, Thai, indigenous
Latvia	Republic	Riga	Latvian, Russian
Lebanon	Republic	Beirut	Arabic, French, Armenian, English
Lesotho	Constitutional monarchy	Maseru	English, Sesotho, Zulu, Xhosa
Liberia	Republic	Monrovia	English, indigenous
Libya	Single-party parliamentary state	Tripoli	Arabic
Liechtenstein	Constitutional monarchy	Vaduz	German
Lithuania	Republic	Vilnius	Lithuanian, Russian, Polish
Luxembourg	Constitutional monarchy	Luxembourg	French, Luxembourgish, German
Macedonia	Republic/transitional	Skopje	Macedonian, Albanian
Madagascar	Military/transitional	Antananarivo	Malagasy, French
Malawi	Single-party republic	Lilongwe	Chichewa, English, Tombuka
Malaysia	Constitutional monarchy	Kuala Lumpur	Malay, Chinese, English
Maldives	Republic	Male	Divehi
Mali	Single-party republic	Bamako	French, Bambara, indigenous
Malta	Parliamentary democracy	Valletta	English, Maltese
Marshall Islands	Constitutional government	Majuro	English, Polynesian dialects, Japanese
Mauritania	Republic/transitional	Nouakchott	Arabic, French, indigenous
Mauritius	Parliamentary state	Port Louis	English, Creole, Bhojpun, Hindi
Mexico	Federal republic	Mexico City	Spanish, indigenous
Micronesia	Republic	Kolonia	English, Malay-Polynesian languages
Moldova	Republic	Kishinev	Moldavian, Russian, Ukrainian
Monaco	Constitutional monarchy	Monaco	French, English, Italian, Monegasque
Mongolia	Single-party communist state	Ulan Bator	Khalkha Mongol, Kazakh, Russian
Morocco	Constitutional monarchy	Rabat	Arabic, Berber dialects, French
Mozambique	Republic	Maputo	Portuguese, indigenous
Myanmar (Burma)	Provisional military	Rangoon	Burmese, indigenous
Namibia	Republic	Windhoek	Afrikaans, English, German, indigenous
Nauru	Republic	Yaren district	Nauruan, English
Nepal	Constitutional monarchy	Kathmandu	Nepali, Maithali, Bhojpuri, indigenous
Netherlands	Constitutional monarchy	Amsterdam	Dutch
New Zealand	Parliamentary state	Wellington	English, Maori
Nicaragua	Republic	Managua	Spanish, English, indigenous
Niger	Provisional military	Niamey	French, Hausa, Djerma, indigenous
Nigeria	Provisional military	Lagos/Abuja	English, Hausa, Fulani, Yorbua, Ibo

(continued on next page)

COUNTRY	GOVERNMENT	CAPITAL	MAJOR LANGUAGES
Norway	Constitutional monarchy	Oslo	Norwegian, Lapp
Oman	Traditional monarchy	Muscat	Arabic, English, Baluchi, Urdu
Pakistan	Federal Islamic republic	Islamabad	English, Urdu, Punjabi, Pashto, Sindhi
Palau	Republic	Koror state	English, Palauan
Panama	Republic	Panama	Spanish, English, indigenous
Papua New Guinea	Parliamentary state	Port Moresby	English, Motu, Pidgin, indigenous
Paraguay	Republic (authoritarian)	Asunción	Spanish, Guarani
Peru	Republic	Lima	Quechua, Spanish, Aymara
Philippines	Republic	Manila	English, Philipino, Tagalog
Poland	Republic	Warsaw	Polish
Portugal	Republic	Lisbon	Portuguese
Qatar	Traditional monarchy	Doha	Arabic, English
Romania	Republic	Bucharest	Romanian, Hungarian, German
Russian Federation	Republic	Moscow	Russian, Tatar, Ukranian
Rwanda	Provisional military	Kigali	French, Kinyarwanda
St. Kitts and Nevis	Parliamentary state	Basseterre	English
St. Lucia	Parliamentary state	Castries	English, French
St. Vincent/Grenadines	Parliamentary state	Kingstown	English, French
Samoa	Constitutional monarchy	Apia	Samoan, English
San Marino	Republic	San Marino	Italian
São Tomé and Principe	Republic	São Tomé	Portuguese, Fang
Saudi Arabia	Islamic monarchy	Riyadh	Arabic
Senegal	Republic	Dakar	French, Wolof, indigenous
Seychelles	Republic	Victoria	English, French, Creole
Sierra Leone	Republic	Freetown	English, Krio, indigenous
Singapore	Republic	Singapore	Mandarin Chinese, English, Malay
Slovak Republic	Parliamentary democracy	Bratislava	Slovak, Hungarian, Polish
Slovenia	Republic/transitional	Ljubljana	Slovene
Solomon Islands	Parliamentary state	Honiara	English, Malay-Polynesian languages
Somalia	Provisional military	Mogadishu	Arabic, Somali, English, Italian
South Africa	Republic	Pretoria	Afrikaans, English, Zulu, Xhosa, other
Spain	Parliamentary monarchy	Madrid	Spanish, Catalán, Galician, Basque
Sri Lanka	Republic	Colombo	English, Sinhala, Tamil
Sudan	Islamic republic	Khartoum	Arabic, Dinka, Nubian
Suriname	Military/transitional	Paramaribo	Dutch, Sranan Tongo, English
Swaziland	Monarchy	Mbabane	English, Swahili
Sweden	Constitutional monarchy	Stockholm	Swedish
Switzerland	Federal republic	Bern	German, French, Italian, Romansch
Syria	Republic (authoritarian)	Damascus	Arabic, Kurdish, Armenian, Aramaic
Taiwan	Single-party republic	Taipei	Chinese dialects
Tajikistan	Republic	Dushanbe	Tajik, Uzbek, Russian
Tanzania	Republic	Dar es Salaam	English, Swahili, indigenous
Thailand	Constitutional monarchy	Bangkok	Thai, indigenous
Togo	Single-party republic	Lomé	French, indigenous
Tonga	Constitutional monarchy	Nuku'alofa	Tongan, English
Trinidad and Tobago	Parliamentary democracy	Port of Spain	English, Hindi, French, Spanish
Tunisia	Republic	Tunis	Arabic, French
Turkey	Parliamentary democracy	Ankara	Turkish, Kurdish, Arabic
Turkmenistan	Republic	Ashkhabad	Turkmen, Russian, Uzbek, Kazakh
Tuvalu	Parliamentary democracy	Funafuti	Tuvaluan, English
Uganda	Republic	Kampala	English, Luganda, Swahili, indigenous
Ukraine	Republic	Kiev	Ukranian, Russian
United Arab Emirates	Federated monarchy	Abu Dhabi	Arabic, English, Farsi, Hindi, Urdu
United Kingdom	Constitutional monarchy	London	English, Welsh, Gaelic
United States	Federal republic	Washington	English, Spanish
Uruguay	Republic	Montevideo	Spanish
Uzbekistan	Republic	Tashkent	Uzbek, Russian, Kazakh, Tajik, Tatar
Vanatu	Republic	Port Vila	English, French, Bislama (pidgin)
Venezuela	Federal republic	Caracas	Spanish, indigenous
Vietnam	Single-party communist state	Hanoi	Vietnamese, French, Chinese, English
Yemen	Republic	San'a	Arabic
Yugoslavia (Serbia-Montenegro)	Republic	Belgrade	Serb, Albanian, Hungarian
Zambia	Single-party republic	Lusaka	English, Tonga, Lozi, other indigenous
Zimbabwe	Republic	Harare	English, ChiShona, SiNdebele

Sources: The World Almanac and Book of Facts, 1998 (St. Martin's Press, New York, 1998); *The New York Times 1998 Almanac* (Penguin Putnam, Inc., New York, 1998); U.S. Census Bureau, *World Population Profile* (1997).

Table C
Defense Expenditures, Armed Forces, Refugees, and the Arms Trade

COUNTRY	DEFENSE EXPENDITURES (% of GNP)	NUMBERS IN ARMED FORCES (in thousands)	REFUGEE POPULATION	ARMS TRADE Exports (% of Total Exports)	Imports (% of Total Imports)
Albania	1.1	52	–	0.0	0.0
Algeria	3.2	120	104,000	0.0	2.2
Angola	3.0	82	9,000	0.0	13.7
Argentina	1.7	65	10,700	0.3	0.2
Armenia	0.9	60	219,150	0.0	4.5
Australia	2.5	58	18,000	0.1	1.5
Austria	0.9	45	11,400	0.1	0.1
Azerbaijan	2.8	87	244,100	0.0	0.0
Bangladesh	1.7	115	40,100	0.0	0.9
Belarus	0.8	115	33,500	4.0	0.0
Belgium	1.7	47	14,100	0.1	0.2
Benin	1.2	6	3,000	0.0	0.0
Bolivia	2.3	28	300	0.0	0.7
Bosnia-Herzegovina	–	50	40,000	0.0	20.0
Botswana	5.3	8	–	0.0	0.0
Brazil	1.7	285	2,300	0.0	0.3
Bulgaria	2.8	86	2,400	2.8	0.0
Burkina Faso	2.9	9	2,000	0.0	0.0
Burundi	4.4	22	12,000	0.0	0.0
Cambodia	3.1	90	–	0.0	3.2
Cameroon	1.9	22	1,000	0.0	0.8
Canada	1.7	70	48,800	0.1	0.1
Central African Republic	2.5	5	38,000	0.0	0.0
Chad	3.1	30	–	0.0	4.5
Chile	3.8	102	300	0.0	2.4
China	2.3	2,930	281,800	–	–

COUNTRY	DEFENSE EXPENDITURES (% of GNP)	NUMBERS IN ARMED FORCES (in thousands)	REFUGEE POPULATION	ARMS TRADE Exports (% of Total Exports)	Imports (% of Total Imports)
Hong Kong, China	–	–	–	–	–
Colombia	2.6	146	200	0.0	0.4
Congo (Zaire)	0.3	49	255,000	0.0	0.0
Congo, Rep.	2.9	10	21,000	0.0	1.5
Costa Rica	0.6	8	23,100	0.0	0.0
Côte d'Ivoire	–	–	202,000	–	–
Croatia	10.5	60	50,000	0.0	1.5
Cuba	1.6	70	1,500	0.0	0.0
Czech Republic	2.3	68	700	0.6	0.0
Denmark	1.8	27	13,000	0.0	0.2
Dominican Republic	1.4	22	600	0.0	0.3
Ecuador	3.7	58	200	0.0	6.2
Egypt	5.7	430	46,000	0.0	16.2
El Salvador	1.1	22	100	0.0	0.7
Eritrea	–	–	3,000	0.0	0.0
Estonia	1.1	6	–	0.0	0.2
Ethiopia	2.2	120	313,000	0.0	0.0
Finland	2.0	32	1,600	0.0	0.1
France	3.1	504	16,000	0.8	0.1
Gabon	2.6	10	1,000	0.0	0.0
Gambia	4.6	1	8,000	0.0	0.0
Georgia	2.4	5	100	0.0	4.0
Germany[a]	–	–	277,000	0.2	0.1
Ghana	1.4	7	20,000	0.0	0.0
Greece	5.5	213	2,100	0.1	2.2
Guatemala	1.3	36	1,300	0.0	0.2

(continued on next page)

COUNTRY	DEFENSE EXPENDITURES (% of GNP)	NUMBERS IN ARMED FORCES (in thousands)	REFUGEE POPULATION	ARMS TRADE Exports (% of Total Exports)	ARMS TRADE Imports (% of Total Imports)
Guinea	1.5	12	430,000	0.0	0.0
Guinea-Bissau	2.8	7	4,000	0.0	0.0
Haiti	2.9	0	–	0.0	0.0
Honduras	1.4	18	–	0.0	0.8
Hungary	1.5	71	3,400	0.2	0.2
India	2.4	1,265	323,500	0.0	1.2
Indonesia	1.8	280	100	0.0	0.4
Iran	2.6	440	1,900,000	1.6	2.2
Iraq	–	390	110,000	0.0	0.0
Ireland	1.3	13	4,300	0.0	0.0
Israel	9.6	185	1,289,000*	4.1	1.1
Italy	1.8	435	20,000	0.1	0.1
Jamaica	0.8	3	–	0.0	0.0
Japan	1.0	240	300	0.0	0.2
Jordan	7.7	112	1,413,800	0.0	1.9
Kazakhstan	0.9	28	14,000	0.4	7.2
Kenya	2.3	22	196,000	0.0	0.3
Korea, North	28.6	1,040		3.6	5.8
Korea, South	3.4	655		0.0	0.8
Kuwait	11.6	20	90,000	0.0	11.6
Kyrgyzstan	0.7	13	15,500	2.5	0.0
Laos	4.2	50	–	0.0	0.0
Latvia	0.9	7	–	0.0	0.3
Lebanon	3.7	55	362,300	0.0	0.5
Lesotho	1.9	2	–	0.0	0.0
Libya	6.0	76	27,000	0.0	0.0
Lithuania	0.5	12	100	0.0	0.2
Macedonia	3.3	16	3,500	0.0	0.0
Madagascar	0.9	21	–	0.0	1.0

COUNTRY	DEFENSE EXPENDITURES (% of GNP)	NUMBERS IN ARMED FORCES (in thousands)	REFUGEE POPULATION	ARMS TRADE Exports (% of Total Exports)	ARMS TRADE Imports (% of Total Imports)
Malawi	1.6	10		0.0	0.0
Malaysia	3.0	122	5,200	0.1	1.0
Mali	1.8	8	17,000	0.0	0.0
Mauritania	3.2	10	5,000	0.0	0.0
Mauritius	0.4	1	–	0.0	0.0
Mexico	1.0	175	30,000	0.0	0.0
Moldova	2.1	12	–	5.6	0.0
Mongolia	2.4	21	–	0.0	0.0
Morocco	4.3	195	–	–	–
Mozambique	5.4	12	–	0.0	0.0
Myanmar (Burma)	–	–	–	–	–
Namibia	2.1	8	1,000	0.0	0.8
Nepal	0.9	40	116,000	0.0	0.0
Netherlands	2.1	67	64,2000	0.1	0.1
New Zealand	1.3	10	–	0.0	0.3
Nicaragua	2.2	14	700	7.7	0.0
Niger	1.2	9	7,000	0.0	0.0
Nigeria	0.8	89	9,000	0.0	0.0
Norway	2.7	38	3,100	0.0	0.4
Oman	16.7	36	–	–	10.8
Pakistan	6.1	587	1,215,650	0.3	4.2
Panama	1.4	12	300	0.0	0.0
Papua New Guinea	1.4	5	8,200	0.0	0.0
Paraguay	1.4	12	–	0.0	0.0
Peru	1.7	115	–	0.0	3.0
Philippines	1.5	110	100	0.0	0.3
Poland	2.3	278	1,200	0.2	0.3
Portugal	2.6	78	150	0.0	0.3
Puerto Rico	–	–	–	–	–

(continued on next page)

COUNTRY	DEFENSE EXPENDITURES (% of GNP)	NUMBERS IN ARMED FORCES (in thousands)	REFUGEE POPULATION	ARMS TRADE Exports (% of Total Exports)	Imports (% of Total Imports)
Romania	2.5	209	2,000	0.3	0.0
Russian Federation	11.4	1,400	324,000	4.3	0.0
Rwanda	5.2	33	28,000	0.0	0.0
Saudi Arabia	13.5	175	116,750	0.0	31.3
Senegal	1.6	14	41,000	0.0	0.4
Sierra Leone	6.1	14	15,000	0.0	0.0
Singapore	4.7	60	–	0.0	0.2
Slovak Republic	3.0	52	100	0.8	3.1
Slovenia	1.5	10	5,300	0.1	0.3
South Africa	2.2	100	28,000	0.4	0.8
Spain	1.6	210	3,300	0.1	0.6
Sri Lanka	4.6	110	–	0.0	3.1
Sudan	6.6	89	365,000	0.0	8.4
Sweden	2.8	51	1,300	0.4	0.0
Switzerland	1.6	29	34,100	0.1	0.0
Syrian Arab Republic	7.2	320	361,000	0.0	1.5
Tajikistan	3.7	8	3,800	1.4	0.0
Tanzania	1.8	35	295,000	0.0	0.0
Thailand	2.5	288	205,600	0.0	1.6
Togo	2.3	12	12,000	0.0	0.0

COUNTRY	DEFENSE EXPENDITURES (% of GNP)	NUMBERS IN ARMED FORCES (in thousands)	REFUGEE POPULATION	ARMS TRADE Exports (% of Total Exports)	Imports (% of Total Imports)
Trinidad and Tobago	1.7	3	–	–	0.0
Tunisia	2.0	35	–	0.0	0.5
Turkey	4.0	805	5,000	0.3	2.0
Turkmenistan	1.7	21	13,000	0.0	4.2
Uganda	2.3	52	185,000	0.0	0.0
Ukraine	2.9	476	4,900	1.4	0.0
United Arab Emirates	4.8	60	500	0.0	1.8
United Kingdom	3.0	233	58,100	2.1	0.1
United States	3.8	1,620	491,000	2.7	0.1
Uruguay	2.4	25	150	0.0	0.2
Uzbekistan	3.8	21	1,250	0.3	0.0
Venezuela	1.1	75	300	0.0	0.8
Vietnam	2.6	550	15,000	0.0	2.7
West Bank and Gaza	–	–	–	–	–
Yemen, Rep.	15.7	68	64,900	0.0	13.9
Yugoslavia (Serbia-Montenegro)	–	–	550,000	–	–
Zambia	2.8	22	118,000	0.0	0.6
Zimbabwe	4.0	40	1,000	0.0	0.0

*figures for Israel includes the Palestinian populations of the Gaza Strip and West Bank.

Note: Data for some countries are based on partial or uncertain data or rough estimates; see ACDA 1997.

aData prior to 1990 refer to the Federal Republic of Germany before unification.

Table D
Armed Conflict in the 1990s

COUNTRY	TYPE OF WAR	LOCATION OF WAR	ADVERSARIES (in interstate wars)	DATE WAR BEGAN	COMBAT STATUS (1/1/1999)
Afghanistan	civil war	general		1978	continuing
Albania	civil war	southern regions		1996	continuing
Algeria	civil war	general		1992	continuing
Angola	civil war	general		1975	continuing
	regional civil war	Cabinda enclave		1978	continuing
Armenia	interstate war	Nagorno-Karabakh	Azerbaijan	1990	suspended by agreement 1994
Azerbaijan	interstate war	Nagorno-Karabakh	Armenia	1990	suspended by agreement 1994
Bangladesh	regional civil war	Chittagong		1973	suspended by agreement 1992
Bosnia-Herzegovina	civil and interstate war	general		1992	suspended by agreement 1995
Burundi	civil war	general		1988	continuing
Cambodia	civil war	general		1970	continuing
Cameroon	interstate war	Bakassi border region	Nigeria	1996	continuing
Chad	civil war	general		1965	continuing
Colombia	civil war	general		1986	continuing
Congo	civil war	general		1993	suspended by agreement 1994
Croatia	civil & interstate war	Slavonia/Krajina	Yugoslavia (Serbia-Montenegro)	1991	suspended by agreement 1992
	regional civil war	Western Slavonia/Krajina		1995	suspended by agreement 1995
Djibouti	regional civil war	Afar		1991	continuing
Ecuador	interstate war	border region	Peru	1995	suspended by agreement 1995
Egypt	civil war	general		1992	continuing
El Salvador	civil war	general		1979	suspended by agreement 1979
Eritrea	war of independence	Eritrea	Ethiopia	1962	suspended by agreement 1991
	interstate war	Hanish Islands	Yemen	1997	suspended by agreement 1998
Ethiopia	against war of independence	Eritrea	Eritrea	1962	suspended by agreement 1991
	civil war	general		1974	suspended by agreement 1991
France	interstate war	Kuwait/Iraq		1991	suspended by agreement 1991
Georgia	regional civil war	western region		1991	break in action 1993
	regional civil war	South Ossetia		1991	suspended by agreement 1996
	regional civil war	Abkhazia		1992	suspended by agreement 1993
Ghana	regional civil war	northern regions		1994	break in action 1995
Guatemala	civil war	general		1968	continuing
Haiti	civil war	general		1991	break in action 1991
India	interstate war	Kashmir	Pakistan	1982	continuing
	regional civil war	Kashmir		1990	continuing
	regional civil war	Andhra Pradesh		1969	continuing
	regional civil war	Punjab		1981	break in action 1993
	regional civil war	Assam		1987	continuing

(continued on next page)

COUNTRY	TYPE OF WAR	LOCATION OF WAR	ADVERSARIES (in interstate wars)	DATE WAR BEGAN	COMBAT STATUS (1/1/1999)
Indonesia	regional civil war	Irian Jaya		1963	continuing
	regional civil war	East Timor		1975	continuing
	regional civil war	Sumatra		1989	break in action 1994
Iran	civil war	general		1978	break in action 1993
	regional civil war	northwestern Kurdish regions		1979	break in action 1995
Iraq	regional civil war	northern regions/Kurdistan		1974	continuing
	interstate war	Iraq/Kuwait	Kuwait, France, Saudi Arabia, Syria, United Kingdom, United States	1990	suspended by agreement 1991
	regional civil war	southern Shia regions		1991	continuing
	interstate war	central Iraq	United States and Great Britain	1998	suspended by agreement 1998
Israel	civil war	general, including occupied territories		1948	continuing
Kurdistan	regional civil war	Turkish border region		1991	continuing
	civil war	general		1993	continuing
Kuwait	interstate war	Kuwait/Iraq	Iraq	1990	suspended by agreement 1991
Laos	civil war	general		1975	break in action 1990
Lebanon	general, then regional civil war	southern zone, from 1990		1975	continuing
Liberia	civil war	general		1989	continuing
Libya	civil war	general		1995	continuing
Mali	regional civil war	northern Tuareg regions		1990	suspended by agreement 1995
Mauritania	interstate war	border regions	Senegal	1989	suspended by agreement 1991
Mexico	regional civil war	Chiapas		1994	suspended by agreement 1995
Moldova	regional civil war	Dniestr Repubic		1991	suspended by agreement 1992
Morocco	against war of independence	western Sahara	Polisario Front (western Sahara)	1975	break in action 1991
Mozambique	civil war	general		1976	suspended by agreement 1992
Myanmar (Burma)	regional civil war	Kachin		1948	suspended by agreement 1994
	regional civil war	Shan		1948	continuing
	regional civil war	Karen		1949	continuing
	civil war	general		1991	break in action 1992
	regional civil war	Arakan		1992	suspended by agreement 1994
	regional civil war	Kaya		1992	continuing
Nicaragua	civil war	general		1970	suspended by agreement 1990
Niger	regional civil war	northern Tuareg regions		1991	continuing
	regional civil war	eastern region		1994	continuing
Nigeria	interstate war	Bakassi border region	Cameroon	1996	continuing
Pakistan	interstate war	Kashmir	India	1982	break in action 1992
	regional civil war	Karachi/Sind		1992	continuing
Papua New Guinea	regional civil war	Bougainville		1988	continuing
Peru	civil war	general		1980	continuing
	interstate war	border region	Ecuador	1995	suspended by agreement 1995
Philippines	civil war	general		1969	continuing

(continued on next page)

COUNTRY	TYPE OF WAR	LOCATION OF WAR	ADVERSARIES (in interstate wars)	DATE WAR BEGAN	COMBAT STATUS (1/1/1999)
	regional civil war	Mindanao		1974	suspended by agreement 1996
Russia	regional civil war	North Ossetia/Ingushetia		1992	break in action 1992
	regional civil war	Moscow		1993	break in action 1993
	regional civil war	Chechnya		1994	suspended by agreement 1996
Rwanda	civil war	general		1990	continuing
Saudi Arabia	interstate war	Kuwait/Iraq	Iraq	1991	suspended by agreement 1991
Senegal	interstate war	border regions	Mauritania	1989	suspended by agreement 1991
	regional civil war	Casamance region		1990	continuing
Sierra Leone	civil war	general		1991	suspended by agreement 1996
Slovenia	interstate war	Slovenia	Yugoslavia (Serbia-Montenegro)	1991	suspended by agreement 1991
Somalia	civil war	general		1977	continuing
Somaliland	civil war	general		1991	break in action 1995
South Africa	civil war	general		1984	suspended by agreement 1994
Spain	regional civil war	Basque region		1968	break in action 1992
Sri Lanka	regional civil war	Tamil areas/northeast		1977	continuing
	civil war	general		1983	break in action 1990
Sudan	regional civil war	southern regions		1955	continuing
	regional civil war	Beja		1994	break in action 1995
Suriname	civil war	general		1986	suspended by agreement 1992
Syria	interstate war	Kuwait/Iraq	Iraq	1991	suspended by agreement 1991
Tajikistan	civil war	general		1992	continuing
Togo	civil war	general		1991	break in action 1991
Trinidad and Tobago	civil war	general		1990	break in action 1990
Turkey	regional civil war	southeastern Kurdish region/northern Iraq		1977	continuing
	regional civil war	western region		1991	break in action 1992
Uganda	regional civil war	northern region		1986	continuing
	regional civil war	central region		1994	break in action 1995
	regional civil war	southeastern region		1995	break in action 1995
United Kingdom	regional civil war	northern Ireland		1969	suspended by agreement 1994
	interstate war	Kuwait/Iraq	Iraq	1991	suspended by agreement 1991
United States	interstate war	Kuwait/Iraq	Iraq	1991	suspended by agreement 1991
Venezuela	civil war	general		1992	break in action 1992
Yemen	civil war	general		1994	suspended by agreement
Yugoslavia (Serbia-Montenegro)	interstate war	Slovenia	Slovenia	1991	suspended by agreement 1991
	interstate war	Croatia	Croatia	1991	suspended by agreement 1992
	interstate war	Kosovo	NATO countries	1999	suspended by agreement 1999
Zaire	civil war	general		1995	continuing

Dan Smith, *The State of War and Peace Atlas*, 3rd edition (Penguin Books: New York, 1997); U.S. Central Intelligence Agency, *The CIA Factbook*, online data 1999, *Encyclopedia Britannica*, online edition.

Table E

World Countries: Basic Economic Indicators 1997

COUNTRY	GROSS NATIONAL PRODUCT (GNP) 1997[b]		PURCHASING POWER PARITY GNP 1997			AVERAGE ANNUAL % GROWTH IN GDP		STRUCTURE OF ECONOMIC OUTPUT (GDP) 1997 (value added in % of GDP)			
	Total ($U.S. billions)	Per Capita ($U.S.)	Total ($U.S. billions)	Per Capita ($U.S.)	Rank	1980–1990	1990–1997	Agriculture	Industry	Manufacturing	Services
Albania	2.5	760	7[c]	2,170[c]	154	1.5	1.8	63	18	—	19
Algeria	43.9	1,500	124[c]	4,250[c]	106	2.7	0.8	11	49	9	39
Angola	3.0	260	10[c]	820[c]	200	3.7	-1.2	9	62	4	29
Argentina	319.3	8,950	360	10,100	64	-0.4	5.4	7	33	22	61
Armenia	2.1	560	10	2,540	143	—	-10.3	41	36	25	23
Australia	382.7	20,650	362	19,510	24	3.4	3.6	3	26	14	71
Austria	225.4	27,920	178	22,010	16	2.2	2.0	1	30	20	68
Azerbaijan	3.9	510	12	1,520	170	—	-15.1	22	18	18	60
Bangladesh	44.1	360	135	1,090	189	4.3	4.7	24	27	17	49
Belarus	22.1	2,150	49	4,820	98	—	-6.1	14	44	37	42
Belgium	272.4	26,730	235	23,090	13	2.0	1.4	1	27	18	72
Benin	2.2	380	7	1,260	182	2.9	4.5	38	14	8	48
Bolivia	7.6	970	22	2,810	139	-0.2	4.1	16	33	19	51
Bosnia-Herzegovina	—	—[d]	—	—	—	—	—	—	—	—	—
Botswana	5.1	3,310	11	7,430	78	10.3	4.5	3	48	5	49
Brazil	784.0	4,790	1,039	6,350	90	2.7	3.4	8	35	23	57
Bulgaria	9.8	1,170	32	3,870	115	3.4	-3.3	23	26	18	50
Burkina Faso	2.6	250	11[c]	1,000[c]	193	3.6	3.3	35	27	20	38
Burundi	0.9	140	4[c]	620[c]	207	4.4	-3.6	53	17	10	30
Cambodia	3.2	300	13[c]	1,290[c]	180	—	5.5	51	15	6	34
Cameroon	8.6	620	25	1,770	159	3.4	-0.1	41	21	10	38
Canada	595.0	19,640	659	21,750	17	3.3	2.2	—	—	—	—
Central African Republic	1.1	320	4[c]	1,310[c]	178	1.4	1.2	54	18	9	28
Chad	1.6	230	7[c]	950[c]	195	3.7	4.6	39	15	12	46
Chile	70.5	4,820	179	12,240	55	4.2	8.3	7	31	15	61
China	1,055.4	860	3,770	3,070	135	10.2	11.6	19	49	37	32
Hong Kong, China	163.8[f]	25,200[f]	158	24,350	9	6.9	5.3	0	15	7	84
Colombia	87.1	2,180	263[c]	6,570[c]	83	3.6	4.4	11	20	17	69
Congo (Zaire)	5.2	110	36[c]	760[c]	201	1.6	-6.0	58	17	—	25
Congo Republic	1.8	670	3	1,290	180	3.3	0.7	10	57	6	33
Costa Rica	9.3	2,680	23	6,510	85	3.0	3.8	15	23	17	62
Côte d'Ivoire	10.2	710	24	1,690	161	0.7	3.0	27	21	18	51
Croatia	19.3	4,060	23	4,930	97	—	-1.0	12	25	20	62
Cuba	—	—[g]	—	—	—	—	—	—	—	—	—
Czech Republic	54.0	5,240	107	10,380	63	1.7	-0.2	—	—	—	—
Denmark	184.3	34,890	124	23,450	12	2.3	2.5	4	27	19	69
Dominican Republic	14.1	1,750	38	4,690	102	3.1	5.1	12	32	17	55
Ecuador	18.8	1,570	56	4,700	101	2.0	3.1	12	35	21	53
Egypt	72.2	1,200	186	3,080	134	5.4	4.0	18	32	25	51
El Salvador	10.7	1,810	17	2,860	138	0.2	5.6	13	28	21	60

(continued on next page)

COUNTRY	GROSS NATIONAL PRODUCT (GNP) 1997[b]		PURCHASING POWER PARITY GNP 1997			AVERAGE ANNUAL % GROWTH IN GDP		STRUCTURE OF ECONOMIC OUTPUT (GDP) 1997 (value added in % of GDP)			
	Total ($U.S. billions)	Per Capita ($U.S.)	Total ($U.S. billions)	Per Capita ($U.S.)	Rank	1980–1990	1990–1997	Agriculture	Industry	Manufacturing	Services
Eritrea	0.9	230	4[c]	1,040[c]	192	—	5.2	9	30	16	61
Estonia	4.9	3,360	7	5,090	94	2.2	-3.8	7	28	17	65
Ethiopia[k]	6.5	110	30	500	209	2.3	4.3	55	7	0	38
Finland	127.4	24,790	101	19,660	23	3.3	1.4	4	34	25	62
France	1,541.6	26,300	1,301	22,210	15	2.3	1.3	2	26	19	72
Gabon	4.8	4,120	8	6,560	84	0.9	3.2	7	55	5	37
Gambia	0.4	340	2[c]	1,440[c]	175	3.6	2.2	30	15	6	55
Georgia	4.7	860	11	1,980	156	0.4	-16.3	32	23	18	45
Germany[l]	2,321.0	28,280	1,737	21,170	19	2.2	1.4	1	—	24	44
Ghana	7.0	390	29[c]	1,610[c]	165	3.0	4.2	36	26	9	39
Greece	122.4	11,640	132	12,540	54	1.8	1.6	11	18	10	71
Guatemala	16.6	1,580	43	4,060	110	0.8	4.1	24	20	14	56
Guinea	3.8	550	12	1,790	158	—	5.0	23	35	4	42
Guinea-Bissau	0.3	230	—	—	—	4.0	3.4	54	11	7	35
Haiti	2.9	380	9[c]	1,260[c]	182	-0.2	-2.5	30	20	—	50
Honduras	4.4	740	14	2,260	150	2.7	3.3	20	28	16	52
Hungary	45.8	4,510	71	6,970	80	1.3	-0.2	6	34	25	60
India	357.4	370	1,599	1,660	163	5.8	6.0	25	30	19	45
Indonesia	221.5	1,110	679	3,390	125	6.1	7.5	16	43	26	41
Iran	108.6	1,780	347	5,690	92	1.7	4.0	25	34	14	40
Iraq	—	—[g]	—	—	—	-6.8	—	—	—	—	—
Ireland	65.1	17,790	64	17,420	31	3.2	7.0	6	—	—	62
Israel	94.4	16,180	103	17,680	30	3.5	5.8	—	—	—	—
Italy	1,160.4	20,170	1,156	20,100	22	2.4	1.1	3	31	20	66
Jamaica	4.0	1,550	9	3,330	129	2.0	0.4	8	35	16	57
Japan	4,812.1	38,160	3,076	24,400	8	4.0	1.5	2	38	24	60
Jordan	6.8	1,520	15	3,350	127	2.5	6.3	3	25	13	71
Kazakhstan	21.3	1,350	56	3,530	124	—	-7.9	12	27	—	61
Kenya	9.7	340	33	1,160	184	4.2	2.1	29	16	10	56
Korea, North	—	—[g]	—	—	—	—	—	—	—	—	—
Korea, South	485.2	10,550[h]	618	13,430	52	9.4	7.2	6	43	26	51
Kuwait	—	—	—	—	—	1.3	—	0	54	11	46
Kyrgyzstan	2.2	480	10	2,180	153	—	-9.5	45	23	18	33
Laos	1.9	400	6	1,300	179	—	6.7	52	21	16	26
Latvia	6.0	2,430	10	3,970	113	3.5	-8.5	7	31	21	62
Lebanon	13.9	3,350	25	6,090	91	—	8.3	12	27	17	61
Lesotho	1.4	680[i]	5[c]	2,490[c]	144	4.4	7.8	11	42	17	47
Libya	—	—[j]	—	—	—	-5.7	—	—	—	—	—
Lithuania	8.4	2,260	15	4,140	107	—	-7.1	13	32	21	55
Macedonia	2.2	1,100	6[c]	3,180[c]	132	—	-0.8	12	27	—	61
Madagascar	3.6	250	13	900	197	1.1	0.9	32	14	11	55
Malawi	2.1	210	7	700	204	2.5	3.6	36	18	14	46

(continued on next page)

— 115 —

COUNTRY	GROSS NATIONAL PRODUCT (GNP) 1997[b]		PURCHASING POWER PARITY GNP 1997			AVERAGE ANNUAL % GROWTH IN GDP		STRUCTURE OF ECONOMIC OUTPUT (GDP) 1997 (value added in % of GDP)			
	Total ($U.S. billions)	Per Capita ($U.S.)	Total ($U.S. billions)	Per Capita ($U.S.)	Rank	1980–1990	1990–1997	Agriculture	Industry	Manufacturing	Services
Malaysia	98.2	4,530	168	7,730	77	5.3	8.6	12	47	34	41
Mali	2.7	260	7	720	202	2.8	3.3	49	17	7	34
Mauritania	1.1	440	4[c]	1,650[c]	164	1.8	4.2	25	29	10	46
Mauritius	4.4	3,870	11	9,230	69	6.2	5.0	9	33	25	58
Mexico	348.6	3,700	765[c]	8,110[c]	73	0.7	2.2	5	26	20	69
Moldova	2.0	460	6	1,450	174	3.0	-14.1	31	35	28	34
Mongolia	1.0	390	4[c]	1,490[c]	171	5.4	-0.6	37	23	—	40
Morocco	34.4	1,260	88	3,210	131	4.2	1.9	15	33	18	51
Mozambique	2.4	140	12[c]	690[c]	205	-0.1	4.9	31	24	10	45
Myanmar (Burma)	—	—[d]	—	—	—	0.6	6.3	59	10	7	31
Namibia	3.4	2,110	8[c]	5,100[c]	93	0.9	3.8	11	33	14	56
Nepal	4.9	220	24	1,090	189	4.6	5.1	41	22	9	36
Netherlands	403.1	25,830	332	21,300	18	2.3	2.4	3	27	18	70
New Zealand	59.5	15,830	59	15,780	38	1.8	3.4	—	—	—	—
Nicaragua	1.9	410	9[c]	1,820[c]	157	-2.0	4.1	34	22	16	44
Niger	2.0	200	8[c]	830[c]	199	-0.1	1.5	38	18	7	44
Nigeria	33.4	280	102	860	198	1.6	2.8	33	47	5	20
Norway	159.0	36,100	107	24,260	10	2.8	4.0	2	32	11	66
Oman	—	—	—	—	—	8.4	5.9	—	—	—	—
Pakistan	64.6	500	202	1,580	168	6.3	4.2	25	25	17	50
Panama	8.4	3,080	19	6,890	81	0.5	4.8	8	18	9	73
Papua New Guinea	4.2	930	—	—	—	1.9	5.7	28	36	9	36
Paraguay	10.2	2,000	20	3,860	116	2.5	3.1	23	22	14	55
Peru	63.7	2,610	112	4,580	103	-0.3	6.2	7	36	23	57
Philippines	88.4	1,200	270	3,670	119	1.0	3.3	19	32	22	49
Poland	138.9	3,590	251	6,510	85	1.8	4.1	6	39	—	55
Portugal	109.5	11,010	141	14,180	47	3.1	2.1	4	32	22	64
Puerto Rico	—	—	—	—	—	4.0	—	—	—	—	—
Romania	31.8	1,410	96	4,270	105	0.5	-0.3	20	45	—	36
Russian Federation	394.9	2,680	631	4,280	104	—	-7.7	8	37	—	55
Rwanda	1.7	210	5	650	206	2.2	-5.7	37	26	19	36
Saudi Arabia	143.4	7,150	211[c]	10,540[c]	61	0.0	1.7	6	45	10	49
Senegal	4.8	540	15	1,690	161	3.1	2.5	18	22	15	59
Sierra Leone	0.8	160	2	410	210	0.3	-4.4	50	21	7	29
Singapore	101.8	32,810	91	29,230	3	6.6	8.5	0	35	24	65
Slovak Republic	19.8	3,680	42	7,680	74	2.0	0.6	5	33	—	62
Slovenia	19.5	9,840	24	11,880	57	—	1.4	5	39	29	57
South Africa	130.2	3,210	292[c]	7,190[c]	79	1.2	1.5	5	39	24	57
Spain	569.6	14,490	617	15,690	39	3.0	1.6	3	—	18	—
Sri Lanka	14.8	800	46	2,460	146	4.0	5.3	22	26	17	52
Sudan	7.9	290	38[c]	1,370[c]	177	0.4	7.7	—	—	—	—
Sweden	231.9	26,210	168	19,010	25	2.3	0.9	—	—	—	—
Switzerland	305.2	43,060	188	26,580	7	2.0	0.2	—	—	—	—
Syria	16.6	1,120	45	3,000	136	1.5	6.3	—	—	—	—
Tajikistan	2.0	330	7	1,100	188	—	-16.4	—	—	—	—
Tanzania	6.6[j]	210[j]	19	620	207	—[j]	2.7[j]	47[j]	21[j]	7[j]	31[j]

(continued on next page)

COUNTRY	GROSS NATIONAL PRODUCT (GNP) 1997[b]		PURCHASING POWER PARITY GNP 1997			AVERAGE ANNUAL % GROWTH IN GDP		STRUCTURE OF ECONOMIC OUTPUT (GDP) 1997 (value added in % of GDP)			
	Total ($U.S. billions)	Per Capita ($U.S.)	Total ($U.S. billions)	Per Capita ($U.S.)	Rank	1980–1990	1990–1997	Agriculture	Industry	Manufacturing	Services
Thailand	165.8	2,740	393	6,490	87	7.6	7.4	11	40	29	49
Togo	1.5	340	6[c]	1,460[c]	173	1.7	1.9	42	21	9	37
Trinidad and Tobago	5.6	4,250	8	6,460	89	-0.8	1.2	2	46	9	52
Tunisia	19.4	2,100	47	5,050	95	3.3	4.3	13	29	19	58
Turkey	199.3	3,130	412	6,470	88	5.4	4.1	15	28	18	57
Turkmenistan	3.0	640	7	1,410	176	—	-9.6	—	—	—	—
Uganda	6.6	330	24[c]	1,160[c]	184	2.9	7.4	44	17	8	39
Ukraine	52.6	1,040	110	2,170	154	—	-13.1	12	40	6	48
United Arab Emirates	—	—[h]	—	—	—	-3.5	—	—	—	—	—
United Kingdom	1,231.3	20,870	1,222	20710	20	3.2	2.0	2	31	21	67
United States	7,783.1	29,080	7,783	29,080	4	3.0	3.0	2	27	18	71
Uruguay	20.0	6,130	30	9,110	70	0.4	4.0	8	27	18	64
Uzbekistan	24.2	1,020	—	—	—	—	-2.4	31	27	9	42
Venezuela	79.3	3,480	197	8,600	71	1.1	2.2	4	41	16	55
Vietnam	24.0	310	122	1,590	167	4.6	8.6	26	31	—	43
West Bank and Gaza	—	—[g]	—	—	—	—	—	—	—	—	—
Yemen, Rep.	4.4	270	12	720	202	—	3.7	18	49	11	34
Yugoslavia (Serbia-Montenegro)	—	—[g]	—	—	—	—	—	—	—	—	—
Zambia	3.5	370	9	910	196	1.0	1.0	16	31	12	52
Zimbabwe	8.2	720	26	2,240	151	3.6	1.8	19	25	18	56

b. Calculated using the World Bank Atlas method.
c. The estimate is based on regression; others are extrapolated from the latest International Comparison Programme benchmark estimates.
d. Estimated to be low income ($785 or less).
f. GNP data refer to GDP.
g. Estimated to be lower middle income ($786 to $3,125).
h. Estimated to be high income ($9,656 or more).
i. Estimated to be upper middle income ($3,126 to $9,655).
j. Data refer to mainland Tanzania only.
k. Data prior to 1992 include Eritrea.
l. Data prior to 1990 refer to the Federal Republic of Germany before unification.

Sources: World Development Indicators (World Bank, 1999)

Table F

World Countries: Population Growth, 1950–2050

COUNTRY	POPULATION (thousands)				AVERAGE ANNUAL POPULATION CHANGE (percent)			AVERAGE ANNUAL INCREMENT TO THE POPULATION (thousands)		
	1950	1998	2025	2050	1985–90	1995–00	2005–10	1985–90	1995–00	2005–10
WORLD	2,513,878	5,929,839	8,039,130	9,366,724	1.7	1.4	1.2	86,966	80,848	80,011
AFRICA	223,974	778,484	1,453,899	2,046,401	2.8	2.6	2.5	16,330	20,063	24,232
Algeria	8,753	30,175	47,322	58,991	2.6	2.3	1.9	610	698	690
Angola	4,131	11,967	25,547	38,897	2.9	3.3	2.9	245	393	461
Benin	2,046	5,681	12,276	18,095	3.0	2.8	2.9	132	163	227
Botswana	389	1,551	2,576	3,320	3.3	2.2	2.0	39	34	39
Burkina Faso	3,654	11,402	23,451	35,419	2.8	2.8	2.8	240	316	414
Burundi	2,456	6,589	12,341	16,937	2.9	2.8	2.4	148	182	205
Cameroon	4,466	14,323	28,521	41,951	2.8	2.7	2.7	301	387	496
Central African Republic	1,314	3,489	6,006	8,215	2.4	2.1	2.1	66	73	89
Chad	2,658	6,892	12,648	18,004	2.0	2.1	2.3	106	187	200
Congo (Zaire)	12,184	49,208	105,925	164,635	3.3	2.6	3.0	1,142	1,259	1,943
Congo Republic	808	2,822	5,747	8,729	3.0	2.8	2.7	62	78	99
Cote d'Ivoire	2,776	14,567	24,397	31,706	3.3	2.0	2.2	349	290	395
Egypt	21,834	65,675	96,766	115,480	2.5	1.9	1.6	1,313	1,205	1,197
Equatorial Guinea	226	430	798	1,144	2.4	2.5	2.4	8	10	13
Eritrea	1,140	3,548	6,504	8,808	1.3	3.7	2.3	37	128	104
Ethiopia	18,434	62,111	136,288	212,732	3.1	3.2	3.0	1,401	1,954	2,480
Gabon	469	1,170	2,118	2,952	3.1	2.8	2.3	26	32	34
Gambia	294	1,194	1,984	2,604	4.2	2.3	2.0	34	27	29
Ghana	4,900	18,857	36,341	51,205	3.1	2.8	2.6	436	518	636
Guinea	2,550	7,673	15,286	22,914	2.9	1.4	2.8	154	102	272
Guinea-Bissau	505	1,134	1,921	2,674	2.0	2.0	2.0	18	22	28
Kenya	6,265	29,020	50,202	66,054	3.3	2.2	2.4	721	638	880
Lesotho	734	2,184	4,031	5,643	2.6	2.5	2.4	44	53	67
Liberia	824	2,748	6,573	9,955	3.2	8.6	3.0	75	227	123
Libya	1,029	5,980	12,885	19,109	3.7	3.3	3.0	152	196	246
Madagascar	4,229	16,348	34,476	50,807	3.4	3.1	3.0	395	504	643
Malawi	2,881	10,377	20,391	39,825	5.1	2.4	2.6	417	262	341
Mali	3,520	11,832	24,575	36,817	3.0	3.0	2.8	259	353	441
Mauritania	825	2,453	4,443	6,007	2.5	2.5	2.4	47	62	73
Mauritius	493	1,154	1,481	1,654	0.8	1.1	1.0	8	12	13
Morocco	8,953	28,012	39,925	47,276	2.1	1.8	1.4	479	492	437
Mozambique	6,198	18,691	35,444	51,774	0.9	2.5	2.5	128	461	582
Namibia	511	1,653	2,999	4,167	2.7	2.4	2.3	35	39	48
Niger	2,400	10,119	22,385	24,576	3.1	3.3	3.1	225	331	418
Nigeria	21,935	121,773	238,397	338,510	2.9	2.8	2.6	2,617	3,413	4,152
Rwanda	2,120	6,528	12,981	16,937	2.8	7.9	2.4	180	498	215
Senegal	2,500	9,001	16,896	23,442	2.8	2.7	2.5	190	237	286
Sierra Leone	1,944	4,577	8,200	11,368	2.2	3.0	2.2	82	134	125
Somalia	3,072	10,653	23,669	36,408	1.8	3.9	3.1	150	408	445
South Africa	13,683	44,295	71,621	91,466	2.3	2.2	2.0	805	958	1,050
Sudan	9,190	28,526	46,850	59,947	2.3	2.2	2.1	520	623	721
Swaziland	264	931	1,675	2,228	2.7	2.8	2.4	19	25	28
Tanzania	7,886	32,189	62,436	88,963	3.1	2.3	2.6	740	732	1,088
Togo	1,329	4,434	8,762	12,655	3.0	2.7	2.6	99	118	150

(continued on next page)

COUNTRY	POPULATION (thousands)				AVERAGE ANNUAL POPULATION CHANGE (percent)			AVERAGE ANNUAL INCREMENT TO THE POPULATION (thousands)		
	1950	1998	2025	2050	1985-90	1995-00	2005-10	1985-90	1995-00	2005-10
Tunisia	3,530	9,497	13,524	15,907	2.1	1.8	1.4	166	170	151
Uganda	4,762	21,318	44,983	66,305	2.4	2.6	2.9	377	554	821
Zambia	2,440	8,690	16,163	21,965	2.4	2.5	2.5	163	210	275
Zimbabwe	2,730	11,924	19,347	24,904	3.2	2.1	2.0	293	237	293
NORTH AND CENTRAL AMERICA										
Belize	69	230	375	480	2.4	2.5	2.0	4	6	6
Canada	13,737	30,194	36,385	36,352	1.4	0.9	0.7	370	255	231
Costa Rica	862	3,650	5,608	6,902	2.8	2.1	1.7	79	75	74
Cuba	5,850	11,115	11,798	13,141	1.0	0.4	0.3	103	47	29
Dominican Republic	2,353	8,232	11,164	13,141	2.2	1.7	1.2	147	134	117
El Salvador	1,951	6,059	9,221	11,364	1.5	2.2	1.7	71	131	121
Guatemala	2,969	11,562	21,668	29,353	2.9	2.8	2.5	247	320	371
Haiti	3,261	7,534	12,513	17,524	2.0	1.9	1.9	122	139	169
Honduras	1,380	6,147	10,656	13,920	3.1	2.8	2.2	139	166	171
Jamaica	1,403	2,539	3,370	3,886	0.5	0.9	1.2	11	24	32
Mexico	27,727	95,831	130,196	154,120	2.0	1.6	1.2	1,552	1,547	1,349
Nicaragua	1,098	4,464	7,639	9,922	2.2	2.6	2.2	73	114	123
Panama	860	2,767	3,779	4,365	2.0	1.6	1.3	46	45	40
Trinidad and Tobago	636	1,318	1,692	1,899	1.0	0.8	1.1	12	11	15
United States	157,813	273,754	332,481	347,543	1.0	0.8	0.8	2,450	2,142	2,204
SOUTH AMERICA										
Argentina	17,150	36,123	47,160	54,522	1.4	1.3	1.1	444	453	434
Bolivia	2,714	7,957	13,131	16,956	2.2	2.3	2.0	136	183	191
Brazil	53,975	165,158	216,596	243,259	1.8	1.2	1.1	2,548	2,037	2,067
Chile	6,082	14,824	19,548	22,215	1.7	1.4	1.1	210	200	175
Colombia	11,945	37,685	52,668	62,284	2.1	1.7	1.3	636	618	579
Ecuador	3,387	12,175	17,796	21,290	2.4	2.0	1.5	233	237	220
Guyana	423	856	1,114	1,239	0.1	1.0	1.0	0	9	10
Paraguay	1,488	5,222	9,355	12,565	3.1	2.6	2.3	122	134	153
Peru	7,632	24,797	35,518	42,292	2.0	1.7	1.4	415	426	416
Suriname	215	442	605	711	1.2	1.2	1.3	5	5	6
Uruguay	2,239	3,239	3,692	4,027	0.6	0.6	0.5	17	18	18
Venezuela	5,094	23,242	34,775	42,152	2.6	2.0	1.6	473	465	450
ASIA										
Afghanistan	8,958	23,364	45,262	61,373	0.3	5.3	2.4	47	1,186	737
Armenia	1,354	3,646	4,185	4,376	1.2	0.2	0.7	41	6	25
Azerbaijan	2,896	7,714	9,714	10,881	1.4	0.8	0.9	98	59	72
Bangladesh	41,783	124,043	179,980	218,188	2.0	1.6	1.6	2,091	2,016	2,396
Bhutan	734	1,917	3,646	5,184	2.5	2.8	2.5	39	52	60
Cambodia	4,346	10,751	16,990	21,394	3.2	2.2	1.8	255	237	226
China	554,760	1,255,091	1,480,430	1,516,664	1.5	0.9	0.7	17,026	11,215	8,676
Georgia	3,527	5,428	5,762	6,028	0.6	(0.1)	0.2	35	(6)	11
India	357,561	975,772	1,330,201	1,532,674	2.1	1.6	1.3	16,571	15,553	14,020
Indonesia	79,538	206,522	275,245	318,264	1.8	1.5	1.1	3,096	3,021	2,488
Iran	16,913	73,057	128,251	170,269	3.8	2.2	2.4	2,061	1,613	2,250
Iraq	5,158	21,795	41,600	56,129	3.3	2.8	2.6	552	603	751

(continued on next page)

COUNTRY	POPULATION (thousands)				AVERAGE ANNUAL POPULATION CHANGE (percent)			AVERAGE ANNUAL INCREMENT TO THE POPULATION (thousands)		
	1950	1998	2025	2050	1985–90	1995–00	2005–10	1985–90	1995–00	2005–10
Israel	1,258	5,883	7,977	9,144	1.9	1.9	1.2	85	110	83
Japan	83,625	125,920	121,348	109,546	0.4	0.2	(0.0)	540	272	(30)
Jordan	1,237	5,956	11,894	16,671	2.1	3.3	2.8	85	191	217
Kazakhstan	6,703	16,854	20,047	22,260	1.1	0.1	0.7	183	22	121
Korea, North	9,488	23,206	30,046	32,873	1.5	1.6	0.9	284	363	232
Korea, South	20,357	46,115	52,533	52,146	1.0	0.9	0.6	413	395	288
Kuwait	152	1,809	2,904	3,406	4.4	3.0	1.7	85	55	40
Kyrgyzstan	1,740	4,497	5,950	7,182	1.8	0.4	1.1	76	17	51
Laos	1,755	5,358	10,202	13,889	3.1	3.1	2.6	122	162	181
Lebanon	1,443	3,194	4,424	5,189	(0.9)	1.8	1.1	(23)	56	41
Malaysia	6,110	21,450	32,577	38,089	2.6	2.0	1.5	443	432	382
Mongolia	761	2,624	4,052	4,986	3.0	2.1	1.8	61	55	58
Myanmar (Burma)	17,832	47,625	67,654	80,896	1.9	1.8	1.4	762	847	796
Nepal	7,862	23,168	40,554	53,621	2.6	2.5	2.3	454	578	657
Oman	456	2,504	6,538	10,930	4.5	4.2	3.8	72	102	137
Pakistan	39,513	147,811	268,904	357,353	3.3	2.7	2.4	3,589	3,950	4,606
Philippines	20,988	72,164	105,194	130,511	2.1	2.0	1.6	1,221	1,440	1,342
Saudi Arabia	3,201	20,207	43,363	59,812	4.8	2.4	2.9	680	681	793
Singapore	1,022	3,491	4,212	4,190	2.2	1.5	0.7	61	52	27
Sri Lanka	7,678	18,450	23,934	26,995	1.2	1.0	1.1	199	179	224
Syria	3,495	15,335	26,303	34,463	3.5	2.5	2.3	398	385	446
Tajikistan	1,532	6,161	9,747	12,366	3.0	1.9	1.9	147	114	141
Thailand	20,010	59,612	69,089	72,969	1.7	0.8	0.6	890	451	391
Turkey	20,809	63,763	85,791	97,911	2.2	1.6	1.2	1,151	979	834
Turkmenistan	1,211	4,316	6,470	7,916	2.6	1.9	1.7	88	81	85
United Arab Emirates	70	2,354	3,297	3,668	4.3	2.0	1.5	74	47	42
Uzbekistan	6,314	24,105	36,500	45,094	2.4	1.9	1.7	468	451	495
Vietnam	29,954	77,896	110,107	129,763	2.2	1.8	1.2	1,358	1,351	1,083
Yemen	4,316	16,891	39,589	61,129	3.6	3.7	3.3	379	618	775
EUROPE										
Albania	1,230	3,445	4,295	4,747	2.1	0.6	0.8	65	22	28
Austria	6,935	8,210	8,305	7,430	0.4	0.6	0.1	29	49	9
Belarus	7,745	10,323	9,641	8,726	0.5	(0.1)	(0.2)	52	(14)	(22)
Belgium	8,639	10,213	10,271	9,763	0.2	0.3	0.0	19	26	4
Bosnia-Herzegovina	2,661	3,994	4,303	3,789	0.9	3.9	0.0	37	154	1
Bulgaria	7,251	8,387	7,453	6,690	(0.6)	(0.5)	(0.4)	(48)	(41)	(31)
Croatia	3,850	4,494	4,243	3,991	0.2	(0.1)	(0.2)	9	(4)	(8)
Czech Republic	8,925	10,223	9,627	8,572	0.0	(0.1)	(0.2)	0	(14)	(16)
Denmark	4,271	5,258	5,324	5,234	0.1	0.2	0.0	5	10	1
Estonia	1,101	1,442	1,256	1,084	0.7	(1.0)	(0.4)	10	(14)	(6)
Finland	4,009	5,156	5,294	5,172	0.3	0.3	0.1	17	14	5
France	41,829	58,733	60,393	58,370	0.6	0.3	0.1	310	191	67
Germany	68,376	82,401	80,877	69,542	0.4	0.3	(0.1)	339	219	(57)
Greece	7,566	10,551	10,074	9,013	0.6	0.3	(0.2)	57	29	(17)
Hungary	9,338	9,930	8,667	7,715	(0.4)	(0.6)	(0.5)	(43)	(59)	(48)
Iceland	143	277	336	363	1.1	1.0	0.8	3	3	2
Ireland	2,969	3,564	3,723	3,809	(0.3)	0.2	0.3	(10)	6	11
Italy	47,104	57,244	51,774	42,092	0.1	0.0	(0.3)	50	(2)	(175)
Latvia	1,949	2,447	2,108	1,891	0.7	(1.1)	(0.5)	18	(28)	(12)

COUNTRY	POPULATION (thousands)				AVERAGE ANNUAL POPULATION CHANGE (percent)			AVERAGE ANNUAL INCREMENT TO THE POPULATION (thousands)		
	1950	1998	2025	2050	1985–90	1995–00	2005–10	1985–90	1995–00	2005–10
Lithuania	2,567	3,710	3,521	3,297	1.0	(0.3)	(0.2)	36	(9)	(6)
Macedonia	1,230	2,205	2,541	2,646	1.2	0.7	0.6	25	15	14
Moldova	2,341	4,451	4,869	5,138	0.7	0.1	0.4	30	4	18
Netherlands	10,114	15,739	16,141	14,956	0.6	0.5	0.1	92	78	20
Norway	3,265	4,379	4,662	4,696	0.4	0.4	0.2	18	15	10
Poland	24,824	38,664	39,973	39,725	0.5	0.1	0.2	183	34	77
Portugal	8,405	9,798	9,438	8,701	(0.1)	(0.1)	(0.1)	(7)	(5)	(8)
Romania	16,311	22,573	21,098	19,009	0.4	(0.2)	(0.2)	96	(45)	(47)
Russian Federation	102,192	147,231	131,995	114,318	0.7	(0.3)	(0.4)	993	(453)	(513)
Slovak Republic	3,463	5,360	5,469	5,260	0.5	0.1	0.2	23	7	8
Slovenia	1,473	1,919	1,738	1,471	0.4	(0.1)	(0.3)	7	(2)	(5)
Spain	28,009	39,754	37,500	31,755	0.4	0.1	(0.1)	160	35	(57)
Sweden	7,014	8,863	9,511	9,574	0.5	0.3	0.2	42	22	22
Switzerland	4,694	7,325	7,581	6,935	0.9	0.7	0.2	60	49	15
Ukraine	37,906	51,218	45,979	40,802	0.4	(0.4)	(0.4)	190	(191)	(175)
United Kingdom	50,616	58,249	59,535	58,733	0.3	0.1	0.1	189	51	37
Yugoslavia (Serbia-Montenegro)	7,131	10,410	10,679	10,979	0.6	0.5	(0.0)	62	50	(1)
OCEANIA										
Australia	8,219	18,445	29,931	25,286	1.5	1.1	1.0	249	194	201
Fiji	289	822	1,170	1,393	0.8	1.6	1.5	5	13	14
New Zealand	1,908	3,680	4,878	5,271	0.7	1.1	1.1	23	40	43
Papua New Guinea	1,613	4,602	7,546	9,637	2.2	2.2	2.0	79	102	113
Solomon Islands	90	417	844	1,192	3.4	3.2	2.8	10	13	16
DEVELOPING COUNTRIES	1,711,191	4,783,310	6,818,880	8,204,983	2.0	1.7	1.4	80,235	77,726	78,204
DEVELOPED COUNTRIES	812,687	1,181,530	1,220,250	1,161,741	0.5	0.3	0.2	6,761	3,121	1,806

Source: United Nations Population Division and International Labour Organisation. World Resources Institute. *World Resources 1998–99.*

Table G

World Countries: Basic Demographic Data, 1975–2000

COUNTRY	CRUDE BIRTH RATE (births per 1,000 population)		LIFE EXPECTANCY AT BIRTH (years)		LIFE EXPECTANCY OF FEMALES AS A PERCENTAGE OF MALES (years)		TOTAL FERTILITY RATE		PERCENTAGE OF POPULATION IN SPECIFIC AGE GROUPS					
									1980			2000		
	1975–1980	1995–00	1975–80	1995–00	1975–80	1995–00	1975–80	1995–00	<15	15–65	>65	<15	15–65	>65
WORLD	28.3	22.6	59.7	65.6	106.0	106.8	3.9	2.8	35.2	58.9	5.9	30.0	63.2	6.8
AFRICA	**46.0**	**39.2**	**47.9**	**53.8**	**106.7**	**105.7**	**6.5**	**5.3**	**44.7**	**52.2**	**3.1**	**43.0**	**53.8**	**3.2**
Algeria	45.0	29.2	57.5	68.9	103.5	104.1	7.2	3.8	46.5	49.6	3.9	36.6	59.6	3.8
Angola	50.2	47.7	40.0	46.5	108.1	107.1	6.8	6.7	44.7	52.4	2.9	47.4	49.8	2.8
Benin	51.4	42.0	47.0	54.8	108.2	109.2	7.1	5.8	45.1	50.8	4.1	46.5	50.7	2.8
Botswana	46.6	235.0	56.5	50.4	106.6	105.7	6.4	4.5	48.7	49.3	2.0	41.9	55.6	2.4
Burkina Faso	50.8	45.9	42.9	46.0	106.0	104.2	7.8	6.6	47.4	49.8	2.8	47.0	50.3	2.7
Burundi	44.7	42.5	46.0	47.2	107.2	107.3	6.8	6.3	44.7	51.8	3.4	45.0	52.3	2.7
Cameroon	45.5	39.3	48.5	55.9	106.4	105.0	6.5	5.3	44.4	52.0	3.6	43.5	52.9	3.6
Central African Republic	44.1	37.6	44.5	48.6	111.9	109.9	5.9	5.0	41.7	54.4	4.0	41.6	54.4	4.0
Chad	44.1	41.6	41.0	47.7	108.1	106.5	5.9	5.5	41.9	54.5	3.6	43.0	53.4	3.6
Congo (Zaire)	47.8	44.9	48.0	52.9	107.1	106.2	6.5	6.2	46.0	51.1	2.8	48.0	49.1	2.9
Congo Republic	45.8	42.5	48.7	50.9	111.3	109.9	6.3	5.9	45.1	51.5	3.4	45.7	51.1	3.3
Cote d'Ivoire	50.7	37.2	47.9	51.0	107.1	104.4	7.4	5.1	46.6	51.0	2.5	43.0	54.0	3.0
Egypt	38.9	26.1	54.1	66.0	104.5	104.0	5.3	3.4	39.5	56.5	4.0	35.0	60.5	4.5
Equatorial Guinea	42.7	40.8	42.0	50.0	107.9	106.6	5.7	5.5	41.0	54.8	4.1	43.1	52.9	4.0
Eritrea	45.1	39.8	45.3	50.6	106.8	106.1	6.1	5.3	44.2	53.1	2.6	43.6	53.3	3.1
Ethiopia	49.0	48.2	42.0	49.9	107.9	106.6	6.8	7.0	46.1	51.2	2.7	47.1	50.2	2.8
Gabon	32.9	37.6	47.0	55.5	107.3	106.3	4.4	5.4	34.4	59.5	6.1	39.8	54.6	5.7
Gambia	48.8	39.9	39.0	47.0	108.3	107.3	6.5	5.2	42.6	54.4	2.8	41.2	55.5	3.1
Ghana	45.1	38.2	51.0	58.0	106.9	106.6	6.5	5.3	44.9	52.3	2.8	43.4	53.6	3.0
Guinea	51.6	48.2	38.8	46.5	102.6	102.2	7.0	6.6	45.8	51.6	2.6	47.0	50.4	2.6
Guinea-Bissau	42.4	40.3	37.5	43.8	108.6	106.6	5.6	5.4	39.0	57.0	4.0	41.7	54.2	4.2
Kenya	53.6	36.9	53.4	54.5	107.8	106.5	8.1	4.9	50.1	46.5	3.4	43.4	53.7	2.9
Lesotho	41.9	35.4	51.8	58.6	107.0	104.5	5.7	4.9	41.9	53.9	4.2	41.0	55.0	4.1
Liberia	47.4	47.5	49.5	51.5	106.3	106.0	6.8	6.3	44.3	52.0	3.7	43.7	52.7	3.6
Libya	47.3	40.0	55.8	65.5	106.3	105.6	7.4	5.9	46.7	51.1	2.2	44.7	52.4	2.9
Madagascar	46.9	41.1	49.5	58.5	106.3	105.3	6.6	5.7	45.9	51.4	2.7	45.8	51.6	2.6
Malawi	57.2	47.7	43.1	40.7	103.3	102.0	7.6	6.7	47.5	50.3	2.3	46.4	50.9	2.7
Mali	50.7	47.4	40.0	48.0	108.1	107.1	7.1	6.6	46.8	50.7	2.5	47.2	50.2	2.5
Mauritania	44.7	38.3	45.5	53.5	107.3	106.2	6.5	5.0	43.7	53.3	3.0	41.5	55.2	3.3
Mauritius	26.7	19.3	64.9	71.6	108.3	109.8	3.1	2.3	35.6	60.8	3.6	26.6	67.3	6.0
Morocco	39.4	25.8	55.8	66.7	106.3	105.7	5.9	3.1	43.2	52.7	4.1	33.8	61.9	4.3
Mozambique	45.4	42.5	43.5	46.9	107.6	106.4	6.5	6.1	43.4	53.4	3.2	44.7	52.1	3.2
Namibia	41.9	35.9	51.3	55.5	105.0	103.5	6.0	4.9	43.1	53.4	3.5	41.6	54.6	3.8
Niger	59.7	50.2	40.5	48.5	108.2	107.0	8.1	7.1	46.8	50.8	2.5	48.6	49.0	2.4
Nigeria	46.6	42.3	45.0	52.4	107.4	106.3	6.5	6.0	44.3	53.1	2.6	45.0	52.1	2.9
Rwanda	52.8	42.8	45.0	42.1	107.4	106.4	8.5	6.0	48.8	48.8	2.4	44.7	53.0	2.4
Senegal	49.3	41.1	42.8	51.3	104.8	104.0	7.0	5.6	45.3	51.8	2.8	43.6	53.4	3.0
Sierra Leone	48.8	46.5	35.2	37.5	108.9	108.6	6.5	6.1	43.0	53.9	3.1	43.9	53.1	3.0
Somalia	50.4	50.0	42.0	49.0	107.9	106.8	7.0	7.0	46.0	51.0	3.0	48.0	49.5	2.6
South Africa	37.3	29.7	55.9	65.2	111.3	109.6	5.1	3.8	40.3	55.9	3.9	36.2	59.3	4.5
Sudan	47.1	33.7	46.7	55.0	106.2	105.2	6.7	4.6	44.9	52.4	2.7	38.7	58.1	3.2

(continued on next page)

COUNTRY	CRUDE BIRTH RATE (births per 1,000 population)		LIFE EXPECTANCY AT BIRTH (years)		LIFE EXPECTANCY OF FEMALES AS A PERCENTAGE OF MALES (years)		TOTAL FERTILITY RATE		PERCENTAGE OF POPULATION IN SPECIFIC AGE GROUPS					
									1980			2000		
	1975–1980	1995–00	1975–80	1995–00	1975–80	1995–00	1975–80	1995–00	<15	15–65	>65	<15	15–65	>65
Swaziland	46.2	36.8	49.9	60.0	109.9	108.0	6.5	4.5	45.9	51.3	2.9	41.7	55.6	2.7
Tanzania	47.5	41.2	49.0	51.4	107.2	105.6	6.8	5.5	47.6	50.1	2.3	45.1	52.3	2.6
Togo	45.2	41.9	48.0	50.1	107.1	105.5	6.6	6.1	44.6	52.3	3.2	45.6	51.3	3.1
Tunisia	36.4	23.9	60.0	69.6	101.7	103.4	5.7	2.9	41.6	54.6	3.8	32.2	62.9	4.9
Uganda	50.3	51.1	47.0	41.4	107.0	104.7	6.9	7.1	47.8	49.7	2.5	49.1	48.6	2.2
Zambia	51.6	42.4	49.3	43.0	106.9	103.6	7.2	5.5	49.4	48.2	2.4	46.3	51.4	2.3
Zimbabwe	44.2	37.1	53.8	48.5	106.9	103.8	6.6	4.7	47.9	49.5	2.6	43.6	53.7	2.7
NORTH AMERICA	**15.1**	**13.6**	**73.3**	**76.9**	**111.2**	**109.1**	**1.8**	**1.9**	**22.5**	**66.4**	**11.0**	**21.2**	**66.4**	**12.4**
Canada	15.4	11.9	74.2	78.9	110.8	107.5	1.8	1.6	22.7	67.9	9.4	19.3	68.1	12.6
United States	15.1	13.8	73.2	76.7	111.2	109.1	1.8	2.0	22.5	66.3	11.2	21.4	66.2	12.4
CENTRAL AMERICA	**38.2**	**26.5**	**63.7**	**71.7**	**110.2**	**108.4**	**5.4**	**3.0**	**45.1**	**51.2**	**3.6**	**34.8**	**60.7**	**4.5**
Belize	40.9	31.3	69.7	74.7	102.5	103.7	6.2	3.7	47.2	48.6	4.8	39.7	55.8	4.1
Costa Rica	31.7	24.0	71.0	76.8	106.4	106.3	3.9	3.0	38.9	57.5	3.6	33.1	61.8	5.1
Cuba	17.2	13.1	73.0	76.0	104.8	105.1	2.1	1.6	32.9	60.5	7.6	21.2	69.2	9.6
Dominican Republic	34.9	24.1	62.0	70.9	106.1	106.1	4.7	2.8	42.3	54.6	3.1	33.1	62.5	4.5
El Salvador	41.5	27.9	57.2	69.5	119.5	109.0	5.7	3.1	46.1	50.8	3.1	35.6	59.7	4.7
Guatemala	44.3	36.3	56.4	67.2	107.2	107.9	6.4	4.9	45.9	51.3	2.8	42.9	53.3	3.7
Haiti	36.8	34.1	50.7	54.5	106.3	106.1	5.4	4.6	40.7	54.8	4.4	40.0	56.2	3.8
Honduras	44.9	33.5	57.7	69.8	107.7	107.1	6.6	4.3	47.2	50.1	2.7	41.6	54.9	3.4
Jamaica	28.8	21.7	70.1	74.6	106.3	106.1	4.0	2.4	40.2	53.0	6.8	30.2	53.4	6.4
Mexico	37.1	24.6	65.3	72.5	110.3	108.6	5.3	2.8	45.1	51.1	3.8	33.1	62.1	4.7
Nicaragua	45.7	33.5	57.6	68.2	108.5	107.3	6.4	3.9	47.7	49.8	2.5	40.8	56.0	3.2
Panama	31.0	22.5	69.0	73.9	105.8	106.4	4.1	2.6	40.5	55.0	4.5	31.3	63.7	5.5
Trinidad and Tobago	29.3	16.6	68.3	73.7	107.6	106.6	3.4	2.1	34.2	60.2	5.5	26.1	67.4	6.5
SOUTH AMERICA	**32.0**	**21.5**	**62.9**	**69.0**	**108.8**	**110.7**	**4.3**	**2.5**	**37.8**	**57.6**	**4.6**	**30.2**	**64.2**	**5.6**
Argentina	25.7	19.9	68.7	73.2	110.4	110.3	3.4	2.6	30.5	61.4	8.1	27.7	62.6	9.7
Bolivia	41.0	33.2	50.1	61.5	108.8	105.7	5.8	4.4	42.6	53.9	3.5	30.5	56.4	4.0
Brazil	32.6	10.6	61.8	67.1	108.1	112.3	4.3	2.2	38.1	57.8	4.2	28.4	66.4	5.2
Chile	24.0	19.9	67.2	75.3	110.5	108.3	3.0	2.4	33.5	60.9	5.6	28.5	64.4	7.2
Colombia	31.7	23.4	64.0	70.9	107.3	108.1	4.1	2.7	40.0	56.2	3.7	32.5	62.8	4.6
Ecuador	38.2	25.6	61.4	69.8	105.9	107.7	5.4	3.1	42.8	53.2	4.0	33.8	61.5	4.7
Guyana	31.5	21.9	60.7	64.4	108.4	111.1	3.9	2.3	40.8	55.2	4.0	29.9	65.9	4.2
Paraguay	35.9	32.3	66.6	69.7	106.6	106.7	5.2	4.2	42.2	53.3	4.5	39.5	57.0	3.5
Peru	38.0	24.9	58.5	68.3	106.7	107.6	5.4	3.0	41.9	54.5	3.6	33.4	61.8	4.8
Suriname	29.5	21.8	65.1	71.5	107.8	107.2	4.2	2.4	39.7	55.8	4.5	32.3	62.4	5.5
Uruguay	20.3	16.8	69.6	72.9	110.2	109.3	2.9	2.3	26.9	62.5	10.5	23.9	63.5	12.7
Venezuela	34.2	24.9	67.6	72.8	109.1	108.1	4.5	3.0	40.7	56.1	3.2	34.0	61.5	4.4
ASIA	**29.6**	**22.3**	**58.5**	**66.2**	**102.6**	**104.5**	**4.2**	**2.7**	**37.6**	**58.0**	**4.4**	**30.1**	**64.1**	**5.8**
Afghanistan	50.8	53.4	40.0	45.5	100.0	102.2	7.2	6.9	43.0	54.5	2.5	41.7	55.6	2.7
Armenia	20.9	13.3	72.3	70.6	109.0	110.1	2.5	1.7	30.4	63.6	6.0	24.5	66.8	8.7
Azerbaijan	24.7	19.2	68.5	70.6	112.1	112.0	3.6	2.3	34.5	60.0	5.4	29.5	63.6	6.9
Bangladesh	47.2	26.8	46.6	58.1	97.9	100.2	6.7	3.1	46.0	50.5	3.4	35.6	61.2	3.3
Bhutan	42.8	41.3	42.6	53.2	104.8	106.4	5.9	5.9	41.3	55.6	3.1	43.0	53.8	3.2
Cambodia	30.0	33.7	31.2	54.1	108.3	105.3	4.1	4.5	39.2	57.9	2.9	40.4	56.6	3.0
China	21.5	16.2	65.3	69.9	103.0	105.1	3.3	1.8	35.5	59.7	4.7	24.9	68.4	6.7

(continued on next page)

COUNTRY	CRUDE BIRTH RATE (births per 1,000 population)		LIFE EXPECTANCY AT BIRTH (years)		LIFE EXPECTANCY OF FEMALES AS A PERCENTAGE OF MALES (years)		TOTAL FERTILITY RATE		PERCENTAGE OF POPULATION IN SPECIFIC AGE GROUPS					
									1980			2000		
	1975–1980	1995–00	1975–80	1995–00	1975–80	1995–00	1975–80	1995–00	<15	15–65	>65	<15	15–65	>65
Georgia	18.1	13.8	70.7	72.7	111.9	112.0	2.4	1.9	25.7	65.1	9.1	22.0	65.4	12.6
India	34.7	25.2	52.9	62.4	96.3	101.0	4.8	3.1	38.5	57.4	4.0	32.7	62.3	5.0
Indonesia	35.4	23.1	52.8	65.1	104.9	105.8	4.7	2.6	41.0	55.6	3.3	30.8	64.6	4.7
Iran	44.7	34.0	58.6	69.2	101.4	102.2	6.5	4.8	44.9	51.8	3.3	43.1	52.8	4.1
Iraq	41.9	36.4	61.4	62.4	103.0	104.9	6.6	5.3	46.0	51.3	2.7	41.4	55.5	3.1
Israel	26.0	20.3	73.1	77.7	104.9	105.0	3.4	2.8	33.2	58.2	8.6	28.1	62.4	9.5
Japan	15.2	10.3	75.5	80.0	107.4	107.8	1.8	1.5	23.6	67.4	9.0	15.2	68.3	16.5
Jordan	45.0	37.5	61.2	69.7	106.1	106.1	7.4	5.1	49.4	47.5	3.1	43.3	53.8	2.9
Kazakhstan	24.9	18.1	65.4	67.6	117.1	115.4	3.1	2.3	32.4	61.5	6.1	27.5	65.4	7.1
Korea, North	22.2	21.3	65.8	72.2	110.3	109.0	3.3	2.1	39.5	57.0	3.5	27.3	57.4	5.3
Korea, South	23.9	15.0	64.8	72.4	111.6	110.5	2.9	1.7	34.0	62.2	3.8	21.4	72.0	6.7
Kuwait	40.1	21.3	69.6	76.0	106.2	105.5	5.9	2.8	40.2	58.3	1.4	33.2	64.8	2.0
Kyrgyzstan	29.9	25.5	64.2	67.6	114.2	113.4	4.1	3.2	37.1	57.1	5.8	35.0	59.0	6.0
Laos	45.1	44.2	43.5	53.5	106.9	105.8	6.7	6.7	42.0	55.2	2.8	45.4	51.7	3.0
Lebanon	30.1	24.2	65.0	69.9	106.2	105.3	4.3	2.8	40.1	54.5	5.4	32.9	61.3	5.8
Malaysia	30.4	25.2	65.3	72.0	105.7	106.3	4.2	3.2	39.3	57.0	3.7	35.3	60.6	4.1
Mongolia	39.2	27.8	56.3	65.8	104.5	104.7	6.7	3.3	43.2	53.9	2.9	36.4	59.8	3.8
Myanmar (Burma)	37.5	27.2	51.2	60.1	106.4	105.6	5.3	3.3	39.6	56.4	4.0	34.0	61.4	4.6
Nepal	43.4	36.3	46.2	57.3	96.6	99.1	6.2	5.0	42.9	54.1	3.0	42.0	54.5	3.5
Oman	46.1	44.1	54.9	70.8	104.3	106.4	7.2	7.2	44.6	52.8	2.6	47.7	49.9	2.3
Pakistan	47.3	36.1	53.4	63.9	101.3	103.5	7.0	5.0	44.4	52.7	2.9	41.8	55.0	3.2
Philippines	35.9	28.4	59.9	68.3	105.5	105.4	5.0	3.6	41.9	55.3	2.8	36.7	59.7	3.6
Saudi Arabia	45.9	34.3	58.8	71.4	104.0	105.0	7.3	5.9	44.3	52.9	2.8	40.7	56.4	2.9
Singapore	17.2	15.7	70.8	77.3	106.6	105.9	1.9	1.8	27.0	68.2	4.7	22.6	70.3	7.1
Sri Lanka	28.5	17.8	66.8	73.1	105.4	106.3	3.8	2.1	35.3	60.4	4.3	26.2	67.2	6.6
Syria	46.0	30.4	60.1	68.9	106.2	106.7	7.4	4.0	48.5	48.3	3.2	40.8	56.1	3.1
Tajikistan	37.2	30.4	64.5	67.2	108.3	109.3	5.9	3.9	42.9	52.5	4.6	36.5	55.9	4.6
Thailand	31.6	16.7	61.2	69.3	106.6	109.0	4.3	1.7	40.0	56.5	3.5	25.2	69.1	5.8
Turkey	32.0	21.9	60.3	69.0	107.8	107.8	4.5	2.5	39.2	56.0	4.7	28.3	65.7	5.9
Turkmenistan	35.3	28.6	61.6	64.6	112.0	111.1	5.3	3.6	41.3	54.4	4.3	37.4	58.3	4.2
United Arab Emirates	30.5	18.7	66.8	74.8	106.5	103.5	5.7	3.5	28.6	70.1	1.3	28.1	69.4	2.5
Uzbekistan	34.4	28.2	65.1	67.5	111.0	110.0	5.1	3.5	40.9	54.0	5.1	37.5	57.9	4.6
Vietnam	38.3	25.1	55.8	67.4	108.2	107.2	5.6	3.0	42.5	52.7	4.8	34.3	60.5	5.2
Yemen	53.7	47.7	44.1	58.0	101.1	101.7	7.6	7.6	50.2	47.2	2.6	48.3	49.3	2.3
EUROPE	**14.8**	**10.5**	**71.3**	**72.6**	**111.4**	**112.7**	**2.0**	**1.5**	**22.2**	**65.5**	**12.3**	**17.5**	**67.9**	**14.6**
Albania	30.3	21.4	68.9	70.9	106.6	106.8	4.2	2.6	35.9	58.9	5.2	29.7	64.4	6.0
Austria	11.5	10.3	72.0	77.0	110.4	108.7	1.7	1.4	20.4	64.2	15.4	17.1	68.5	14.4
Belarus	16.1	10.0	71.1	69.6	114.7	116.1	2.1	1.4	22.9	66.4	10.7	18.8	67.3	13.8
Belgium	12.4	11.2	72.3	77.3	109.6	109.1	1.7	1.6	20.2	65.5	14.3	17.4	66.2	16.4
Bosnia-Herzegovina	19.6	10.8	69.9	73.2	107.0	107.7	2.2	1.4	27.3	66.7	6.1	18.9	71.2	9.8
Bulgaria	15.8	10.3	71.3	71.3	107.9	110.5	2.2	1.5	22.1	66.0	11.9	16.9	67.2	15.8
Croatia	15.6	10.8	70.6	72.2	110.4	112.3	2.0	1.6	21.2	67.2	11.7	17.3	68.0	14.6
Czech Republic	17.4	10.7	70.6	72.9	110.4	108.9	2.3	1.4	23.5	63.2	13.4	17.6	69.8	12.6
Denmark	12.3	13.0	74.2	75.6	108.4	107.3	1.7	1.8	20.8	64.7	14.4	18.6	66.7	14.7
Estonia	15.0	9.0	69.7	69.4	115.3	117.4	2.1	1.3	21.7	65.8	12.5	17.6	68.5	13.9
Finland	13.6	11.6	72.7	76.6	112.6	109.7	1.6	1.8	20.3	67.7	12.0	18.4	67.1	14.6
France	14.0	11.6	73.7	76.8	111.6	111.1	1.9	1.6	22.3	63.8	14.0	18.3	65.4	16.2
Germany	10.4	9.3	72.5	76.7	109.4	108.9	1.5	1.3	18.5	65.9	15.6	15.4	68.8	15.9

COUNTRY	CRUDE BIRTH RATE (births per 1,000 population)		LIFE EXPECTANCY AT BIRTH (years)		LIFE EXPECTANCY OF FEMALES AS A PERCENTAGE OF MALES (years)		TOTAL FERTILITY RATE		PERCENTAGE OF POPULATION IN SPECIFIC AGE GROUPS					
									1980			2000		
	1975–1980	1995–00	1975–80	1995–00	1975–80	1995–00	1975–80	1995–00	<15	15–65	>65	<15	15–65	>65
Greece	15.6	10.0	73.7	78.1	105.7	106.8	2.3	1.4	22.8	64.0	13.1	15.3	66.9	17.8
Hungary	16.2	10.2	69.4	69.0	109.8	114.4	2.1	1.4	21.9	64.6	13.4	17.0	68.5	14.5
Iceland	19.2	16.5	76.3	79.3	108.0	104.9	2.3	2.2	27.6	62.7	10.1	23.8	64.9	11.3
Ireland	21.2	13.0	72.0	76.6	107.2	107.3	3.5	1.8	30.6	58.7	10.7	21.2	67.5	11.4
Italy	13.0	9.1	73.6	78.3	109.2	108.4	1.9	1.2	22.3	64.6	13.1	14.2	68.1	17.7
Latvia	14.0	9.8	69.2	68.4	115.6	118.9	2.0	1.4	20.4	66.5	13.0	18.2	67.5	14.4
Lithuania	15.4	10.8	70.8	70.4	114.2	117.1	2.1	1.5	23.6	65.1	11.3	19.5	67.0	13.5
Macedonia	22.6	14.5	69.6	72.5	105.2	106.3	2.7	1.9	28.6	64.5	6.9	22.3	68.3	9.4
Moldova	19.6	13.6	64.8	67.5	111.2	112.6	2.4	1.8	26.7	65.5	7.8	23.4	66.8	9.8
Netherlands	12.7	11.9	75.3	77.9	109.0	107.5	1.6	1.6	22.3	66.2	11.5	18.2	68.2	13.6
Norway	12.9	13.4	75.3	77.6	108.9	107.8	1.8	1.9	22.2	63.1	14.8	19.8	65.1	15.0
Poland	19.2	11.9	70.9	71.1	111.9	113.5	2.3	1.7	24.3	65.6	10.1	19.8	68.4	11.8
Portugal	18.2	11.2	70.2	75.4	110.6	109.9	2.4	1.5	25.9	63.6	10.5	16.7	67.5	15.7
Romania	19.1	11.0	69.6	69.5	107.0	110.9	2.6	1.4	26.7	63.1	10.3	18.5	68.4	13.2
Russian Federation	15.8	9.6	67.4	64.4	118.1	123.3	1.9	1.4	21.6	68.1	10.2	18.0	69.3	12.7
Slovak Republic	20.6	11.7	70.4	71.3	110.9	113.1	2.5	1.5	26.1	63.5	10.4	20.0	68.8	11.1
Slovenia	16.6	9.5	71.0	73.5	111.6	112.4	2.2	1.3	23.4	65.3	11.4	15.7	70.2	14.2
Spain	17.4	9.7	74.3	78.0	108.4	109.4	2.6	1.2	26.6	62.7	10.7	15.0	68.4	16.5
Sweden	11.7	11.9	75.2	78.5	109.3	106.0	1.7	1.8	19.6	64.1	16.3	19.2	64.3	16.7
Switzerland	11.6	10.9	75.2	78.6	109.2	108.6	1.5	1.5	19.7	66.4	13.8	17.2	68.1	14.7
Ukraine	14.9	9.7	69.3	68.8	114.8	116.4	2.0	1.4	21.4	66.7	11.9	17.8	67.9	14.3
United Kingdom	12.4	11.9	72.8	77.1	109.0	107.1	1.7	1.7	20.9	64.0	15.1	18.9	65.5	15.8
Yugoslavia (Serbia-Montenegro)	18.4	12.6	70.3	72.5	106.5	107.9	2.4	1.8	24.1	66.1	9.8	19.8	66.9	13.3
OCEANIA	**20.9**	**18.4**	**68.2**	**73.9**	**108.7**	**106.9**	**2.8**	**2.5**	**29.3**	**62.7**	**8.0**	**25.5**	**64.9**	**9.7**
Australia	16.0	14.3	73.4	78.3	109.8	107.7	2.1	1.9	25.3	65.1	9.6	21.0	67.1	11.9
Fiji	33.2	22.6	67.1	72.6	105.3	106.1	4.0	2.8	39.1	58.0	2.8	31.3	64.3	4.5
New Zealand	17.2	15.4	72.4	77.2	109.2	106.7	2.2	2.0	26.7	63.3	10.0	23.0	65.6	11.3
Papua New Guinea	39.6	32.3	49.7	57.9	101.0	102.6	5.9	4.7	43.0	55.5	1.6	38.7	58.3	3.0
Solomon Islands	45.0	36.1	65.3	71.6	106.2	106.2	7.1	5.0	47.6	49.3	3.1	43.0	54.1	2.9
DEVELOPING COUNTRIES	**32.8**	**25.4**	**56.7**	**63.6**	**103.8**	**105.0**	**4.7**	**3.1**	**39.3**	**56.6**	**4.1**	**32.8**	**62.2**	**5.0**
DEVELOPED COUNTRIES	**14.9**	**11.4**	**72.2**	**74.5**	**110.8**	**111.0**	**1.9**	**1.6**	**22.5**	**65.9**	**11.6**	**18.3**	**67.5**	**14.2**

Source: United Nations Population Division, *World Resources 1998–99.*

Table H

World Countries: Mortality, Health, and Nutrition, 1997

COUNTRY	MORTALITY						HEALTH			NUTRITION
			Adult Mortality							
			Male (per 1,000)		Female (per 1,000)					
	Infant Mortality 1997 (per 1,000 live births)	Under-five Mortality 1997 (per 1,000)	1980	1997	1980	1997	Health Expenditure Per Capita ($US)	Physicians Per 1,000 People	Hospital Beds Per 1,000 People	Calories Available as a Percentage of Need
Albania	26	40	140	122	82	65	..	1.4	3.2	107
Algeria	32	39	226	160	197	125	85	0.8	2.1	123
Angola	125	209	569	412	458	355	..	0.1	1.3	8
Argentina	22	24	205	165	102	80	799	2.7	4.6	131
Armenia	15	..	158	164	85	81	27	3.1	7.6	..
Australia	5	7	178	110	85	57	1,798	2.2	8.9	124
Austria	5	7	197	123	92	61	2,012	3.5	9.3	133
Azerbaijan	20	23	262	213	127	101	31	3.9	9.9	..
Bangladesh	75	104	383	285	388	309	6	0.2	0.3	88
Belarus	12	..	255	333	95	115	134	4.2	12.3	..
Belgium	6	7	173	134	90	62	1,816	3.8	7.6	149
Benin	88	149	486	362	397	304	..	0.1	0.2	104
Bolivia	66	96	357	269	273	220	54	0.4	1.4	84
Bosnia- Herzegovina	13	..	181	170	108	93	..	0.9	3.1	..
Botswana	58	88	341	600	278	552	..	0.3	1.6	97
Brazil	34	44	221	202	161	139	351	1.4	3.0	114
Bulgaria	18	24	190	213	106	106	68	3.5	10.6	148
Burkina Faso	99	169	467	540	362	520	17	0.0	0.3	94
Burundi	119	200	489	550	400	491	..	0.1	0.7	84
Cambodia	103	147	473	349	355	303	18	0.1	2.1	96
Cameroon	52	78	489	390	415	352	7	0.1	2.6	95
Canada	6	8	161	106	85	52	1,829	2.2	5.1	122
Central African Republic	98	160	540	567	424	476	..	0.0	0.9	82
Chad	100	182	556	448	449	383	6	0.0	0.7	73
Chile	11	13	218	143	120	73	295	1.1	3.2	102
China	32	39	185	165	148	137	19	1.6	2.4	112
Hong Kong, China	5	..	150	109	87	56	1,134	1.3	..	106
Colombia	24	30	237	210	162	115	140	0.9	1.3	106
Congo (Zaire)	92	148	408	464	298	402	..	0.1	1.4	96
Congo, Rep.	90	145	..	..	..	..	77	0.3	3.3	103
Costa Rica	12	15	159	117	100	70	215	0.9	2.5	121
Côte d'Ivoire	87	140	421	510	346	490	25	0.1	0.8	..
Croatia	9	10	233	176	106	78	302	2.1	5.9	135
Cuba	7	9	135	125	94	80	..	3.6	5.4	..
Czech Republic	6	8	225	181	102	82	360	3.0	6.7	135
Denmark	6	6	163	144	102	81	2,388	2.9	4.9	135
Dominican Republic	40	47	183	150	138	94	77	1.1	2.0	102
Ecuador	33	39	229	180	176	104	78	1.5	1.6	105

(continued on next page)

COUNTRY	Infant Mortality 1997 (per 1,000 live births)	Under-five Mortality 1997 (per 1,000)	Adult Mortality Male (per 1,000) 1980	Adult Mortality Male (per 1,000) 1997	Adult Mortality Female (per 1,000) 1980	Adult Mortality Female (per 1,000) 1997	Health Expenditure Per Capita ($US)	Physicians Per 1,000 People	Hospital Beds Per 1,000 People	Calories Available as a Percentage of Need
Egypt	51	66	257	198	204	174	38	1.8	2.1	132
El Salvador	32	39	410	207	178	117	86	0.7	1.4	102
Eritrea	62	95	..	450	..	403	..	0.0	..	..
Estonia	10	13	291	284	110	95	..	3.0	8.1	..
Ethiopia	107	175	491	550	401	510	3	0.0	0.2	73
Finland	4	5	206	141	74	61	1,666	2.8	9.3	113
France	5	6	190	130	85	51	2,349	2.8	8.9	143
Gabon	87	136	474	380	387	340	..	0.5	3.2	104
Gambia	78	..	584	404	466	339	..	0.0	0.6	..
Georgia	17	21	210	197	94	83	..	3.5	4.8	..
Germany	5	6	177	133	90	66	2,677	3.4	9.7	..
Ghana	66	102	400	278	334	226	6	0.1	1.5	93
Greece	7	9	134	114	86	61	803	3.9	5.0	151
Guatemala	43	55	336	296	266	193	41	0.3	1.2	103
Guinea	120	182	589	399	507	400	..	0.1	0.6	97
Guinea-Bissau	130	220	535	469	517	416	..	0.2	1.5	97
Haiti	71	125	348	427	275	332	14	0.1	0.8	89
Honduras	36	48	306	193	237	115	33	0.4	1.1	96
Hungary	10	12	270	330	130	138	291	3.4	9.0	137
India	71	88	261	212	279	202	18	0.4	0.8	101
Indonesia	47	60	368	240	308	188	17	0.2	0.7	121
Iran	32	35	221	165	190	162	89	0.3	1.4	125
Iraq	112	140	207	198	191	174	..	0.6	1.7	128
Ireland	5	7	175	135	103	73	1,337	2.1	5.0	157
Israel	7	8	138	111	85	69	551	3.8	6.0	125
Italy	5	7	163	117	80	54	1,515	1.7	6.4	139
Jamaica	12	14	186	141	121	86	76	0.5	2.1	114
Japan	4	6	129	100	70	46	2,442	1.8	16.2	125
Jordan	29	35	..	160	..	121	117	1.6	1.6	110
Kazakhstan	24	29	312	383	140	168	42	3.6	10.3	..
Kenya	74	112	417	425	339	397	8	0.1	1.6	89
Korea, North	56	74	270	268	156	207	..	..	..	121
Korea, South	9	11	270	209	156	97	397	1.2	4.4	120
Kuwait	12	13	172	124	116	65	..	0.2	..	..
Kyrgyzstan	28	..	296	305	131	143	..	3.3	8.8	..
Laos	98	..	531	378	439	323	10	0.2	2.6	111
Latvia	15	19	281	306	106	100	..	3.0	10.3	..
Lebanon	28	32	241	177	181	134	87	1.9	3.1	127
Lesotho	93	137	371	320	279	282	..	0.1	..	93
Libya	24	30	276	187	218	135	..	1.1	4.2	140
Lithuania	10	13	243	269	92	88	..	4.0	10.6	..
Macedonia	16	17	..	164	..	107	171	2.3	5.2	..

(continued on next page)

COUNTRY	Infant Mortality 1997 (per 1,000 live births)	Under-five Mortality 1997 (per 1,000)	Adult Mortality Male (per 1,000) 1980	Male 1997	Adult Mortality Female (per 1,000) 1980	Female 1997	Health Expenditure Per Capita ($US)	Physicians Per 1,000 People	Hospital Beds Per 1,000 People	Calories Available as a Percentage of Need
Madagascar	94	158	353	332	278	295	..	0.1	0.9	95
Malawi	133	224	429	454	349	471	..	0.0	1.6	88
Malaysia	11	14	230	187	149	114	140	0.4	2.0	120
Mali	118	235	454	416	362	334	8	0.1	..	96
Mauritania	92	149	505	344	416	294	28	0.1	0.7	106
Mauritius	20	23	277	205	181	97	116	0.9	3.1	128
Mexico	31	38	205	166	121	83	200	1.3	1.2	..
Moldova	20	24	289	316	173	177	..	3.6	12.1	..
Mongolia	52	68	320	203	273	170	26	2.7	11.5	97
Morocco	51	67	264	207	207	150	49	0.4	1.1	125
Mozambique	135	201	468	400	361	354	..	..	0.9	77
Myanmar (Burma)	79	131	284	263	313	217	127	0.1	0.6	114
Namibia	65	101	427	366	366	341	..	0.3	..	100
Nepal	83	117	376	274	395	314	10	0.1	0.2	114
Netherlands	5	7	133	121	74	62	1,978	2.5	11.3	..
New Zealand	7	7	177	132	91	68	1,348	2.1	7.3	99
Nicaragua	43	57	277	202	189	126	37	0.6	1.8	95
Niger	118	..	562	450	453	342	..	0.0	..	93
Nigeria	77	122	535	398	453	335	5	0.2	1.7	120
Norway	4	6	144	114	71	59	2,622	3.1	13.3	..
Oman	18	28	389	143	326	108	..	0.9	2.1	99
Pakistan	95	136	283	175	291	158	13	0.5	0.7	98
Panama	21	26	172	137	117	81	199	1.8	2.5	131
Papua New Guinea	61	82	514	348	478	333	..	0.1	4.0	116
Paraguay	23	28	198	185	144	124	86	0.3	0.6	87
Peru	40	52	287	200	229	124	80	1.0	1.4	104
Philippines	35	41	323	238	259	153	17	0.1	1.1	131
Poland	10	12	254	238	105	91	182	2.3	6.2	136
Portugal	6	8	199	154	95	72	805	3.0	4.1	..
Puerto Rico	11	..	159	158	78	63	..	..	..	116
Romania	22	26	216	270	119	119	..	1.8	7.6	82
Russian Federation	17	25	341	370	120	130	117	4.1	11.7	..
Rwanda	124	209	503	585	409	534	..	0.0	1.7	..
Saudi Arabia	21	28	283	171	241	147	161	1.3	2.5	120
Senegal	70	110	586	453	516	381	..	0.1	0.7	98
Sierra Leone	170	286	540	544	527	483	..	..	..	83
Singapore	4	6	199	136	115	77	943	1.4	3.6	136
Slovak Republic	9	..	226	208	105	90	..	3.0	7.5	..
Slovenia	5	6	250	173	105	76	..	2.1	5.7	..
South Africa	48	65	..	261	..	160	258	0.6	..	126
Spain	5	7	144	124	69	56	1,003	4.1	4.0	141
Sri Lanka	14	19	210	156	152	99	11	0.1	2.7	101

COUNTRY	Infant Mortality 1997 (per 1,000 live births)	Under-five Mortality 1997 (per 1,000)	Adult Mortality Male (per 1,000) 1980	Male 1997	Female (per 1,000) 1980	Female 1997	Health Expenditure Per Capita ($US)	Physicians Per 1,000 People	Hospital Beds Per 1,000 People	Calories Available as a Percentage of Need
Sudan	71	115	537	373	462	328	4	::	1.1	87
Sweden	4	5	142	105	76	54	2,222	3.1	6.3	111
Switzerland	5	6	145	106	70	50	3,603	3.2	20.8	136
Syria	31	38	::	206	::	141	::	0.8	1.1	126
Tajikistan	30	36	190	234	129	143	::	2.0	8.8	::
Tanzania	85	136	451	502	370	460	::	0.0	0.9	::
Thailand	33	38	280	219	210	122	96	0.2	1.7	103
Togo	86	138	457	477	375	432	15	0.1	1.5	99
Trinidad and Tobago	12	15	234	168	166	103	131	0.7	3.2	114
Tunisia	30	33	227	171	224	153	99	0.6	1.8	131
Turkey	40	50	::	165	::	120	113	1.1	2.5	127
Turkmenistan	40	50	263	282	154	159	::	3.2	11.5	::
Uganda	99	162	463	580	395	590	9	::	0.9	93
Ukraine	14	17	282	350	112	135	::	4.5	9.9	::
United Arab Emirates	8	11	153	127	106	93	379	0.8	3.1	::
United Kingdom	6	7	160	123	96	67	1,454	1.5	4.7	130
United States	7	::	194	150	102	80	4,093	2.5	4.1	138
Uruguay	16	20	176	171	91	76	440	3.2	4.5	101
Uzbekistan	::	31	219	230	116	128	::	3.2	8.3	::
Venezuela	21	25	219	160	123	91	213	1.6	2.6	99
Vietnam	29	40	262	205	204	150	9	0.4	3.8	103
West Bank and Gaza	25	28	::	170	::	112	114	::	::	
Yemen	96	137	382	340	304	330	39	0.1	0.8	
Yugoslavia (Serbia-Montenegro)	14	20	164	180	106	108	::	2.0	5.3	
Zambia	113	189	482	512	413	524	17	0.1	::	87
Zimbabwe	69	108	389	449	321	388	41	0.1	0.5	94

Sources: United Nations Children's Fund; United Nations Development Program; UNESCO; *World Resources 1996–97*; *World Almanac and Book of Facts 1996*.

Table 1

World Countries: Education and Literacy, 1970–1997

	EDUCATION												
	Inputs						Outcomes						
COUNTRY	ADULT ILLITERACY (% above age 15)				Public Expenditure on Education 1996 (% of GNP)	Primary Pupil-Teacher Ratio 1996 (pupils per teacher)	Primary School Enrollment 1996 (% of age group)	Secondary School Enrollment 1996 (% of age group)	Tertiary School Enrollment 1996 (% of age group)	Youth Illiteracy Rate (% aged 15–24)			
	Male		Female							Male		Female	
	1970	1995	1970	1995						1980	1997	1980	1997
Albania	:	:	:	:	3.1	18	107	38	11	:	:	:	:
Algeria	61	26	88	51	5.1	27	108	63	13	26	14	55	32
Angola	84	:	93	:		:	:	:	1	:	:	:	:
Argentina	7	4	8	4	3.5	16	113	77	42	3	2	3	1
Armenia	:	:	:	:	2.0	19	87	90	12	:	:	:	:
Australia	:	:	:	:	5.6	18	101	148[a]	76	:	:	:	:
Austria	:	:	:	:	5.6	12	101	104	48	:	:	:	:
Azerbaijan	:	:	:	:	3.3	21	106	77	18	:	:	:	:
Bangladesh	64	51	88	74	2.9	:	98	:	6	52	42	74	63
Belarus	:	:	:	:	6.1	20	:	93	44	0	0	0	0
Belgium	1	:	1	:	3.2	12	103	146[a]	57	:	:	:	:
Benin	83	51	96	74	3.2	52	78	17	3	57	33	84	67
Bolivia	29	10	54	24	5.6	:	:	:	24	7	3	21	8
Bosnia- Herzegovina	:	:	:	:		:	:	:	:	:	:	:	:
Botswana	40	20	69	40	10.4	25	108	65	6	32	17	25	9
Brazil	28	17	35	27	5.5	23	120	45	12	15	10	13	7
Bulgaria	6	:	:	:	3.3	17	99	77	41	1	0	1	1
Burkina Faso	87	71	98	91	1.5	51	40	8	1	73	58	92	81
Burundi	70	51	93	78	3.1	50	51	7	1	49	36	72	43
Cambodia	:	20	77	47	2.9	44	110	29	:	18	7	34	43
Cameroon	53	25	82	48	2.9	:	89	27	4	:	:	:	10
Canada	:	:	:	:	7.0	16	102	105	90	:	:	:	:
Central African Republic	79	32	95	48		67	58	:	1	44	27	76	48
Chad	64	38	88	65	2.4	30	:	10	:	:	:	:	:
Chile	11	5	13	5	3.1	24	101	75	30	3	2	3	1
China	33	10	64	27	2.3	24	120	70	6	4	1	16	4
Hong Kong, China	:	:	:	:	2.9	:	94	73	28	3	1	4	0
Colombia	18	9	21	9	4.4	25	113	67	19	8	4	7	3
Congo (Zaire)	39	13	72	32		45	72	26	2	12	3	27	5
Congo Republic	51	17	79	33	6.2	70	114	53	8	4	2	3	2
Costa Rica	12	5	13	5	5.3	30	103	47	33	52	33	76	46
Côte d'Ivoire	75	50	94	70	5.0	41	71	24	5	52	33	76	46
Croatia	:	:	:	:	5.3	19	87	82	28	0	0	1	0
Cuba	15	4	22	5		12	106	81	12	2	0	2	0
Czech Republic	:	:	:	:	5.4	19	104	99	23	:	:	:	:
Denmark	:	:	:	:	8.2	10	102	121	46	:	:	:	:
Dominican Republic	30	18	34	18	2.0	35	103	41	23	18	10	17	9

(continued on next page)

	ADULT ILLITERACY (% above age 15)				Inputs			Outcomes		Youth Illiteracy Rate (% aged 15–24)			
	Male		Female		Public Expenditure on Education 1996 (% of GNP)	Primary Pupil-Teacher Ratio 1996 (pupils per teacher)	Primary School Enrollment 1996 (% of age group)	Secondary School Enrollment 1996 (% of age group)	Tertiary School Enrollment 1996 (% of age group)	Male		Female	
COUNTRY	1970	1995	1970	1995						1980	1997	1980	1997
Ecuador	21	8	30	12	3.5	25	127	50	26	6	3	9	3
Egypt	53	36	82	61	4.8	23	101	75	23	36	25	62	41
El Salvador	39	27	48	30	2.2	33	93	34	17	19	12	24	14
Eritrea	..	..	..	..	1.8	44	53	20	1	..	..	..	..
Estonia	..	..	..	..	7.3	17	94	104	42	..	..	..	..
Ethiopia	76	55	91	75	4.0	38	38	12	1	59	47	78	51
Finland	1	..	2	..	7.6		99	116	71	..	..	..	..
France	..	..	..	..	6.1	19	106	111	52	..	..	..	..
Gabon	61	26	86	47	2.8	51				..	..	..	..
Gambia	72	47	93	75	6.0	30	77	25	2	64	39	79	55
Georgia	..	..	..	..	5.2	18	88	77	40	..	..	..	..
Germany	..	..	..	..	4.8	17	102	104	45	..	..	..	..
Ghana	55	24	83	47	3.0	15	94		1	22	9	48	17
Greece	7	..	24	..			88	95	43	1	0	1	0
Guatemala	49	38	64	51	1.7	35	88	26	8	26	16	43	29
Guinea	75	50	94	78		49	48	12	1	..	..	..	..
Guinea-Bissau	57	32	83	58			62			50	32	86	66
Haiti	72	52	80	58					1	53	40	57	41
Honduras	43	27	49	27	3.6	35	111	32	11	29	22	29	21
Hungary	2	..	2	..	4.7	11	103	98	25	0	0	0	0
India	52	35	82	62	3.4	64	100	49	7	32	23	61	44
Indonesia	31	10	56	22	1.4	23	115	48	11	7	2	15	4
Iran	..	22	..	34	4.0	31	98	77	17	16	5	35	10
Iraq	56	29	85	55		20	85	42	11	..	..	..	..
Ireland	..	..	..	..	5.8	23	104	116	40	..	..	..	..
Israel	..	..	..	..	7.2	16	98	88	44	1	0	3	1
Italy	1	..	1	..	4.7	11	101	94	43	0	0	0	0
Jamaica	34	19	27	11	7.4		100		8	17	11	8	4
Japan	1	..	1	..	3.6	19	102	103	43	..	..	..	..
Jordan	27	7	66	21	7.3	21				4	2	14	0
Kazakhstan	..	..	..	..	4.7	18	98	87	32	..	..	..	..
Kenya	41	14	73	30	6.6	30	85	24	2	13	5	32	8
Korea, North	..	1	..	3						..	..	..	..
Korea, South	6	1	20	3	3.7	31	94	102	60	0	0	0	0
Kuwait	35	18	55	25	5.7	15	75	65	27	17	9	23	8
Kyrgyzstan	..	..	..	..	5.7	20	104	79	12	..	..	..	..
Laos	55	31	82	56	2.5	30	112	29	3	..	..	..	..
Latvia	..	..	..	..	6.5	13	96	84	33	0	0	0	0
Lebanon	13	10	27	20	2.5		111	81	27	7	3	18	8
Lesotho	38	19	66	38	7.0	47	108	31	2	29	18	5	2

(continued on next page)

EDUCATION

Country	ADULT ILLITERACY (% above age 15) Male 1970	Male 1995	Female 1970	Female 1995	Inputs — Public Expenditure on Education 1996 (% of GNP)	Primary Pupil-Teacher Ratio 1996 (pupils per teacher)	Outcomes — Primary School Enrollment 1996 (% of age group)	Secondary School Enrollment 1996 (% of age group)	Tertiary School Enrollment 1996 (% of age group)	Youth Illiteracy Rate (% aged 15–24) Male 1980	Male 1997	Female 1980	Female 1997
Libya	43	12	89	37	..	..	111	..	20	5	0	39	10
Lithuania	..	..	..	..	5.6	16	98	86	31	0	0	0	0
Macedonia	..	..	57	..	5.6	19	99	63	18	..	..	..	..
Madagascar	34	..	57	58	1.9	37	92	16	2	..	..	..	..
Malawi	42	28	80	58	5.5	59	89	17	1	29	20	60	42
Malaysia	31	11	56	22	5.2	20	102	61	11	8	3	15	3
Mali	89	61	96	77	2.2	70	45	10	1	66	34	83	49
Mauritania	63	50	83	74	5.1	50	79	16	4	53	44	84	62
Mauritius	24	13	45	21	4.3	24	107	65	7	11	8	16	7
Mexico	20	8	30	13	4.9	28	115	61	16	6	3	9	5
Moldova	..	..	..	..	9.7	23	97	81	26	0	0	0	0
Mongolia	25	..	48	..	6.4	31	88	56	17	..	..	..	..
Morocco	67	43	91	69	5.3	28	86	39	11	43	26	72	47
Mozambique	74	42	94	77	..	58	60	7	1	38	28	79	59
Myanmar (Burma)	16	11	40	22	1.2	..	121	30	6	11	11	19	11
Namibia	..	..	..	..	9.1	..	131	61	9	18	11	20	8
Nepal	76	59	96	86	2.8	..	109	38	5	48	27	86	62
Netherlands	..	..	..	..	5.2	..	107	137[a]	50	..	..	..	..
New Zealand	..	..	..	..	7.3	19	99	114	59	..	..	..	..
Nicaragua	42	35	44	33	3.7	38	103	44	13	37	33	37	32
Niger	89	79	99	93	..	41	29	7	1	82	71	95	88
Nigeria	68	33	89	53	0.9	37	98	33	4	32	13	57	20
Norway	..	..	..	..	7.5	..	99	116	62	..	..	..	..
Oman	..	..	..	..	4.4	26	78	66	6	18	1	64	7
Pakistan	69	50	91	76	3.0	..	74	..	3	48	31	79	61
Panama	20	9	22	10	4.6	..	104	68	32	5	3	7	4
Papua New Guinea	40	19	67	37	..	38	80	14	3	..	..	..	..
Paraguay	14	7	24	9	3.9	21	112	44	11	6	3	7	3
Peru	17	6	40	17	2.9	28	123	70	31	5	2	13	6
Philippines	14	5	17	6	2.2	35	116	77	35	5	2	5	2
Poland	1	..	3	..	5.2	15	96	98	24	0	0	0	0
Portugal	22	..	35	..	5.5	12	128	106[a]	38	2	0	2	0
Puerto Rico	..	..	..	..	..	..	..	48	48	6	3	4	2
Romania	4	..	..	..	3.6	20	104	78	23	1	1	1	0
Russian Federation	..	..	..	..	4.1	20	107	87	41	0	0	0	0
Rwanda	55	30	82	48	..	..	..	..	1	32	16	51	21
Saudi Arabia	51	29	79	50	5.5	13	76	61	16	16	6	40	12
Senegal	76	57	93	77	3.5	58	68	16	3	59	43	79	62
Sierra Leone	78	55	95	82	..	..	..	..	2	..	..	3	..
Singapore	13	7	39	14	3.0	22	101	67	39	2	1	3	0

COUNTRY	ADULT ILLITERACY (% above age 15) Male 1970	Male 1995	Female 1970	Female 1995	Public Expenditure on Education 1996 (% of GNP)	Primary Pupil-Teacher Ratio 1996 (pupils per teacher)	Primary School Enrollment 1996 (% of age group)	Secondary School Enrollment 1996 (% of age group)	Tertiary School Enrollment 1996 (% of age group)	Youth Illiteracy Rate (% aged 15–24) Male 1980	Male 1997	Female 1980	Female 1997
Slovak Republic	:	:	:	:	4.9	19	102	94	22	:	:	:	0
Slovenia	:	:	:	:	5.8	14	98	92	36	0	0	0	0
South Africa	28	18	32	18	7.9	36	131	94	19	15	10	15	10
Spain	6	:	14	:	4.9	17	109	122	51	1	0	1	0
Sri Lanka	12	7	29	13	3.4	28	109	75	5	6	3	9	4
Sudan	67	42	91	65	:	29	51	21	4	36	19	66	33
Sweden	:	:	:	:	8.3	11	106	137[a]	49	:	:	:	:
Switzerland	:	:	:	:	5.3	12	:	:	:	:	:	:	:
Syria	39	14	79	44	4.2	23	101	43	15	13	5	47	25
Tajikistan	:	:	:	:	2.2	24	95	78	20	0	0	0	0
Tanzania	45	21	79	43	:	36	66	5	1	18	8	43	15
Thailand	14	4	30	8	4.1	:	87	56	21	3	1	4	2
Togo	64	33	90	63	4.7	51	120	27	4	32	15	68	11
Trinidad and Tobago	5	1	11	3	3.7	25	98	74	8	1	0	1	0
Tunisia	58	21	83	45	6.7	24	117	65	14	12	4	41	15
Turkey	27	8	60	28	2.2	28	105	56	18	6	2	25	8
Turkmenistan	:	:	:	:	:	:	:	:	20	:	:	:	:
Uganda	47	26	78	50	2.6	35	74	12	2	27	16	53	31
Ukraine	:	:	:	:	7.2	20	87	91	42	:	:	:	:
United Arab Emirates	39	21	60	20	1.8	16	94	80	12	26	14	22	7
United Kingdom	:	:	:	:	5.4	18	115	133[a]	50	:	:	:	:
United States	1	:	1	:	5.4	16	102	97	81	:	:	:	:
Uruguay	8	3	7	2	3.3	20	109	85	29	2	1	1	0
Uzbekistan	:	:	:	:	8.1	21	78	94	36	:	:	:	:
Venezuela	20	8	27	10	5.2	:	91	40	25	6	3	6	2
Vietnam	18	:	35	:	2.6	:	114	47	5	4	3	7	3
West Bank and Gaza	:	:	:	:	:	:	:	:	:	:	:	:	:
Yemen	:	:	:	:	6.5	30	70	34	4	45	19	89	61
Yugoslavia (Serbia-Montenegro)	:	:	:	:	:	:	69	62	23	:	:	:	:
Zambia	36	14	68	29	2.2	39	89	27	3	18	10	35	18
Zimbabwe	25	10	62	20	8.3	39	113	49	7	7	0	14	2

[a]Includes training for the unemployed.

Source: World Development Indicators (World Bank, 1998, 1999).

World Countries: Agricultural Operations, 1994–1997

COUNTRY	AGRICULTURAL INPUTS				Agricultural Machinery		AGRICULTURAL OUTPUT AND PRODUCTIVITY			
	Arable Land (hectares per capita)	Irrigated Land (% of cropland)	Land under Cereal Production (thousand hectares)	Fertilizer Consumption (hundreds of grams per hectare of arable land)	Tractors Per Thousand Agricultural Workers	Tractors Per Hundred Hectares of Agricultural Land	Crop Production Index (1989–91 = 100)	Food Production Index (1989–91 = 100)	Livestock Production Index (1989–91 = 100)	Agricultural Productivity (agricultural value added per worker in 1995$)
	1994–96	1994–96	1995–97	1995–97	1994–96	1994–96	1995–97	1995–97	1995–97	1995–97
Albania	0.18	48.4	227	207	10	150	::	::	::	1,717
Algeria	0.27	6.9	2,453	100	43	125	119.1	118.2	109.2	1,903
Angola	0.27	2.1	789	33	3	34	147.0	130.1	106.4	117
Argentina	0.71	6.3	10,126	254	190	112	133.2	121.9	106.1	13,833
Armenia	0.16	43.7	181	130	64	306	114.4	82.3	62.4	4,477
Australia	2.70	4.8	15,854	376	698	65	141.2	126.9	103.5	29,044
Austria	0.18	0.3	829	1,704	1,492	2,481	93.0	100.0	105.4	15,474
Azerbaijan	0.21	50.0	617	244	31	181	54.5	55.6	65.0	847
Bangladesh	0.07	39.1	10,825	1,374	0	6	101.7	106.0	132.3	221
Belarus	0.60	1.9	2,508	969	131	184	101.2	58.9	56.0	3,461
Belgium	::	0.1	334	4,245	1,130	1,465	122.3	114.4	113.6	::
Benin	0.26	0.5	718	214	0	1	156.0	129.5	113.9	504
Bolivia	0.27	3.7	726	41	4	27	137.5	126.7	114.8	::
Bosnia-Herzegovina	0.21	0.3	227	210	228	548	::	::	::	::
Botswana	0.23	0.3	178	62	21	163	88.4	104.2	106.8	647
Brazil	0.33	4.9	19,554	898	51	142	115.9	122.2	126.9	3,931
Bulgaria	0.49	18.7	1,975	459	61	64	70.0	68.3	59.4	4,351
Burkina Faso	0.34	0.7	2,998	70	0	5	122.2	122.4	120.2	159
Burundi	0.12	1.3	206	61	0	2	94.7	96.4	93.4	139
Cambodia	0.37	4.5	1,950	30	0	3	126.3	124.8	121.2	407
Cameroon	0.45	0.3	935	53	0	1	119.8	118.7	107.9	958
Canada	1.52	1.6	19,330	545	1,683	163	115.2	112.7	115.0	::
Central African Republic	0.58	::	140	6	0	1	121.4	122.7	123.5	439
Chad	0.48	0.4	1,523	27	0	1	123.4	117.5	108.7	212
Chile	0.24	32.6	621	1,131	44	119	123.5	128.7	136.3	5,211
China	0.10	37.0	91,370	2,732	1	56	132.3	155.8	202.6	296
Hong Kong, China	0.00	28.6	0	::	0	7	77.1	56.7	45.3	::
Colombia	0.05	23.4	1,239	2,853	7	118	101.3	110.8	117.2	2,890
Congo (Zaire)	0.16	0.1	2,063	16	0	4	103.4	104.9	104.6	285
Congo Republic	0.05	0.6	26	170	1	52	113.8	114.5	116.9	470
Costa Rica	0.08	23.8	70	3,636	23	246	127.8	128.4	120.6	4,627
Côte d'Ivoire	0.21	1.0	1,556	229	1	13	110.7	119.2	119.7	1,005
Croatia	0.25	0.2	626	1,577	14	31	80.2	57.7	46.2	7,144
Cuba	0.34	20.2	182	546	94	207	58.5	62.8	66.5	::
Czech Republic	0.30	0.7	1,618	1,122	148	252	86.4	81.9	77.8	::
Denmark	0.44	20.3	1,522	1,914	1,088	624	92.8	102.5	110.5	46,621
Dominican Republic	0.17	13.7	140	722	3	18	92.2	109.1	133.9	2,454

(continued on next page)

Country	Arable Land (hectares per capita) 1994-96	Irrigated Land (% of cropland) 1994-96	Land under Cereal Production (thousand hectares) 1995-97	Fertilizer Consumption (hundreds of grams per hectare of arable land) 1995-97	Tractors Per Thousand Agricultural Workers 1994-96	Tractors Per Hundred Hectares of Agricultural Land 1994-96	Crop Production Index (1989-91=100) 1995-97	Food Production Index (1989-91=100) 1995-97	Livestock Production Index (1989-91=100) 1995-97	Agricultural Productivity (agricultural value added per worker in 1995$) 1995-97
Ecuador	0.14	8.1	1,038	752	7	56	134.0	136.9	140.5	1,764
Egypt	0.05	100.0	2,632	3,750	10	304	129.4	129.8	122.2	1,163
El Salvador	0.11	14.2	431	1,261	5	54	104.0	109.5	123.4	1,705
Eritrea	0.12	5.4	292	78	1	19	119.3	102.3	91.3	..
Estonia	0.76	..	305	268	475	440	69.2	49.3	43.1	3,342
Ethiopia	0.20	1.6	7,790	126	0	3	..	92.4	91.6	..
Finland	0.49	..	1,059	1,397	1,301	911	95.1	103.6	105.0	28,296
France	0.31	8.2	8,780	2,679	1,189	721	104.8	105.2	107.5	34,760
Gabon	0.29	0.8	18	13	7	48	107.0	81.6	108.9	1,809
Gambia	0.16	..	99	49	0	3	77.4	74.6	80.9	216
Georgia	0.14	42.2	346	422	28	219	63.3	90.9	84.8	1,838
Germany	0.14	3.9	6,753	2,410	954	1,041	105.6	98.4	102.8	19,930
Ghana	0.16	0.1	1,291	44	1	15	158.2	147.7	98.7	533
Greece	0.27	33.8	1,306	1,895	267	805	102.6	114.0	117.6	12,611
Guatemala	0.13	6.5	629	1,324	2	32	107.9	129.2	129.5	1,902
Guinea	0.09	10.9	692	47	0	9	127.0	111.3	111.6	262
Guinea-Bissau	0.27	5.0	133	43	0	1	111.2	90.5	113.7	326
Haiti	0.08	9.7	418	89	0	4	84.2	104.7	112.5	407
Honduras	0.30	3.6	492	380	7	29	111.0	76.8	72.3	1,018
Hungary	0.47	4.2	2,840	836	54	68	79.0	117.1	122.8	4,655
India	0.17	32.0	100,140	856	5	82	116.5	122.4	137.1	343
Indonesia	0.09	15.0	14,942	1,468	1	34	120.0	136.8	132.7	745
Iran	0.30	38.0	8,921	600	39	133	135.5	92.8	56.3	3,831
Iraq	0.26	61.0	3,090	637	54	67	104.7	106.2	106.0	..
Ireland	0.37	..	289	5,514	978	1,265	109.2	114.1	114.2	..
Israel	0.06	45.3	86	2,963	336	731	109.5	99.7	102.9	..
Italy	0.14	24.9	4,210	2,280	867	1,797	98.1	117.9	98.9	19,001
Jamaica	0.07	14.0	3	1,547	11	181	132.9	96.9	96.5	1,294
Japan	0.03	62.7	2,257	4,168	593	5,359	94.0	157.3	162.1	28,665
Jordan	0.08	18.2	109	544	42	206	159.7	68.5	63.8	1,634
Kazakhstan	1.99	6.9	17,158	34	106	51	56.6	102.9	99.2	1,477
Kenya	0.15	1.5	1,805	278	19	35	109.8	119.1	146.3	230
Korea, North	0.08	73.0	1,410	2,418	19	441	107.0	139.3	148.5	..
Korea, South	0.04	60.7	1,174	5,291	34	563	101.6	123.8	92.0	10,962
Kuwait	0.00	..	0	2,000	14	200	87.2	112.4	127.7	..
Kyrgyzstan	0.19	76.8	596	295	44	238	107.9	49.8	41.2	2,917
Laos	0.17	20.3	597	58	0	11	75.6	117.6	132.1	526
Latvia	0.68	..	445	655	284	316	114.4	104.4	114.2	3,125
Lebanon	0.05	28.4	39	2,507	77	219	102.6	..	..	..
Lesotho	0.16	..	178	207	6	61	..	104.4	114.2	319

(continued on next page)

COUNTRY	AGRICULTURAL INPUTS				Agricultural Machinery		AGRICULTURAL OUTPUT AND PRODUCTIVITY			
	Arable Land (hectares per capita)	Irrigated Land (% of cropland)	Land under Cereal Production (thousand hectares)	Fertilizer Consumption (hundreds of grams per hectare of arable land)	Tractors Per Thousand Agricultural Workers	Tractors Per Hundred Hectares of Agricultural Land	Crop Production Index (1989–91 = 100)	Food Production Index (1989–91 = 100)	Livestock Production Index (1989–91 = 100)	Agricultural Productivity (agricultural value added per worker in 1995$)
	1994–96	1994–96	1995–97	1995–97	1994–96	1994–96	1995–97	1995–97	1995–97	1995–97
Libya	0.36	22.2	466	449	275	187	88.2	97.4	97.1	..
Lithuania	0.79	..	1,101	410	239	236	91.3	69.8	58.7	2,907
Macedonia	0.31	9.4	228	751	323	877	94.4	95.9	96.7	1,528
Madagascar	0.19	35.0	1,350	48	1	13	102.7	105.3	105.5	180
Malawi	0.16	1.6	1,391	213	0	9	114.0	105.3	100.0	122
Malaysia	0.09	4.5	696	6,375	23	230	109.0	124.0	141.2	6,267
Mali	0.40	2.3	2,538	79	1	7	131.1	118.7	116.4	241
Mauritania	0.20	10.3	253	93	1	7	134.6	103.2	99.0	439
Mauritius	0.09	17.0	0	3,174	6	37	97.3	106.1	137.4	5,400
Mexico	0.28	23.1	10,923	538	20	71	113.1	120.6	124.1	1,690
Moldova	0.41	14.1	900	652	82	281	75.2	58.3	46.3	1,473
Mongolia	0.53	6.1	304	19	22	56	31.9	81.6	86.6	1,085
Morocco	0.33	13.0	4,967	331	10	48	91.6	94.9	100.8	1,593
Mozambique	0.18	3.4	1,756	31	1	19	126.1	119.5	96.1	76
Myanmar (Burma)	0.22	15.9	6,303	163	1	10	135.7	133.5	122.9	..
Namibia	0.52	0.8	332	..	11	40	104.8	118.8	121.1	1,235
Nepal	0.14	30.6	3,249	336	0	16	114.9	113.5	110.1	187
Netherlands	0.06	61.5	198	5,923	646	2,060	111.0	106.1	102.8	43,836
New Zealand	0.43	8.9	167	4,247	451	488	129.1	120.3	113.4	..
Nicaragua	0.55	3.3	383	147	7	11	119.4	123.7	115.1	1,407
Niger	0.54	1.4	6,860	19	0	0	120.3	118.4	115.1	190
Nigeria	0.27	0.7	18,139	68	1	4	135.5	134.2	127.1	541
Norway	0.23	..	336	2,138	1,251	1,539	93.5	99.7	102.9	31,577
Oman	0.01	98.4	3	7,083	1	94	110.0	96.1	92.1	..
Pakistan	0.17	80.2	12,285	1,115	12	144	114.2	130.5	138.1	585
Panama	0.19	4.9	169	720	20	100	96.0	102.5	113.7	2,463
Papua New Guinea	0.01	..	2	2,311	1	203	106.3	106.8	105.4	827
Paraguay	0.45	3.0	596	120	25	75	103.9	116.7	112.3	3,295
Peru	0.16	41.8	874	453	3	25	132.8	131.5	124.9	1,619
Philippines	0.07	16.7	6,608	1,193	1	22	111.6	120.6	145.7	1,379
Poland	0.37	0.7	8,730	1,074	277	923	89.3	84.8	79.2	1,647
Portugal	0.22	21.7	706	1,198	203	692	93.1	99.8	109.9	5,574
Puerto Rico	0.01	57.8	0	..	..	..	66.4	83.7	89.2	..
Romania	0.41	31.4	6,202	483	80	175	102.7	100.5	94.5	3,170
Russian Federation	0.89	4.0	52,759	129	122	88	80.9	69.5	62.1	2,540
Rwanda	0.13	0.3	140	1	0	1	73.9	76.9	85.5	201
Saudi Arabia	0.19	38.7	621	873	11	26	99.1	90.8	118.8	10,507
Senegal	0.27	3.1	1,204	74	0	2	99.5	109.1	132.6	321
Sierra Leone	0.11	5.4	361	62	1	11	93.1	94.7	107.4	404
Singapore	0.00	..	..	50,940	16	650	56.6	37.9	38.0	39,851

(continued on next page)

COUNTRY	Arable Land (hectares per capita) 1994–96	Irrigated Land (% of cropland) 1994–96	Land under Cereal Production (thousand hectares) 1995–97	Fertilizer Consumption (hundreds of grams per hectare of arable land) 1995–97	Agricultural Machinery — Tractors Per Thousand Agricultural Workers 1994–96	Agricultural Machinery — Tractors Per Hundred Hectares of Agricultural Land 1994–96	Crop Production Index (1989–91 = 100) 1995–97	Food Production Index (1989–91 = 100) 1995–97	Livestock Production Index (1989–91 = 100) 1995–97	Agricultural Productivity (agricultural value added per worker in 1995$) 1995–97
Slovak Republic	0.28	13.4	851	660	100	199	92.0	74.4	65.1	3,347
Slovenia	0.12	0.7	99	3,116	2,762	3,800	120.3	100.9	99.3	26,006
South Africa	0.38	8.1	6,176	511	69	87	99.9	97.5	91.0	3,355
Spain	0.39	17.7	6,788	1,285	513	525	95.6	99.4	108.3	12,022
Sri Lanka	0.05	29.2	775	2,324	9	356	110.5	113.0	133.5	732
Sudan	0.48	15.0	8,377	52	2	8	160.1	139.8	122.2	..
Sweden	0.32	..	1,186	1,121	931	592	92.2	95.1	101.1	..
Switzerland	0.06	5.9	195	3,058	616	2,815	94.7	96.2	95.9	..
Syria	0.32	20.4	3,449	761	65	178	146.2	136.7	105.2	..
Tajikistan	0.14	80.6	353	850	37	366	57.8	67.9	61.4	..
Tanzania	0.10	4.6	3,171	113	1	23	93.1	97.2	110.5	159
Thailand	0.29	23.2	11,215	873	7	82	112.4	107.2	112.5	928
Togo	0.50	0.3	771	73	0	2	128.4	129.9	121.8	510
Trinidad and Tobago	0.06	18.0	4	1,022	49	353	103.0	110.7	110.9	1,838
Tunisia	0.32	7.5	1,223	312	39	121	99.4	108.3	129.9	2,750
Turkey	0.40	15.4	13,958	678	57	318	108.7	106.3	102.6	1,835
Turkmenistan	0.32	87.8	390	919	83	347	80.0	108.7	119.6	..
Uganda	0.26	0.1	1,315	6	1	9	110.9	107.7	112.9	326
Ukraine	0.65	7.5	12,789	277	92	123	69.5	69.9	62.3	2,259
United Arab Emirates	0.01	89.9	1	9,672	4	68	204.1	182.2	140.2	..
United Kingdom	0.10	1.8	3,346	3,700	871	837	103.1	100.5	99.2	..
United States	0.67	12.0	63,137	1,134	1,452	271	113.7	113.7	112.9	34,727
Uruguay	0.39	10.7	628	777	172	262	142.2	128.8	120.0	9,384
Uzbekistan	0.20	81.6	1,729	1,089	59	376	86.1	100.7	103.1	2,085
Venezuela	0.12	5.2	772	1,024	58	182	108.2	114.0	117.4	4,931
Vietnam	0.07	29.6	7,568	2,593	4	172	134.3	132.7	135.2	226
West Bank and Gaza	..	..	..	..	..	..	..	..	..	..
Yemen	0.09	31.3	719	85	2	41	111.8	115.5	121.5	305
Yugoslavia (Serbia- Montenegro)	0.35	1.6	..	437	..	..	..	..	..	..
Zambia	0.58	0.9	748	96	2	11	93.3	95.6	98.4	226
Zimbabwe	0.28	4.6	2,205	554	7,074	81	105.5	94.8	97.1	316

Source: *World Development Indicators* (World Bank, 1999).

Table K

Land Use and Deforestation, 1980–1996

COUNTRY	Land Area (thousands of sq. km.) 1996	Rural Population Density (people per sq. km. of arable land) 1996	Land Use Arable Land (% of land area) 1980	1996	Permanent Cropland (% of land area) 1980	1996	Other (% of land area) 1980	1996	Forest Area (thousands of sq. km.) 1995	Average Annual Deforestation (% change) 1990–1995
Albania	27	355	21.4	21.1	4.3	4.6	74.4	74.4	10	0.0
Algeria	2,382	166	2.9	3.2	0.3	0.2	96.8	96.6	19	1.2
Angola	1,247	258	2.3	2.4	0.4	0.4	97.3	97.2	222	1.0
Argentina	2,737	16	9.1	8.1	0.8	0.8	90.1	90.1	339	0.3
Armenia	28	197	..	21.2	..	3.5	..	78.7	3	-2.7
Australia	7,682	6	5.7	6.5	0.0	0.0	94.2	93.9	409	0.0
Austria	83	202	18.6	17.2	1.2	1.1	80.2	81.7	39	0.0
Azerbaijan	87	208	..	18.5	..	4.6	..	76.9	10	0.0
Bangladesh	130	1,161	68.3	65.3	2.0	2.5	29.6	32.4	10	0.8
Belarus	207	47	..	30.0	..	0.7	..	69.3	74	-1.0
Belgium[a]	33	..	23.2	22.0	0.4	0.5	76.4	75.8	7	0.0
Benin	111	240	12.2	12.9	4.0	4.1	83.8	83.0	46	1.2
Bolivia	1,084	147	1.7	1.8	0.2	0.2	98.1	97.9	483	1.2
Bosnia-Herzegovina	51	264	..	9.8	..	2.9	..	84.3	27	0.0
Botswana	567	161	0.7	0.6	0.0	0.0	99.3	0.0	139	0.5
Brazil	8,457	64	4.6	6.3	1.2	1.4	94.2	92.9	5,511	0.5
Bulgaria	111	62	34.6	38.0	3.2	1.8	62.2	61.8	32	0.0
Burkina Faso	274	252	10.0	12.4	0.1	0.1	89.8	87.5	43	0.7
Burundi	26	753	35.8	30.0	10.1	12.9	54.0	56.8	3	0.4
Cambodia	177	217	11.3	21.1	0.4	0.6	88.3	78.4	98	1.6
Cameroon	465	124	12.7	12.8	2.2	2.3	85.1	84.9	196	0.6
Canada	9,221	15	4.9	4.9	0.0	0.0	95.0	95.1	2,446	-0.1
Central African Republic	623	105	3.0	3.1	0.1	0.1	96.9	96.8	299	0.4
Chad	1,259	166	2.5	2.6	0.0	0.0	97.5	97.4	110	0.8
Chile	749	68	5.4	4.5	0.3	0.4	94.3	94.6	79	0.4
China[b]	9,326	675	10.4	13.3	0.4	1.2	89.3	85.7	1,333	0.1
Hong Kong, China	1	5,085	7.0	6.1	1.0	1.0	92.0	92.9	..	..
Colombia	1,039	549	3.6	1.9	1.4	2.4	95.0	95.7	530	0.5
Congo (Zaire)	2,267	464	3.0	3.1	0.3	0.4	96.6	96.5	..	..
Congo, Rep.	342	796	0.4	0.4	0.1	0.1	99.6	99.5	195	0.2
Costa Rica	51	602	5.5	5.6	4.4	4.8	90.1	89.6	12	3.0
Côte d'Ivoire	318	268	6.1	9.1	7.2	13.5	86.6	78.9	55	0.6
Croatia	56	169	..	22.2	..	2.2	..	78.2	18	0.0
Cuba	110	70	23.9	34.3	6.4	6.8	69.7	58.9	18	1.2
Czech Republic	77	115	..	40.1	..	3.1	..	56.2	26	0.0
Denmark	42	33	62.3	54.7	0.3	0.2	37.4	44.0	4	0.0
Dominican Republic	48	221	22.1	27.9	7.2	11.4	70.6	62.4	16	1.6
Ecuador	277	300	5.6	5.7	3.3	5.2	91.1	89.0	111	1.6
Egypt	995	1,167	2.3	2.8	0.2	0.5	97.5	96.7	0	0.0
El Salvador	21	498	27.0	30.7	8.0	10.5	65.0	59.9	1	3.3
Eritrea	101	689	..	4.4	..	0.8	..	94.9	3	0.0

(continued on next page)

COUNTRY	Land Area (thousands of sq. km.)	Rural Population Density (people per sq. km. of arable land)	Land Use						Forest Area (thousands of sq. km.)	Average Annual Deforestation (% change)
			Arable Land (% of land area)		Permanent Cropland (% of land area)		Other (% of land area)			
	1996	1996	1980	1996	1980	1996	1980	1996	1995	1990–1995
Estonia	42	35	..	26.7	..	0.4	..	72.9	20	-1.0
Ethiopia	1,000	434	..	11.3	..	0.7	..	88.9	136	0.5
Finland	305	76	8.4	8.1	..	..	..	0.0	200	0.1
France	550	80	31.8	33.2	2.5	2.1	65.7	64.7	150	-1.1
Gabon	258	169	1.1	1.3	0.6	0.7	98.2	98.2	179	0.5
Gambia	10	460	15.9	17.5	..	..	..	0.0	1	0.9
Georgia	70	288	..	11.1	..	4.7	..	83.8	30	0.0
Germany	349	92	34.4	33.9	1.4	0.7	64.1	65.5	107	0.0
Ghana	228	398	8.4	12.3	7.5	7.5	84.2	80.2	90	1.3
Greece	129	148	22.5	22.2	7.9	8.4	69.6	69.1	65	-2.3
Guatemala	108	458	11.7	12.6	4.4	5.1	83.9	82.4	38	2.0
Guinea	246	796	2.0	2.4	0.9	1.2	97.1	96.7	64	1.1
Guinea-Bissau	28	289	9.1	10.7	1.1	1.4	89.9	87.9	23	0.4
Haiti	28	885	19.8	20.3	12.5	12.7	67.7	67.0	0	3.4
Honduras	112	191	13.9	15.1	1.8	3.1	84.3	81.9	41	2.3
Hungary	92	74	54.4	52.1	3.3	2.4	42.2	46.1	17	-0.5
India	2,973	424	54.8	54.7	1.8	2.4	43.4	42.9	650	0.0
Indonesia	1,812	699	9.9	9.9	4.4	7.2	85.6	83.3	1,098	1.0
Iran	1,622	137	8.0	10.9	0.5	1.0	91.5	88.3	15	1.7
Iraq	437	97	12.0	12.6	0.4	0.6	87.6	86.8	1	0.0
Ireland	69	116	16.1	19.3	0.0	0.0	83.9	80.9	6	-2.7
Israel	21	149	15.8	17.0	4.3	4.2	80.0	78.9	1	0.0
Italy	294	236	32.2	27.6	10.0	9.1	57.7	62.1	65	-0.1
Jamaica	11	646	16.6	16.6	5.5	6.1	77.8	79.8	2	7.2
Japan	377	693	11.4	10.5	1.6	1.0	87.0	88.3	251	0.1
Jordan	89	378	3.4	3.6	0.4	1.0	96.2	95.4	0	2.5
Kazakhstan	2,671	20	..	11.9	..	0.1	..	86.9	105	-1.9
Kenya	569	492	6.7	7.0	0.8	0.9	92.5	92.1	13	0.3
Korea, North	120	511	13.4	14.1	2.4	2.5	84.2	83.4	62	0.0
Korea, South	99	462	20.9	17.7	1.4	2.0	77.8	79.4	76	0.2
Kuwait	18	977	0.1	0.3	0.0	0.1	..	0.0	0	0.0
Kyrgyzstan	192	310	..	4.7	..	2.7	..	92.6	7	0.0
Laos	231	463	2.9	3.5	0.1	0.2	97.0	96.3	..	..
Latvia	62	40	..	27.3	..	0.5	..	72.0	29	-0.9
Lebanon	10	264	20.5	18.2	8.9	12.5	70.6	70.0	1	7.8
Lesotho	30	463	9.6	10.5	..	0.0	..	0.0	0	0.0
Libya	1,760	40	1.0	1.0	0.2	0.2	98.8	98.8	4	0.0
Lithuania	65	35	..	45.5	..	0.9	..	53.4	20	-0.6
Macedonia	25	129	..	23.9	..	1.9	..	74.0	10	0.0
Madagascar	582	391	4.3	4.4	0.9	0.9	94.8	94.7	151	0.8
Malawi	94	540	13.3	17.0	0.9	1.1	85.8	81.9	33	1.6
Malaysia	329	530	3.0	5.5	11.6	17.6	85.4	76.9	155	2.4
Mali	1,220	157	1.6	3.8	0.0	0.0	98.3	97.5	116	1.0
Mauritania	1,025	233	0.2	0.5	0.0	0.0	99.8	99.6	6	0.0
Mauritius	2	673	49.3	49.3	3.4	3.0	47.3	47.8	0	0.0

(continued on next page)

COUNTRY	Land Area (thousands of sq. km.)	Rural Population Density (people per sq. km. of arable land)	Land Use — Arable Land (% of land area)		Land Use — Permanent Cropland (% of land area)		Land Use — Other (% of land area)		Forest Area (thousands of sq. km.)	Average Annual Deforestation (% change)
	1996	1996	1980	1996	1980	1996	1980	1996	1995	1990–1995
Mexico	1,909	97	12.1	13.2	0.8	1.1	87.1	87.0	554	0.9
Moldova	33	116	..	53.8	..	12.5	..	33.6	4	0.0
Mongolia	1,567	73	0.8	0.8	0.0	0.0	99.2	99.2	94	0.0
Morocco	446	145	16.6	19.7	1.1	1.9	82.3	78.2	38	0.3
Mozambique	784	357	3.6	3.8	0.3	0.3	96.1	95.9	169	0.7
Myanmar (Burma)	658	336	14.6	14.5	0.7	0.9	84.8	84.7	272	1.4
Namibia	823	122	0.8	1.0	0.0	0.0	99.2	99.1	124	0.3
Nepal	143	668	16.0	20.4	0.2	0.4	83.8	80.8	48	1.1
Netherlands	34	192	23.3	26.1	0.9	1.0	75.8	72.9	3	0.0
New Zealand	268	33	9.3	5.8	3.7	6.4	86.9	88.5	79	-0.6
Nicaragua	121	69	9.5	20.2	1.5	2.4	89.1	78.8	56	2.5
Niger	1,267	154	2.8	3.9	0.0	0.0	97.2	96.4	26	0.0
Nigeria	911	225	30.6	33.3	2.8	2.8	66.6	64.1	138	0.9
Norway	307	117	2.7	3.3	..	..	97.3	96.7	81	-0.2
Oman	212	3,086	0.1	0.1	0.1	0.2	99.8	99.7	0	..
Pakistan	771	388	25.9	27.3	0.4	0.7	73.7	72.1	17	2.9
Panama	74	235	5.8	6.7	1.6	2.1	92.5	91.1	28	2.1
Papua New Guinea	453	6,140	0.0	0.1	0.9	1.1	99.0	98.8	369	0.4
Paraguay	397	106	4.1	5.5	0.3	0.2	95.6	94.3	115	2.6
Peru	1,280	186	2.5	2.9	0.3	0.4	97.2	96.8	676	0.3
Philippines	298	621	14.5	17.5	14.8	14.4	70.8	68.6	68	3.5
Poland	304	98	48.0	46.3	1.1	1.2	50.9	51.9	87	-0.1
Portugal	92	295	26.5	23.5	7.8	8.2	65.7	67.7	29	-0.9
Puerto Rico	9	4,526	5.6	2.5	5.6	4.4	88.7	91.3	3	0.9
Romania	230	106	42.7	40.5	2.9	2.4	54.4	56.9	62	0.0
Russian Federation	16,889	27	..	7.8	..	0.1	..	92.2	7,635	0.0
Rwanda	25	746	30.8	34.5	10.3	12.2	58.9	53.4	3	0.2
Saudi Arabia	2,150	87	0.9	1.7	0.0	0.1	99.1	98.2	2	0.8
Senegal	193	212	12.2	11.7	0.0	0.1	87.8	87.7	74	0.7
Sierra Leone	72	629	6.3	6.8	0.7	0.8	93.0	92.5	13	3.0
Singapore	1	0	3.3	1.6	9.8	0.0	86.9	98.4	0	0.0
Slovak Republic	48	147	..	30.8	..	2.7	..	66.5	20	-0.1
Slovenia	20	418	..	11.5	..	2.7	..	85.8	11	0.0
South Africa	1,221	134	10.2	12.3	0.7	0.7	89.1	87.3	85	0.2
Spain	499	60	31.1	30.5	9.9	9.8	59.0	59.7	84	0.0
Sri Lanka	65	1,601	13.2	13.7	15.9	15.5	70.8	70.9	18	1.1
Sudan	2,376	142	5.2	5.4	0.0	0.0	94.8	94.5	416	0.8
Sweden	412	53	7.2	6.8	0.5	0.6	92.3	92.6	244	0.0
Switzerland	40	686	9.9	10.1	2.5	0.6	89.6	89.0	11	0.0
Syria	184	153	28.5	24.4	2.5	3.9	69.1	70.1	2	2.2
Tajikistan	141	488	..	5.8	..	0.5	..	93.7	4	0.0
Tanzania	884	738	2.5	3.5	1.0	1.0	96.5	95.6	325	1.0
Thailand	511	280	32.3	33.4	3.5	6.6	64.2	60.0	116	2.6

(continued on next page)

| COUNTRY | Land Area (thousands of sq. km.) | Rural Population Density (people per sq. km. of arable land) | Land Use | | | | | | Forest Area (thousands of sq. km.) | Average Annual Deforestation (% change) |
| | | | Arable Land (% of land area) | | Permanent Cropland (% of land area) | | Other (% of land area) | | | |
	1996	1996	1980	1996	1980	1996	1980	1996	1995	1990–1995
Togo	54	141	36.8	38.1	6.6	6.6	56.6	55.9	12	1.4
Trinidad and Tobago	5	481	13.6	14.6	9.0	9.2	77.4	76.2	2	1.5
Tunisia	155	119	20.5	18.3	9.7	13.1	69.7	69.0	6	0.5
Turkey	770	76	32.9	31.8	4.1	3.2	63.0	63.9	89	0.0
Turkmenistan	470	176	..	3.1	..	0.1	..	96.9	38	0.0
Uganda	200	340	20.4	25.3	8.0	8.8	71.6	65.9	61	0.9
Ukraine	579	45	..	57.3	..	1.8	..	40.7	92	-0.1
United Arab Emirates	84	1,108	0.2	0.4	0.1	0.5	99.7	99.0	1	0.0
United Kingdom	242	104	28.7	25.2	0.3	0.2	71.1	75.4	24	-0.5
United States	9,159	36	20.6	19.1	0.2	0.2	79.2	80.2	2,125	-0.3
Uruguay	175	24	8.0	7.2	0.3	0.3	91.7	92.5	8	0.0
Uzbekistan	414	301	..	10.9	..	0.9	..	88.2	91	-2.7
Venezuela	882	117	3.2	3.0	0.9	1.0	95.9	95.9	440	1.1
Vietnam	325	1,102	18.2	16.9	1.9	3.8	79.8	79.2	91	1.4
West Bank and Gaza	..	..	..	..	..	..	..	0.0	..	..
Yemen	528	714	2.6	2.7	0.2	0.2	97.2	97.1	0	0.0
Yugoslavia (Serbia-Montenegro)	102	122	..	36.4	..	3.5	..	60.0	18	0.0
Zambia	743	99	6.9	7.1	0.0	0.0	93.1	92.9	314	0.8
Zimbabwe	387	246	6.4	8.0	0.3	0.3	93.4	92.6	87	0.6

[a]Includes Luxembourg.
[b]Includes Taiwan, China.

Source: World Development Indicators (World Bank, 1999).

Table L

World Countries: Energy Production and Use, 1980–1996

COUNTRY	Commercial Energy Production — Thousand Metric Tons of Oil Equivalent		Commercial Energy Use — Thousand Metric Tons of Oil Equivalent			Commercial Energy Use Per Capita — Kg. of Oil Equivalent			Net Energy Imports — % of Commercial Energy Use	
	1980	1996	1980	1996	Average Annual % Growth 1980–96	1980	1996	Average Annual % Growth 1980–96	1980	1996
Albania	3,428	1,079	3,049	1,188	-6.6	1,142	362	-8.0	-12	9
Algeria	67,061	116,207	12,410	24,150	3.7	665	842	1.0	-440	-381
Angola	11,301	40,485	4,538	6,017	1.8	647	532	-1.2	-149	-573
Argentina	38,813	74,860	41,868	58,921	2.1	1,490	1,673	0.7	7	-27
Armenia	1,263	742	1,070	1,790	-3.7	346	474	-4.9	-18	59
Australia	86,096	189,045	70,372	100,612	2.3	4,790	5,494	0.9	-22	-88
Austria	7,655	7,788	23,450	27,187	1.3	3,105	3,373	0.9	67	71
Azerbaijan	14,821	14,387	15,002	11,862	-4.4	2,433	1,570	-5.6	1	-21
Bangladesh	13,224	21,501	14,920	23,928	3.1	172	197	0.9	11	10
Belarus	2,566	3,147	2,385	24,566	3.1	247	2,386	7.5	-8	87
Belgium	7,445	11,881	46,100	56,399	1.7	4,682	5,552	1.4	84	79
Benin	1,212	1,951	1,363	1,920	2.1	394	341	-0.1	11	-2
Bolivia	4,289	5,239	2,335	3,633	2.2	436	479	0.0	-84	-44
Bosnia and Herzegovina	..	626	..	1,750	..	..	777	..	..	64
Botswana	..	..	..	..	..	..	..	..	..	..
Brazil	62,069	112,319	108,997	163,374	2.8	896	1,012	1.0	43	31
Bulgaria	7,737	10,348	28,673	22,605	-2.4	3,235	2,705	-2.0	73	54
Burkina Faso	..	..	..	..	..	..	..	..	..	..
Burundi	..	..	..	..	..	..	..	..	..	..
Cambodia	..	..	..	..	..	..	..	..	..	..
Cameroon	5,824	10,016	3,687	5,000	1.7	426	369	-1.1	-58	-100
Canada	207,417	357,279	193,000	236,170	1.6	7,848	7,880	0.3	-7	-51
Central African Republic	..	..	..	..	..	..	..	..	..	..
Chad	..	..	..	..	..	..	..	..	..	..
Chile	5,664	7,843	9,525	20,456	5.4	855	1,419	3.7	41	62
China	608,625	1,100,390	593,109	1,096,800	4.1	604	902	2.6	-3	0
Hong Kong, China	39	47	5,681	12,190	5.7	1,127	1,931	4.4	99	100
Colombia	18,212	66,739	19,127	31,393	3.1	672	799	1.0	5	-113
Congo (Zaire)	8,697	13,689	8,706	13,799	3.1	322	305	-0.2	0	1
Congo, Rep.	3,970	11,493	845	1,205	2.2	506	457	-0.6	-370	-854
Costa Rica	767	736	1,527	2,248	3.4	669	657	0.7	50	67
Côte d'Ivoire	2,419	4,762	3,662	5,301	2.8	447	382	-0.6	34	10
Croatia	..	3,908	..	6,765	..	..	1,418	..	..	42
Cuba	3,891	6,709	14,570	15,953	0.4	1,501	1,448	-0.5	73	58
Czech Republic	42,697	31,528	46,910	40,404	-1.7	4,585	3,917	-1.7	9	22
Denmark	896	17,549	19,734	22,870	0.9	3,852	4,346	0.8	95	23
Dominican Republic	1,332	1,462	3,464	5,191	2.2	608	652	0.1	62	72
Ecuador	11,756	21,869	5,191	8,548	2.6	652	731	0.2	-126	-156
Egypt	34,168	59,759	15,970	37,790	5.1	391	638	2.6	-114	-58
El Salvador	1,915	2,607	2,540	4,058	2.5	554	700	1.0	25	36
Eritrea	..	..	..	..	..	..	..	..	..	..
Estonia	..	3,853	..	5,621	..	..	3,834	..	..	31
Ethiopia	10,588	15,536	11,157	16,566	2.7	296	284	-0.1	5	6
Finland	6,912	13,570	25,413	31,482	1.5	5,316	6,143	1.1	73	57
France	45,603	129,811	190,111	254,196	2.1	3,528	4,355	1.6	76	49
Gabon	9,441	19,706	1,493	1,578	-0.9	2,160	1,403	-3.9	-532	1,149

(continued on next page)

COUNTRY	Commercial Energy Production — Thousand Metric Tons of Oil Equivalent		Commercial Energy Use — Thousand Metric Tons of Oil Equivalent		Commercial Energy Use — Average Annual % Growth	Commercial Energy Use Per Capita — Kg. of Oil Equivalent		Commercial Energy Use Per Capita — Average Annual % Growth	Net Energy Imports — % of Commercial Energy Use	
	1980	1996	1980	1996	1980–96	1980	1996	1980–96	1980	1996
Gambia, The	..	..	..	..	..	..	..	..	..	..
Georgia	4,706	701	4,474	1,576	-5.4	882	291	-5.8	-5	55
Germany	185,628	140,455	360,441	349,552	-0.2	4,603	4,267	-0.5	48	60
Ghana	3,305	5,604	4,071	6,657	3.6	379	380	0.4	19	16
Greece	3,696	8,810	15,960	24,389	3.1	1,655	2,328	2.5	77	64
Guatemala	2,503	3,997	3,754	5,224	2.6	550	510	0.0	33	23
Guinea	..	..	..	..	..	..	..	..	..	..
Guinea-Bissau	..	..	..	..	..	..	..	..	..	..
Haiti	1,877	1,598	2,099	1,968	-0.9	392	268	2.8	11	19
Honduras	1,315	1,763	1,877	2,925	2.9	526	503	-0.2	30	40
Hungary	14,886	12,843	28,895	25,470	-1.2	2,699	2,499	-0.8	48	40
India	221,887	390,602	242,024	450,287	4.0	352	476	1.9	8	13
Indonesia	128,403	219,187	59,561	132,419	5.4	402	672	3.5	-116	-66
Iran	84,001	220,894	38,918	89,340	6.0	995	1,491	3.2	-116	-147
Iraq	136,643	32,584	12,030	25,027	4.0	925	1,174	0.8	-1,036	-30
Ireland	1,894	3,470	8,484	11,961	2.3	2,495	3,293	2.0	78	71
Israel	153	573	8,609	16,185	5.1	2,220	2,843	2.6	98	96
Italy	19,644	29,305	138,629	161,140	1.4	2,456	2,808	1.3	86	82
Jamaica	224	547	2,378	3,718	3.4	1,115	1,465	2.3	91	85
Japan	43,193	102,377	346,491	510,359	2.8	2,967	4,058	2.4	88	80
Jordan	1	181	1,714	4,487	5.1	786	1,040	0.6	100	96
Kazakhstan	76,799	62,628	76,799	43,376	-4.4	5,163	2,724	-4.9	0	-44
Kenya	7,891	11,245	9,791	13,279	2.2	589	476	-1.1	19	15
Korea, North	29,136	21,052	31,793	24,002	-1.6	1,799	1,063	-3.1	8	12
Korea, South	12,162	22,752	43,756	162,874	9.3	1,148	3,576	8.1	72	86
Kuwait	94,085	112,600	9,564	13,859	1.0	6,956	8,167	0.7	-884	-712
Kyrgyzstan	2,190	1,442	1,717	2,952	5.6	473	645	4.1	-27	51
Laos	..	..	..	..	..	..	..	..	..	..
Latvia	261	998	..	4,171	..	..	1,674	..	54	76
Lebanon	178	195	2,483	4,747	3.7	827	1,164	1.7	93	96
Lesotho	..	..	..	..	..	..	..	..	..	..
Libya	96,662	77,742	7,173	14,911	4.4	2,357	2,935	1.1	-1,248	-421
Lithuania	534	4,168	11,701	8,953	-3.4	3,428	2,414	-4.0	95	53
Macedonia	..	..	..	..	..	..	..	..	..	..
Madagascar	..	..	..	..	..	..	..	..	..	..
Malawi	..	..	..	..	..	..	..	..	..	..
Malaysia	16,644	69,559	11,128	41,209	9.0	809	1,950	6.0	-50	-69
Mali	..	..	..	..	..	..	..	..	..	..
Mauritania	..	..	..	..	..	..	..	..	..	..
Mauritius	..	..	..	..	..	..	..	..	..	..
Mexico	149,365	213,524	98,904	141,384	2.2	1,464	1,525	0.2	-51	-51
Moldova	35	53	..	4,601	..	..	1,064	..	106	99
Mongolia	..	..	..	..	..	..	..	..	..	..
Morocco	877	868	4,778	8,822	4.2	247	329	2.1	82	90
Mozambique	8,556	7,249	8,386	7,813	-0.4	693	481	-2.0	-2	7
Myanmar	9,513	11,835	9,430	12,767	1.8	279	294	0.3	-1	7
Namibia	..	..	..	..	..	..	..	..	..	..
Nepal	4,504	6,374	4,663	6,974	2.7	322	320	0.1	3	9
Netherlands	71,830	73,384	65,000	75,797	1.5	4,594	4,885	0.9	-11	3
New Zealand	5,488	13,585	9,251	16,295	3.8	2,972	4,388	2.9	41	17
Nicaragua	910	1,495	1,562	2,391	2.6	535	525	-0.1	42	37

(continued on next page)

COUNTRY	Commercial Energy Production — Thousand Metric Tons of Oil Equivalent		Commercial Energy Use — Thousand Metric Tons of Oil Equivalent			Commercial Energy Use Per Capita — Kg. of Oil Equivalent			Net Energy Imports — % of Commercial Energy Use	
	1980	1996	1980	1996	Average Annual % Growth 1980-96	1980	1996	Average Annual % Growth 1980-96	1980	1996
Niger										
Nigeria	148,479	170,453	52,846	82,669	2.9	743	722	-0.1	-181	-106
Norway	55,743	208,145	18,819	23,150	1.7	4,600	5,284	1.2	-196	-799
Oman	15,175	47,310	1,387	4,848	10.0	1,260	2,231	5.4	-994	-876
Pakistan	20,998	41,494	25,479	55,903	5.0	308	446	2.3	18	26
Panama	529	756	1,865	2,280	1.7	957	853	-0.3	72	67
Papua New Guinea										
Paraguay	1,605	6,678	2,094	4,285	4.6	672	865	1.5	23	-56
Peru	14,655	12,354	11,700	13,933	0.8	675	582	-1.2	-25	11
Philippines	10,670	17,232	21,212	37,992	3.7	439	528	1.1	50	55
Poland	121,848	102,363	124,806	108,411	-1.5	3,508	2,807	-2.0	2	6
Portugal	1,481	2,432	10,291	19,148	4.5	1,054	1,928	4.5	86	87
Puerto Rico										
Romania	52,587	31,317	64,694	45,824	-2.8	2,914	2,027	-2.9	19	32
Russian Federation	749,289	948,631	764,349	615,899	-3.3	5,499	4,169	-3.6	2	-54
Rwanda										
Saudi Arabia	533,071	474,997	35,357	92,243	5.2	3,773	4,753	0.4	-1,408	-415
Senegal	1,046	1,566	1,921	2,588	2.0	347	302	-0.7	46	39
Sierra Leone		55								
Singapore			6,054	23,851	10.0	2,653	7,835	8.1	100	100
Slovak Republic	3,416	4,818	20,810	17,449	-1.4	4,175	3,266	-1.8	84	72
Slovenia	1,623	2,762	4,313	6,167	1.2	2,269	3,098	1.0	62	55
South Africa	73,068	127,859	65,355	99,079	2.0	2,370	2,482	-0.4	-12	-29
Spain	15,644	32,622	68,583	101,411	3.1	1,834	2,583	2.8	77	68
Sri Lanka	3,209	4,204	4,493	6,792	2.1	305	371	0.7	29	38
Sudan	7,089	9,486	8,169	10,787	1.8	437	397	-0.5	13	12
Sweden	16,134	31,804	40,984	52,567	1.3	4,932	5,944	0.9	61	39
Switzerland	7,030	10,479	20,861	25,622	1.6	3,301	3,622	0.8	66	59
Syria	9,502	33,705	5,348	14,541	5.7	614	1,002	2.4	-78	-132
Tajikistan	1,986	1,343	1,650	3,513	7.7	416	594	5.1	-20	62
Tanzania	9,502	13,073	10,280	13,798	2.0	553	453	-1.1	8	5
Thailand	11,183	43,954	22,740	79,987	9.0	487	1,333	7.3	51	45
Togo										
Trinidad and Tobago	13,141	13,575	3,873	7,887	4.2	3,580	6,081	3.1	-239	-72
Tunisia	6,966	6,289	3,900	6,676	3.7	611	735	1.4	-79	6
Turkey	17,190	26,783	31,314	65,520	4.9	704	1,045	2.6	45	59
Turkmenistan	8,034	32,623	7,948	12,164	-7.6	2,778	2,646	-10.5	-1	-168
Uganda										
Ukraine	109,708	79,042	97,893	153,937	1.2	1,956	3,012	1.0	-12	49
United Arab Emirates	93,915	148,818	8,576	32,336	7.3	8,222	13,155	1.7	-995	-360
United Kingdom	196,792	288,126	201,299	234,719	1.1	3,574	3,992	0.8	2	-14
United States	1,553,260	1,687,300	1,811,650	2,134,960	1.4	7,973	8,051	0.4	14	21
Uruguay	664	1,021	2,637	2,955	0.9	905	912	0.2	75	65
Uzbekistan	4,615	47,406	4,821	42,406	9.5	302	1,826	7.0	4	-12
Venezuela	132,934	193,993	35,026	54,962	2.1	2,321	2,463	-0.4	-280	-253
Vietnam	18,052	38,437	19,348	33,750	2.9	360	448	0.7	7	-14
West Bank and Gaza										
Yemen	60	18,181	1,424	2,936	4.7	167	187	0.6	96	-519
Yugoslavia (Serbia-Montenegro)		10,987		14,420			1,364			24
Zambia	4,198	5,357	4,551	5,790	1.2	793	628	-1.7	8	7
Zimbabwe	5,688	8,721	6,511	10,442	3.4	929	929	0.4	13	16

COUNTRY	Commercial Energy Production Thousand Metric Tons of Oil Equivalent		Commercial Energy Use Thousand Metric Tons of Oil Equivalent		Average Annual % Growth	Commercial Energy Use Per Capita Kg. of Oil Equivalent		Average Annual % Growth	Net Energy Imports % of Commercial Energy Use	
	1980	1996	1980	1996	1980–96	1980	1996	1980–96	1980	1996
World	6,911,503t	9,438,480t	6,943,349t	9,317,404t	2.9w	1,623w	1,684w	1.1w	..w	..w
Low income	563,859	916,261	493,168	837,277	3.6	390	461	1.2	–14	–9
Middle income	3,552,971	4,833,815	2,635,621	3,652,666	4.6	1,205	1,305	2.7	–35	–32
Lower middle income	2,200,925	3,205,571	1,954,874	2,667,023	5.8	1,103	1,190	3.9	–13	–20
Upper middle income	1,352,046	1,628,244	680,747	985,643	2.1	1,643	1,766	0.2	–99	–65
Low & middle income	4,116,830	5,750,076	3,128,789	4,489,943	4.4	906	973	2.3	–32	–28
East Asia & Pacific	832,224	1,521,645	768,319	1,458,927	4.2	572	855	2.6	7	::
Europe & Central Asia	1,240,595	1,437,762	1,338,028	1,287,193	7.6	3,300	2,732	3.9	::	–12
Latin America & Carib.	468,430	751,684	376,913	557,686	2.4	1,062	1,163	0.5	–24	–35
Middle East & N. Africa	989,486	1,096,558	146,618	337,967	5.1	842	1,246	2.2	–577	–225
South Asia	263,822	464,175	291,579	543,884	4.0	329	441	1.8	10	15
Sub-Saharan Africa	322,273	478,251	207,332	304,286	2.3	720	670	–0.6	::	::
High income	2,794,673	3,688,405	3,814,560	4,827,461	1.8	4,625	5,259	1.1	27	24
Europe EMU	363,765	444,746	940,145	1,091,718	1.2	3,408	3,768	0.9	61	59

Source: *World Development Indicators* (World Bank, 1999).

Table M

World Countries: Water Resources

COUNTRY	Annual Renewable Water Resources[a]		Annual Average Groundwater Resources[b]		Sectoral Withdrawals (%)[c]					
	Supply Per Capita (cubic meters) 1998 est.	Withdrawal Per Capita (cubic meters) 1998	Recharge Per Capita (cubic meters) 1998 est.	Withdrawal Per Capita (cubic meters) 1998	Domestic Surface	Domestic Ground	Industry Surface	Industry Ground	Agriculture Surface	Agriculture Ground
WORLD	6,918	645	..	..	8	..	23	..	69	..
AFRICA	5,133	202	..	..	7	..	5	..	88	..
Algeria	460	180	56	91	25	..	15	..	60	..
Angola	15,376	57	6,017	..	14	..	10	..	76	..
Benin	1,751	28	306	..	23	..	10	..	67	..
Botswana	1,870	84	1,096	..	32	..	20	x	48	..
Burkina Faso	1,535	39	833	..	19	..	0	..	81	..
Burundi	546	20	319	..	36	..	0	..	64	..
Cameroon	18,711	38	6,982	..	46	..	19	..	35	..
Central African Republic	40,413	26	16,050	..	21	..	5	..	74	..
Chad	2,176	34	1,669	15.3	16	29.4	2	0.0	82	70.6
Congo (Zaire)	19,001	10	149,185	..	61	..	16	..	23	..
Congo Republic	78,668	20	70,163	..	62	..	27	..	11	100.0
Cote d'Ivoire	5,265	67	2,588	..	22	..	11	..	67	..
Egypt	43	921	20	68.3	6	..	8	..	86	..
Equatorial Guinea	69,767	15	24,256	..	81	..	13	..	6	..
Eritrea	789	..	..	..	..	..	..	..	..	..
Ethiopia	1,771	51	708	..	11	..	3	..	86	..
Gabon	140,171	70	52,991	0.36	72	100.0	22	0.0	6	0.0
Gambia	2,513	29	419	..	7	..	2	..	91	..
Ghana	1,607	35	1,326	..	35	..	13	..	52	..
Guinea	29,454	142	4,952	..	10	..	3	..	87	..
Guinea-Bissau	14,109	17	142,346	..	60	..	4	..	36	..
Kenya	696	87	103	..	20	x	4	..	76	..
Lesotho	2,395	30	229	..	22	..	22	..	56	..
Liberia	72,780	54	21,834	..	27	..	13	..	60	..
Libya	100	880	84	554.7	11	13.3	2	4.3	87	82.5
Madagascar	20,614	1,579	3,364	461.2	1	100.0	0	0.0	99	0.0
Malawi	1,690	98	135	..	10	..	3	..	86	..
Mali	5,071	162	1,690	11.2	2	7.1	1	0.0	97	92.9
Mauritania	163	923	122	498.3	6	..	2	..	92	..
Mauritius	1,915	410	589	..	16	..	7	..	77	..
Morocco	1,071	433	268	138.6	5	..	3	..	92	..

(continued on next page)

COUNTRY	Annual Renewable Water Resources[a]		Annual Average Groundwater Resources[b]		Sectoral Withdrawals (%)[c]					
	Supply Per Capita (cubic meters) 1998 est.	Withdrawal Per Capita (cubic meters) 1998	Recharge Per Capita (cubic meters) 1998 est.	Withdrawal Per Capita (cubic meters) 1998	Domestic		Industry		Agriculture	
					Surface	Ground	Surface	Ground	Surface	Ground
Mozambique	5,350	40	910	..	9	..	2	..	89	..
Namibia	3,751	179	1,270	..	29	..	3	..	68	..
Niger	346	69	247	17.9	16	57.7	2	3.8	82	38.5
Nigeria	1,815	41	714	..	31	..	15	..	54	..
Rwanda	965	135	551	..	5	..	2	..	94	..
Senegal	2,933	202	844	39.2	5	25.0	3	0.0	92	75.0
Sierra Leone	34,957	98	10,924	..	7	..	4	..	89	..
Somalia	563	99	310	38.1	3	..	0	..	97	..
South Africa	1,011	359	108	61.4	17	10.6	11	5.6	72	83.8
Sudan	1,227	666	245	13.0	4	..	1	..	94	..
Swaziland	2,836	1,171	..	..	2	..	2	..	96	..
Tanzania	2,485	40	932	..	9	..	2	..	89	..
Togo	2,594	28	1,286	..	62	..	16	..	25	..
Tunisia	371	376	127	167.7	9	13.6	6	0.0	89	86.4
Uganda	1,829	20	1,360	..	32	..	8	..	60	..
Zambia	9,229	216	5,420	..	16	..	7	..	77	..
Zimbabwe	1,182	136	419	..	14	..	7	..	79	..
NORTH AMERICA	**17,458**	1,798	..	..	**13**	..	**47**	..	**39**	..
Canada	94,373	1,602	12,241	38.8	18	43.3	70	14.2	12	42.5
United States	8,983	1,839	5,531	432.9	13	22.7	45	6.1	42	71.1
CENTRAL AMERICA	**8,084**	916	..	..	**6**	..	**8**	..	**86**	..
Belize	69,565	109	..	..	10	..	0	..	90	..
Costa Rica	26,027	780	5,753	..	4	..	7	..	89	..
Cuba	3,104	870	720	408.3	9	..	2	..	89	..
Dominican Republic	2,430	446	364	..	5	..	6	..	89	..
El Salvador	3,128	244	..	..	7	..	4	..	89	..
Guatemala	10,033	139	2,681	..	9	..	17	..	74	..
Haiti	1,460	7	382	..	24	..	8	..	68	..
Honduras	9,015	294	6,345	..	4	..	5	..	91	..
Jamaica	3,269	159	..	..	7	..	7	..	86	..
Mexico	3,729	915	1,450	311.4	6	13.2	8	23.0	86	63.8
Nicaragua	39,203	368	13,217	..	25	..	21	..	54	..
Panama	52,042	754	15,179	..	12	..	11	..	77	..
Trinidad and Tobago	3,869	148	..	..	27	..	38	..	35	..

(continued on next page)

COUNTRY	Annual Renewable Water Resources[a]		Annual Average Groundwater Resources[b]		Sectoral Withdrawals (%)[c]					
					Domestic		Industry		Agriculture	
	Supply Per Capita (cubic meters) 1998 est.	Withdrawal Per Capita (cubic meters) 1998	Recharge Per Capita (cubic meters) 1998 est.	Withdrawal Per Capita (cubic meters) 1998	Surface	Ground	Surface	Ground	Surface	Ground
SOUTH AMERICA	**28,072**	**335**	..	..	**18**	..	**23**	..	**59**	..
Argentina	19,212	1,043	3,543	180.4	9	10.6	18	19.1	73	70.2
Bolivia	37,703	201	16,338	..	10	..	5	..	85	..
Brazil	31,424	246	11,347	..	22	..	19	..	59	..
Chile	31,570	1,625	9,444	..	6	..	5	..	89	..
Colombia	28,393	174	13,533	..	41	..	16	..	43	..
Ecuador	25,791	581	11,006	..	7	..	3	..	90	..
Guyana	281,542	1,819	120,327	..	1	..	0	..	99	..
Paraguay	18,001	112	7,851	..	15	..	7	..	78	..
Peru	1,613	300	12,219	139.4	19	25.0	9	15.0	72	60.0
Suriname	452,489	1,192	180,995	..	6	..	5	..	89	..
Uruguay	18,215	241	7,101	..	6	..	3	..	91	..
Venezuela	36,830	382	9,767	..	43	..	11	..	46	..
ASIA	**3,680**	**542**	..	..	**6**	..	**9**	..	**85**	..
Afghanistan	2,354	1,825	1,241	..	1	..	0	..	99	..
Armenia	2,493	804	1,154	..	30	..	4	..	66	..
Azerbaijan	1,069	2,177	856	..	5	..	25	..	70	..
Bangladesh	10,940	217	274	39.6	3	12.9	1	0.9	96	86.2
Bhutan	49,557	13	..	..	36	..	10	..	54	..
Cambodia	8,195	66	2,790	..	5	..	1	..	94	..
China	2,231	461	693	69.7	6	..	7	46.4	87	53.6
Georgia	10,682	637	3,166	..	21	..	20	..	59	..
India	1,896	612	359	222.4	3	3.1	4	1.3	93	95.7
Indonesia	12,251	96	1,094	..	13	..	11	..	76	..
Iran	1,755	1,079	671	738.8	6	..	2	..	92	..
Iraq	1,615	2,368	55	13.1	3	55.6	5	44.4	92	0.0
Israel	289	407	187	279.1	16	..	5	..	79	..
Japan	4,344	735	1,469	104.3	17	29.3	33	40.7	50	30.1
Jordan	114	201	97	107.0	22	..	3	..	75	..
Kazakhstan	4,484	2,002	2,133	..	2	..	17	..	81	..
Korea, North	2,887	727	..	..	11	..	16	..	73	..
Korea, South	1,434	632	..	29.4	19	0.0	35	83.3	46	16.7
Kuwait	11	307	..	..	37	..	2	..	60	..
Kyrgyzstan	10,394	2,257	3,043	..	3	..	3	..	94	..
Laos	50,392	259	9,332	..	8	..	10	..	82	..
Lebanon	1,315	444	1,002	224.9	28	..	4	..	68	..
Malaysia	21,259	768	3,310	..	23	..	30	..	47	..

(continued on next page)

COUNTRY	Annual Renewable Water Resources[a]		Annual Average Groundwater Resources[b]		Sectoral Withdrawals (%)[c]					
	Supply Per Capita (cubic meters) 1998 est.	Withdrawal Per Capita (cubic meters) 1998	Recharge Per Capita (cubic meters) 1998 est.	Withdrawal Per Capita (cubic meters) 1998	Domestic		Industry		Agriculture	
					Surface	Ground	Surface	Ground	Surface	Ground
Mongolia	9,375	271	8,765	∶	11	∶	27	∶	62	∶
Myanmar (Burma)	22,719	101	3,276	∶	7	∶	3	∶	90	∶
Nepal	7,338	154	∶	∶	4	∶	1	∶	95	∶
Oman	393	656	381	280.7	5	∶	2	∶	94	∶
Pakistan	1,678	1,269	372	527.6	2	∶	2	11.1	97	88.9
Philippines	4,476	686	2,494	82.8	18	0.0	21	50.0	61	50.0
Saudi Arabia	119	1,003	109	587.4	9	5.4	1	8.1	90	86.5
Singapore	172	84	∶	∶	45	∶	51	∶	4	∶
Sri Lanka	2,341	503	921	∶	2	∶	2	∶	96	∶
Syria	456	1,069	280	353.0	4	∶	2	∶	94	∶
Tajikistan	11,171	2,001	1,011	∶	3	∶	4	∶	92	∶
Thailand	1,845	602	721	15.0	4	60.0	6	25.7	90	14.3
Turkey	3,074	544	314	112.3	16	42.9	11	0.0	72	57.1
Turkmenistan	232	5,723	778	∶	1	∶	1	∶	98	∶
United Arab Emirates	64	954	51	251.3	7	∶	1	∶	62	∶
Uzbekistan	704	2,501	848	∶	4	∶	5	∶	94	∶
Vietnam	4,827	416	1,078	∶	13	∶	9	∶	78	∶
Yemen	243	253	89	139.2	7	∶	1	∶	92	∶
EUROPE	**8,547**	**625**	∶	∶	**14**	∶	**55**	∶	**31**	∶
Albania	2,903	94	2,032	∶	6	∶	18	∶	76	∶
Austria	6,857	304	2,716	144.7	33	52.1	58	42.7	9	5.1
Belarus	3,595	264	1,740	106.0	22	55.6	43	14.1	35	30.3
Belgium	822	917	84	79.2	11	68.3	85	27.0	4	4.8
Bosnia-Herzegovina	∶	∶	∶	∶	∶	∶	∶	∶	∶	∶
Bulgaria	2,146	1,574	1,598	566.0	3	∶	76	∶	22	∶
Croatia	13,663	∶	∶	∶	∶	∶	∶	∶	∶	∶
Czech Republic	5,694	266	∶	77.9	41	∶	57	∶	2	∶
Denmark	2,092	233	5,706	215.1	30	40.2	27	22.0	43	37.9
Estonia	8,642	107	2,718	∶	56	∶	39	∶	5	∶
Finland	21,334	440	369	47.3	12	64.9	85	10.8	3	24.3
France	3,065	665	1,703	109.5	16	52.5	69	30.2	15	17.3
Germany	1,165	580	555	97.4	11	48.6	70	47.5	20	3.9
Greece	4,279	523	237	193.9	8	12.8	29	2.7	63	84.5
Hungary	604	660	685	99.1	9	35.0	55	47.5	36	17.5
Iceland	606,498	636	86,643	394.2	31	∶	63	∶	6	∶
Ireland	13,187	233	971	50.0	16	34.5	74	36.8	10	28.7
Italy	2,785	986	524	211.4	14	53.1	27	13.3	59	33.7

(continued on next page)

COUNTRY	Annual Renewable Water Resources[a]		Annual Average Groundwater Resources[b]		Sectoral Withdrawals (%)[c]					
	Supply Per Capita (cubic meters) 1998 est.	Withdrawal Per Capita (cubic meters) 1998	Recharge Per Capita (cubic meters) 1998 est.	Withdrawal Per Capita (cubic meters) 1998	Domestic		Industry		Agriculture	
					Surface	Ground	Surface	Ground	Surface	Ground
Latvia	6,685	114	879	..	55	..	32	..	13	..
Lithuania	4,174	68	322	..	81	..	16	..	3	..
Macedonia	..	..	..	..	..	..	..	..	..	..
Moldova	225	667	90	..	9	..	65	..	26	..
Netherlands	635	518	286	78.7	5	32.0	61	44.5	34	23.4
Norway	87,691	488	21,923	26.5	20	27.3	72	72.7	8	0.0
Poland	1,278	321	931	63.2	13	70.0	76	30.0	11	0.0
Portugal	3,878	738	521	210.6	15	38.6	37	22.8	48	38.6
Romania	1,639	1,139	368	55.5	8	61.0	33	38.1	59	0.8
Russian Federation	29,115	521	5,320	..	19	..	62	..	20	..
Slovak Republic	5,745	337	..	142.5	..	..	..	..	..	..
Slovenia	..	..	..	..	..	..	..	..	..	..
Spain	2,775	781	521	140.0	12	..	26	22.2	62	77.8
Sweden	19,858	340	2,257	69.8	36	91.7	55	8.3	9	0.0
Switzerland	5,802	173	369	138.6	23	94.7	73	5.3	4	0.0
Ukraine	1,029	504	388	82.8	18	30.3	52	17.5	30	52.1
United Kingdom	1,219	204	168	47.1	20	51.3	77	46.6	3	2.1
Yugoslavia (Serbia-Montenegro)	..	..	..	..	..	..	..	..	..	..
OCEANIA	**54,795**	591	..	..	**64**	..	**2**	..	**34**	..
Australia	18,596	933	..	162.2	65	..	2	22.6	33	77.4
Fiji	34,732	42	87,591	..	20	..	20	..	60	..
New Zealand	88,859	589	53,804	..	46	..	10	..	44	..
Papua New Guinea	174,055	28	..	..	29	..	22	..	49	..
Solomon Islands	107,194	0	..	..	40	..	20	..	40	..

[a] Annual renewable water resources usually include river flows from other countries.

[b] Withdrawal data from most recent year available; varies by country from 1987 to 1995.

[c] Total withdrawals may exceed 100% because of groundwater withdrawals or river inflows.

Source: *World Resources 1998–99* (World Resources Institute).

Table N

World Countries: Energy Efficiency and Emissions, 1980–1996

COUNTRY	GDP per Unit of Energy Use 1995 $US Per Kg. of Oil Equivalent		Traditional Fuel Use % of Total Energy Use		Carbon Dioxide Emissions Total Million Metric Tons		Per Capita Metric Tons		Kg. Per 1995 $US of GDP	
	1980	1996	1980	1996	1980	1996	1980	1996	1980	1996
Albania	0.8	2.2	12.3	8.6	4.8	1.9	1.8	0.6	2.0	0.7
Algeria	2.5	1.8	2.7	2.0	66.2	94.3	3.5	3.3	2.1	2.2
Angola	..	0.9	47.1	59.5	5.3	5.1	0.8	0.5	..	0.9
Argentina	5.7	5.0	6.5	4.0	107.5	129.9	3.8	3.7	0.5	0.4
Armenia	5.2	1.7	..	..	..	3.7	..	1.0	..	1.2
Australia	3.3	3.7	2.1	3.8	202.8	306.6	13.8	16.7	0.9	0.8
Austria	7.1	8.7	1.4	2.8	52.2	59.3	6.9	7.4	0.3	0.3
Azerbaijan	..	0.3	..	..	..	30.0	..	4.0	..	8.5
Bangladesh	1.3	1.7	67.8	49.9	7.6	23.0	0.1	0.2	0.4	0.6
Belarus	..	0.8	..	0.8	..	61.7	..	6.0	..	3.2
Belgium	4.6	4.9	0.2	0.9	127.2	106.0	12.9	10.4	0.6	0.4
Benin	0.9	1.1	84.9	92.5	0.5	0.7	0.1	0.1	0.4	0.3
Bolivia	2.3	1.9	19.8	12.8	4.5	10.1	0.8	1.3	0.8	1.4
Bosnia-Herzegovina	..	..	..	..	..	3.1	..	1.4	..	0.4
Botswana	..	..	35.7	9.9	1.0	2.1	1.1	1.4	0.7	0.4
Brazil	4.7	4.4	41.2	27.5	183.4	273.4	1.5	1.7	0.4	0.4
Bulgaria	0.4	0.5	0.7	0.8	75.3	55.3	8.5	6.6	6.4	4.7
Burkina Faso	..	..	91.4	93.3	0.4	1.0	0.1	0.1	0.3	0.4
Burundi	..	..	92.7	88.8	0.1	0.2	0.0	0.0	0.2	0.2
Cambodia	..	..	71.2	75.3	0.3	0.5	0.0	0.0	..	0.2
Cameroon	1.7	1.7	69.4	77.3	3.9	3.5	0.4	0.3	0.6	0.4
Canada	2.1	2.5	0.6	0.6	420.9	409.4	17.1	13.7	1.0	0.7
Central African Republic	..	..	90.8	89.0	0.1	0.2	0.0	0.1	0.1	0.2
Chad	..	..	87.4	90.2	0.2	0.1	0.0	0.0	0.2	0.1
Chile	2.8	3.1	14.5	13.3	27.9	48.8	2.5	3.4	1.0	0.8
China	0.3	0.7	8.0	5.6	1,476.8	3,363.5	1.5	2.8	8.9	4.4
Hong Kong, China	10.0	12.0	0.9	0.3	16.3	23.1	3.2	3.7	0.3	0.2
Colombia	2.4	2.6	21.4	21.1	39.8	65.3	1.4	1.7	0.9	0.8
Congo (Zaire)	1.0	0.5	79.5	83.9	3.5	2.3	0.1	0.1	0.4	0.4
Congo. Rep.	1.5	1.9	55.9	61.0	0.4	5.0	0.2	1.9	0.3	2.2
Costa Rica	3.7	4.0	40.4	12.7	2.5	4.7	1.1	1.4	0.4	0.5
Côte d'Ivoire	2.3	2.0	53.5	67.2	4.6	13.1	0.6	0.9	0.5	1.2
Croatia	..	2.8	..	3.0	..	17.5	..	3.7	..	0.9
Cuba	..	..	28.1	19.7	31.0	31.2	3.2	2.8	..	..
Czech Republic	..	1.3	..	0.5	..	126.7	..	12.3	..	2.4
Denmark	6.8	8.2	0.3	3.3	62.9	56.6	12.3	10.7	0.5	0.3
Dominican Republic	2.2	2.5	28.3	12.1	6.4	12.9	1.1	1.6	0.8	1.0
Ecuador	2.4	2.1	26.5	14.8	13.4	24.5	1.7	2.1	1.1	1.3
Egypt	1.8	1.6	5.0	3.3	45.2	97.9	1.1	1.7	1.5	1.6
El Salvador	2.9	2.4	50.3	42.9	2.1	4.0	0.5	0.7	0.3	0.4
Eritrea	..	..	..	..	..	..	..	..	..	..
Estonia	..	0.9	..	2.3	..	16.4	..	11.2	..	3.3

(continued on next page)

COUNTRY	GDP per Unit of Energy Use (1995 $US Per Kg. of Oil Equivalent)		Traditional Fuel Use (% of Total Energy Use)		Carbon Dioxide Emissions					
					Total Million Metric Tons		Per Capita Metric Tons		Kg. Per 1995 $US of GDP	
	1980	1996	1980	1996	1980	1996	1980	1996	1980	1996
Ethiopia	0.4	0.4	92.4	90.1	1.8	3.4	0.0	0.1	0.4	0.5
Finland	3.7	4.1	3.8	5.1	54.9	59.2	11.5	11.5	0.6	0.5
France	6.1	6.1	1.3	1.0	482.7	361.8	9.0	6.2	0.4	0.2
Gabon	2.4	3.3	33.6	51.8	4.9	3.7	7.1	3.3	1.4	0.7
Gambia	..	..	79.7	81.2	0.2	0.2	0.2	0.2	0.7	0.6
Georgia	2.7	2.1	..	1.3	..	3.0	..	0.5	..	0.9
Germany	..	7.0	..	0.7	..	861.2	..	10.5	..	0.4
Ghana	1.0	1.0	68.2	79.0	2.4	4.0	0.2	0.2	0.6	0.6
Greece	5.7	4.8	2.8	1.5	51.7	80.6	5.4	7.7	0.6	0.7
Guatemala	2.9	2.9	53.1	59.9	4.5	6.8	0.7	0.7	0.4	0.4
Guinea	..	..	68.4	69.9	0.9	1.1	0.2	0.2	..	0.3
Guinea-Bissau	..	..	76.1	70.5	0.1	0.2	0.2	0.2	1.0	0.9
Haiti	1.5	1.4	82.4	80.3	0.8	1.1	0.1	0.1	0.2	0.4
Honduras	1.4	1.4	61.2	49.3	2.1	4.0	0.6	0.7	0.8	1.0
Hungary	1.6	1.8	2.1	1.8	82.5	59.5	7.7	5.8	1.8	1.3
India	0.6	0.8	34.7	23.3	347.3	997.4	0.5	1.1	2.4	2.8
Indonesia	1.3	1.6	51.6	29.9	94.6	245.1	0.6	1.2	1.3	1.1
Iran	1.4	1.1	1.6	0.8	116.1	266.7	3.0	4.4	2.1	2.9
Iraq	4.0	..	0.2	0.1	44.0	91.4	3.4	4.3	..	..
Ireland	..	5.9	0.1	0.2	25.2	34.9	7.4	9.6	0.7	0.5
Israel	5.1	5.6	0.0	..	21.1	52.3	5.4	9.2	0.5	0.6
Italy	6.0	6.8	0.7	1.9	371.9	403.2	6.6	7.0	0.5	0.4
Jamaica	1.3	1.1	6.2	8.0	8.4	10.1	4.0	4.0	2.7	2.4
Japan	9.3	10.5	0.1	0.5	920.4	1,167.7	7.9	9.3	0.3	0.2
Jordan	2.2	1.5	0.0	..	..	..	..	..	..	..
Kazakhstan	..	0.5	..	0.1	..	173.8	..	10.9	..	8.7
Kenya	0.6	0.7	75.4	76.1	6.2	6.8	0.4	0.2	1.1	0.7
Korea, North	3.1	..	2.7	3.9	124.9	254.3	7.1	11.3	..	..
Korea, South	2.4	3.0	5.7	0.7	125.2	408.1	3.3	9.0	0.9	0.8
Kuwait	..	1.7	0.0	..	..	..	..	..	..	..
Kyrgyzstan	..	1.2	..	..	..	6.1	..	1.3	..	1.7
Laos	..	..	86.6	85.1	0.2	0.3	0.1	0.1	..	0.2
Latvia	16.0	1.5	..	18.0	..	9.3	..	3.7	..	1.4
Lebanon	..	..	4.3	2.6	6.2	14.2	2.1	3.5	..	..
Lesotho	..	..	..	..	..	..	..	..	..	..
Libya	..	..	1.7	0.8	26.9	40.6	8.8	8.0	..	..
Lithuania	..	0.8	..	5.6	..	13.8	..	3.7	..	1.9
Macedonia	..	..	..	6.9	..	12.7	..	6.4	..	6.1
Madagascar	..	..	77.1	83.8	1.6	1.2	0.2	0.1	0.5	0.4
Malawi	..	..	89.1	86.8	0.7	0.7	0.1	0.1	0.7	0.5
Malaysia	2.9	2.3	14.4	6.6	28.0	119.1	2.0	5.6	0.9	1.3
Mali	..	..	85.2	87.4	0.4	0.5	0.1	0.0	0.2	0.2
Mauritania	..	..	0.7	..	0.6	2.9	0.4	1.2	0.8	2.6
Mauritius	..	..	44.1	41.6	0.6	1.7	0.6	1.5	0.3	0.4
Mexico	2.3	2.1	4.4	4.4	251.6	348.1	3.7	3.8	1.1	1.2
Moldova	..	0.6	..	0.5	..	12.1	..	2.8	..	4.2

COUNTRY	GDP per Unit of Energy Use		Traditional Fuel Use		Carbon Dioxide Emissions					
	1995 $US Per Kg. of Oil Equivalent		% of Total Energy Use		Total Million Metric Tons		Per Capita Metric Tons		Kg. Per 1995 $US of GDP	
	1980	1996	1980	1996	1980	1996	1980	1996	1980	1996
Mongolia	∴	∴	14.0	3.6	6.8	8.9	4.1	3.6	9.2	9.1
Morocco	4.5	4.2	5.4	4.7	15.9	27.9	0.8	1.0	0.7	0.8
Mozambique	0.2	0.3	72.6	86.0	3.2	1.0	0.3	0.1	2.0	0.5
Myanmar (Burma)	∴	∴	66.5	69.4	4.8	7.3	0.1	0.2	∴	∴
Namibia	∴	∴	∴	∴	∴	∴	∴	∴	∴	∴
Nepal	0.5	0.7	94.8	88.9	0.5	1.6	0.0	0.1	0.3	0.3
Netherlands	4.4	5.4	0.0	0.5	152.6	155.2	10.8	10.0	0.5	0.4
New Zealand	4.7	3.8	0.2	∴	17.6	29.8	5.6	8.0	0.4	0.5
Nicaragua	1.3	1.0	50.4	45.8	2.0	2.9	0.7	0.6	1.0	1.2
Niger	∴	∴	78.0	79.6	0.6	1.1	0.1	0.1	0.3	0.6
Nigeria	0.4	0.4	63.7	56.6	68.1	83.3	1.0	0.7	3.0	2.8
Norway	5.1	6.7	0.8	1.1	90.4	67.0	22.1	15.3	0.9	0.4
Oman	2.8	2.6	0.0	∴	5.9	15.1	5.3	7.0	1.5	1.3
Pakistan	1.0	1.1	27.2	20.2	31.6	94.3	0.4	0.8	1.2	1.5
Panama	2.8	3.6	26.4	19.4	3.5	6.7	1.8	2.5	0.7	0.8
Papua New Guinea	∴	∴	64.1	58.9	1.8	2.4	0.6	0.5	0.6	0.5
Paraguay	2.8	2.1	66.1	51.5	1.5	3.7	0.5	0.7	0.3	0.4
Peru	4.1	4.3	18.7	22.9	23.6	26.2	1.4	1.1	0.5	0.4
Philippines	2.7	2.1	35.8	30.5	36.5	63.2	0.8	0.9	0.6	0.8
Poland	0.9	1.2	0.4	1.1	456.2	356.8	12.8	9.2	4.2	2.8
Portugal	6.8	5.6	1.1	0.7	27.2	47.9	2.8	4.8	0.4	0.4
Puerto Rico	0.6	0.7	0.0	∴	14.0	15.8	4.4	4.2	∴	∴
Romania	0.6	0.7	1.5	21.5	191.8	119.3	8.6	5.3	5.3	3.5
Russian Federation	0.5	0.5	∴	1.1	∴	1,579.5	∴	10.7	∴	4.7
Rwanda	∴	∴	84.8	85.7	0.3	0.5	0.1	0.1	0.2	0.3
Saudi Arabia	3.0	1.4	0.0	∴	130.7	267.8	14.0	13.8	1.2	2.1
Senegal	1.6	1.8	48.6	55.9	2.8	3.1	0.5	0.4	0.9	0.6
Sierra Leone	∴	∴	63.5	69.4	0.6	0.4	0.2	0.1	0.6	0.5
Singapore	4.6	3.8	0.0	∴	30.1	65.8	13.2	21.6	1.1	0.7
Slovak Republic	∴	1.1	∴	0.5	∴	39.6	∴	7.4	∴	2.1
Slovenia	∴	3.1	∴	0.8	∴	13.0	∴	6.5	∴	0.7
South Africa	1.7	1.4	4.5	3.9	211.3	292.7	7.7	7.3	1.9	2.1
Spain	5.7	5.6	0.5	0.6	200.0	232.5	5.3	5.9	0.5	0.4
Sri Lanka	1.5	2.0	54.3	48.4	3.4	7.1	0.2	0.4	0.5	0.5
Sudan	0.5	0.7	76.4	76.4	3.3	3.5	0.2	0.1	0.7	0.4
Sweden	4.5	4.5	3.9	2.5	71.4	54.1	8.6	6.1	0.4	0.2
Switzerland	12.1	12.0	1.1	2.1	40.9	44.2	6.5	6.3	0.2	0.1
Syria	1.7	1.2	0.1	∴	19.3	44.3	2.2	3.1	2.1	2.6
Tajikistan	∴	0.5	∴	∴	∴	5.8	∴	1.0	∴	3.6
Tanzania	∴	0.3	83.7	89.6	1.9	2.4	0.1	0.1	0.5	0.5
Thailand	2.3	2.2	48.3	32.7	40.0	205.4	0.9	3.4	0.8	1.2
Togo	∴	∴	38.3	73.1	0.6	0.8	0.2	0.2	0.5	0.5
Trinidad and Tobago	1.3	0.7	1.8	1.0	16.7	22.2	15.4	17.1	3.4	4.0
Tunisia	2.7	2.9	15.4	12.9	9.4	16.2	1.5	1.8	0.9	0.8
Turkey	2.8	2.8	18.0	3.1	76.3	178.3	1.7	2.8	0.9	1.0
Turkmenistan	∴	0.3	∴	∴	∴	34.2	∴	7.4	∴	8.2

(continued on next page)

COUNTRY	GDP per Unit of Energy Use — 1995 $US Per Kg. of Oil Equivalent		Traditional Fuel Use — % of Total Energy Use		Carbon Dioxide Emissions					
					Total Million Metric Tons		Per Capita Metric Tons		Kg. Per 1995 $US of GDP	
	1980	1996	1980	1996	1980	1996	1980	1996	1980	1996
Uganda	..	..	87.2	89.2	0.6	1.0	0.1	0.1	0.2	0.2
Ukraine	..	0.5	..	0.4	..	397.3	..	7.8	..	5.1
United Arab Emirates	..	..	0.0	..	36.3	81.8	34.8	33.3	..	0.5
United Kingdom	4.0	4.8	0.0	1.1	583.8	557.0	10.4	9.5	0.7	0.7
United States	2.7	3.4	1.2	4.2	4,575.4	5,301.0	20.1	20.0	0.9	0.7
Uruguay	5.8	6.4	20.4	26.7	5.8	5.6	2.0	1.7	0.4	0.3
Uzbekistan	..	0.5	..	..	..	95.0	..	4.1	..	4.2
Venezuela	1.7	1.4	1.0	1.2	89.6	144.5	5.9	6.5	1.5	1.9
Vietnam	..	0.7	53.5	49.1	16.8	37.6	0.3	0.5	..	1.7
West Bank and Gaza	..	..	..	..	..	..	..	..	..	..
Yemen	..	1.3	0.0	..	..	..	..	..	..	..
Yugoslavia (Serbia-Montenegro)	..	..	100.0	..	..	..	..	..	..	..
Zambia	0.7	0.6	54.6	71.2	3.5	2.4	0.6	0.3	1.1	0.7
Zimbabwe	0.7	0.7	33.6	27.4	9.6	18.4	1.4	1.6	2.1	2.4
WORLD	..w	3.2w	7.1w	6.9w	13,640.7t	22,653.9t	3.4w	4.0w	0.8w	0.7w
Low income	..	0.8	50.1	38.0	559.4	1,448.1	0.4	0.7	1.7	2.1
Middle income	..	1.3	12.3	7.3	4,247.0	10,068.9	2.2	3.6	1.7	2.1
Lower middle income	..	0.9	12.9	7.2	2,509.0	7,512.7	1.6	3.4	3.0	3.1
Upper middle income	..	2.4	11.5	7.5	1,738.0	2,556.2	4.3	4.5	1.1	1.1
Low & middle income	..	1.2	18.8	12.0	4,806.4	11,517.0	1.5	2.4	1.7	2.1
East Asia & Pacific	..	1.0	15.8	11.6	1,833.3	4,309.5	1.3	2.5	4.3	2.9
Europe & Central Asia	..	0.8	3.5	2.1	886.9	3,412.7	..	7.4	..	3.4
Latin America & Carib.	..	3.2	20.3	15.6	848.5	1,209.1	2.4	2.5	0.6	0.7
Middle East & N. Africa	..	1.6	2.0	1.2	494.6	988.6	3.0	3.9	1.5	1.8
South Asia	..	0.9	37.5	25.6	392.4	1,125.1	0.4	0.9	1.9	2.3
Sub-Saharan Africa	..	0.9	46.6	47.4	350.7	472.1	0.9	0.8	1.6	1.5
High Income	..	5.0	1.0	2.5	8,834.4	11,136.9	11.9	12.1	0.6	0.5
Europe EMU	5.6	6.3	0.9	1.1	1,504.4	2,329.5	7.6	8.0	0.5	0.3

Source: World Development Indicators (World Bank, 1999).

Part IX

Geographic Index

The geographic index contains approximately 1500 names of cities, states, countries, rivers, lakes, mountain ranges, oceans, capes, bays, and other geographic features. The name of each geographical feature in the index is accompanied by a geographical coordinate (latitude and longitude) in degrees and by the page number of the primary map on which the geographical feature appears. Where the geographical coordinates are for specific places or *points,* such as a city or a mountain peak, then the latitude and longitude figures give the location of the map symbol denoting that point. Thus, Los Angeles, California, is at 34N and 118W and the location of Mt. Everest is 28N and 87E. The coordinates for political features (countries or states) or physical features (oceans, deserts) that are *areas* rather than *points* are given according to the location of the name of the feature on the map, except in those cases where the name of the feature is separated from the feature (a country's name appearing over an adjacent ocean area because of space requirements). In such cases, the feature's coordinates will indicate the location of the center of the feature. The coordinates for the Sahara Desert will lead the reader to the place name "Sahara Desert" on the map; the coordinates for North Carolina will show the center location of the state since the name appears over the adjacent Atlantic Ocean. Finally, the coordinates for geographical features that are *lines* rather than *points* or *areas* will also appear near the center of the text identifying the geographical feature. Alphabetizing follows general conventions; the names of physical features such as lakes, rivers, mountains are given as: proper name, followed by the generic name. Thus "Mount Everest" is listed as "Everest, Mt." Where an article such as "the," "le," or "al" appears in a geographic name, the name is alphabetized according to the article. Hence, "La Paz" is found under "L" and not under "P."

Name/Description	Latitude & Longitude	Page	Name/Description	Latitude & Longitude	Page
Abidjan, Cote d'Ivoire *(city, nat. cap.)*	5N 4W	97	Aguascalientes, Aguas. *(city, st. cap., Mex.)*	22N 102W	90
Abu Dhabi, U.A.E. *(city, nat. cap.)*	24N 54E	95	Agulhas, Cape	35S 20E	96
Accra, Ghana *(city, nat. cap.)*	64N 0	97	Ahaggar Range	23N 6E	96
Aconcagua, Mt. 22,881	38S 78W	90	Ahmadabad, India *(city)*	23N 73E	95
Acre *(st., Brazil)*	9S 70W	91	Akmola, Kazakhstan *(city)*	51N 72E	95
Addis Ababa, Ethiopia *(city, nat. cap.)*	9N 39E	97	Al Fashir, Sudan *(city)*	14N 25E	97
Adelaide, S. Australia *(city, st. cap., Aust.)*	35S 139E	99	Al Fayyum, Egypt *(city)*	29N 31E	97
Aden, Gulf of	12N 46E	94	Al Hijaz Range	30N 40E	94
Aden, Yemen *(city)*	13N 45E	95	Al Khufra Oasis	24N 23E	96
Admiralty Islands	1S 146E	98	Alabama *(st., US)*	33N 87W	89
Adriatic Sea	44N 14E	92	Alagoas *(st., Brazil)*	9S 37W	91
Aegean Sea	39N 25E	92	Alaska *(st., US)*	63N 153W	89 inset
Afghanistan *(country)*	35N 65E	95	Alaska, Gulf of	58N 150W	89 inset
Aguascalientes *(st., Mex.)*	22N 110W	90	Alaska Peninsula	57N 155W	88 inset

Name/Description	Latitude & Longitude	Page	Name/Description	Latitude & Longitude	Page
Alaska Range	60N 150W	88 inset	Ashkhabad, Turkmenistan (city, nat. cap.)	38N 58E	95
Albania (country)	41N 20E	93	Asia Minor	39N 33E	97
Albany, Australia (city)	35S 118E	99	Asmera, Eritrea (city, nat. cap.)	15N 39E	97
Albany, New York (city, st. cap., US)	43N 74W	89	Astrakhan, Russia (city)	46N 48E	93
Albert Edward, Mt. 13,090	8S 147E	98	Asuncion, Paraguay (city, nat. cap.)	25S 57W	91
Albert, Lake	2N 30E	96	Aswan, Egypt (city)	24N 33E	97
Alberta (prov., Can.)	55N 117W	89	Asyuf, Egypt (city)	27N 31E	97
Albuquerque, NM (city)	35N 107W	89	Atacama Desert	23S 70W	90
Aldabra Islands	9S 44E	96	Athabasca (lake, N.Am.)	60N 109W	88
Aleppo, Syria (city)	36N 37E	95	Athabaska (riv., N.Am.)	58N 114W	88
Aleutian Islands	55N 175W	88	Athens, Greece (city, nat. cap.)	38N 24E	93
Alexandria, Egypt (city)	31N 30E	97	Atlanta, Georgia (city, st. cap., US)	34N 84W	89
Algeria (country)	28N 15E	97	Atlantic Ocean	30N 40W	88
Algiers, Algeria (city, nat. cap.)	37N 3E	97	Atlas Mountains	31N 6W	96
Alice Springs, Aust. (city)	24S 134E	99	Auckland, New Zealand (city)	37S 175E	99
Alma Ata, Kazakhstan (city, nat. cap.)	43N 77E	95	Augusta, Maine (city, st. cap., US)	44N 70W	89
Alps Mountains	46N 6E	92	Austin, Texas (city, st. cap., US)	30N 98W	89
Altai Mountains	49N 87E	94	Australia (country)	20S 135W	99
Altun Shan	45N 90E	94	Austria (country)	47N 14E	93
Amapa (st., Brazil)	2N 52W	91	Ayers Rock 2844	25S 131E	98
Amazon Riv.	2S 53W	90	Azerbaijan (country)	38N 48E	93
Amazonas (st., Brazil)	2S 64W	91	Azov, Sea of	48N 36E	92
Amman, Jordan (city, nat. cap.)	32N 36E	95	Bab el Mandeb (strait)	13N 42E	96
Amsterdam, Netherlands (city)	52N 5E	93	Baffin Bay	74N 65W	88
Amu Darya (riv., Asia)	40N 62E	94	Baffin Island	70N 72W	88
Amur (riv., Asia)	52N 156E	94	Baghdad, Iraq (city, nat. cap.)	33N 44E	92
Anchorage, AK (city)	61N 150W	89 inset	Bahamas (island)	25N 75W	88
Andaman Islands	12N 92E	95	Bahia (st., Brazil)	13S 42W	91
Andes Mountains	25S 70W	90	Bahia Blanca, Argentina (city)	39S 62W	91
Angara (riv., Asia)	60N 100E	94	Baikal, Lake	52N 105E	94
Angola (country)	11S 18E	97	Baja California (st., Mex.)	30N 110W	89
Ankara, Turkey (city, nat. cap.)	40N 33E	95	Baja California Sur (st., Mex.)	25N 110W	89
Annapolis, Maryland (city, st. cap., US)	39N 76W	89	Baku, Azerbaijan (city, nat. cap.)	40N 50E	93
Antananarivo, Madagascar (city, nat. cap.)	19S 48E	97	Balearic Islands	29N 3E	93
Antofagasta, Chile (city)	24S 70W	91	Balkash, Lake	47N 75E	94
Antwerp, Belgium (city)	51N 4E	93	Ballarat, Aust. (city)	38S 144E	99
Appalachian Mountains	37N 80W	88	Baltic Sea	56N 18E	92
Appenines Mountains	32N 14E	92	Baltimore, MD (city)	39N 77W	94
Arabian Desert	25N 33E	92	Bamako, Mali (city, nat. cap.)	13N 8W	97
Arabian Peninsula	23N 40E	98	Bandiera Peak 9,843	20S 42W	90
Arabian Sea	18N 61E	94	Bangalore, India (city)	13N 75E	95
Aracaju, Sergipe (city, st. cap., Braz.)	11S 37W	91	Bangeta, Mt. 13,520	6S 147E	98
Arafura Sea	9S 133E	98	Banghazi, Libya (city)	32N 20E	97
Araguaia, Rio (riv., Brazil)	13S 50W	90	Bangkok, Thailand (city, nat. cap.)	14N 100E	95
Aral Sea	45N 60E	94	Bangladesh (country)	23N 92E	95
Arctic Ocean	75N 160W	91	Bangui, Cent. African Rep. (city, nat. cap.)	4N 19E	97
Arequipa, Peru (city)	16S 71W	91	Banjul, Gambia (city, nat. cap.)	13N 17W	97
Argentina (country)	39S 67W	91	Banks Island	73N 125W	88
Aripuana, Rio (riv., S.Am.)	11S 60W	90	Barbados (island)	13N 60W	91
Arizona (st., US)	34N 112W	89	Barcelona, Spain (city)	41N 2E	93
Arkansas (riv., N.Am.)	38N 100W	88	Barents Sea	69N 40E	94
Arkansas (st., US)	37N 94W	89	Bartle Frere, Mt. 5322	18S 145W	98
Arkhangelsk, Russia (city)	75N 160W	93	Barwon (riv., Australasia)	29S 148E	98
Armenia (country)	40N 45E	93	Bass Strait	40S 146E	98
Arnhem, Cape	11S 139E	98	Baton Rouge, Louisiana (city, st. cap., US)	30N 91W	89
Arnhem Land	12S 133E	98	Beaufort Sea	72N 135W	88
As Sudd	9N 26E	96	Beijing, China (city, nat. cap.)	40N 116E	95
Ascension (island)	9S 13W	96	Beirut, Lebanon (city, nat. cap.)	34N 35E	93
Ashburton (riv., Australasia)	23S 115W	94	Belarus (country)	52N 27E	93

Name/Description	Latitude & Longitude	Page	Name/Description	Latitude & Longitude	Page
Belem, Para (city, st. cap., Braz.)	1S 48W	91	Bristol Bay	58N 159W	88 inset
Belfast, Northern Ireland (city)	55N 6W	93	British Columbia (prov., Can.)	54N 130W	89
Belgium (country)	51N 4E	93	Brooks Range	67N 155W	88
Belgrade, Yugoslavia (city, nat. cap.)	45N 21E	93	Bruce, Mt. 4052	22S 117W	98
Belhuka, Mt. 14,483	50N 86E	94	Brussels, Belgium (city, nat. cap.)	51N 4E	93
Belize (country)	18S 88W	89	Bucharest, Romania (city, nat. cap.)	44N 26E	93
Belle Isle, Strait of	52N 57W	88	Budapest, Hungary (city, nat. cap.)	47N 19E	93
Belmopan, Belize (city, nat. cap.)	18S 89W	89	Buenos Aires, Argentina (city, nat. cap.)	34S 58W	91
Belo Horizonte, M.G. (city, st. cap., Braz.)	20S 43W	91	Buenos Aires (st., Argentina)	36S 60W	91
Belyando (riv., Australasia)	22S 147W	98	Buffalo, NY (city)	43N 79W	89
Ben, Rio (riv., S.Am.)	14S 67W	90	Bujumbura, Burundi (city, nat. cap.)	3S 29E	97
Bengal, Bay of	15N 90E	94	Bulgaria (country)	44N 26E	93
Benguela, Angola (city)	13S 13E	97	Bur Sudan, Sudan (city)	19N 37E	97
Benin (country)	10N 4E	97	Burdekin (riv., Australasia)	19S 146W	98
Benin City, Nigeria (city)	6N 6E	97	Burkina Faso (country)	11N 2W	97
Benue (riv., Africa)	8N 9E	96	Buru (island)	4S 127E	98
Bergen, Norway (city)	60N 5E	93	Burundi (country)	4S 30E	97
Bering Sea	57N 175W	94	Cairns, Aust. (city)	17S 145E	99
Bering Strait	65N 168W	94	Cairo, Egypt (city, nat. cap.)	30N 31E	97
Berlin, Germany (city)	52N 13E	93	Calcutta, India (city)	23N 88E	95
Bermeo, Rio (riv., S.Am.)	25S 61W	90	Calgary, Canada (city)	51N 114W	89
Bermuda (island)	30S 66W	89	Calicut, India (city)	11N 76E	95
Bhutan (country)	28N 110E	95	California (st., US)	35N 120W	89
Billings, MT (city)	46N 108W	89	California, Gulf of	29N 110W	89
Birmingham, AL (city)	34N 87W	89	Callao, Peru (city)	13S 77W	91
Birmingham, UK (city)	52N 2W	93	Cambodia (country)	10N 106E	95
Biscay, Bay of	45N 5W	92	Cameroon (country)	5N 13E	97
Bishkek, Kyrgyzstan (city, nat. cap.)	43N 75E	95	Campeche (st., Mex.)	19N 90W	89
Bismarck Archipelago	4S 147E	98	Campeche Bay	20N 92W	88
Bismarck, North Dakota (city, st. cap., US)	47N 101W	89	Campeche, Campeche (city, st. cap., Mex.)	19N 90W	89
Bismarck Range	6S 145E	98	Campo Grande, M.G.S. (city, st. cap., Braz.)	20S 55W	91
Bissau, Guinea-Bissau (city, nat. cap.)	12N 16W	97	Canada (country)	52N 100W	89
Black Sea	46N 34E	92	Canadian (riv., N.Am.)	30N 100W	88
Blanc, Cape	21N 18W	96	Canary Islands	29N 18W	96
Blue Nile (riv., Africa)	10N 36E	96	Canberra, Australia (city, nat. cap.)	35S 149E	99
Blue Mountains	33S 150E	98	Cape Breton Island	46N 60W	88
Boa Vista do Rio Branco, Roraima (city, st. cap., Braz.)	3N 61W	91	Cape Town, South Africa (city)	34S 18E	97
Boise, Idaho (city, st. cap., US)	44N 116W	89	Caracas, Venezuela (city, nat. cap.)	10N 67W	91
Bolivia (country)	17S 65W	91	Caribbean Sea	18N 75W	91
Boma, Congo Republic (city)	5S 13E	97	Carnarvon, Australia (city)	25S 113E	99
Bombay, India (city)	19N 73E	95	Carpathian Mountains	48N 24E	92
Bonn, Germany (city, nat. cap.)	51N 7E	93	Carpentaria, Gulf of	14S 140E	98
Boothia Peninsula	71N 94W	88	Carson City, Nevada (city, st. cap., US)	39N 120W	89
Borneo (island)	0 11E	95	Cartagena, Colombia (city)	10N 76W	91
Bosnia-Herzegovina (country)	45N 18E	93	Cascade Range	45N 120W	88
Bosporus, Strait of	41N 29E	92	Casiquiare, Rio (riv., S.Am.)	4N 67W	90
Boston, Massachusetts (city, st. cap., US)	42N 71W	89	Caspian Depression	49N 48E	92
Botany Bay	35S 153E	99	Caspian Sea	42N 48E	92
Bothnia, Gulf of	62N 20E	92	Catamarca (st., Argentina)	25S 70W	91
Botswana (country)	23S 25E	97	Catamarca, Catamarca (city, st. cap., Argen.)	28S 66W	91
Brahmaputra (riv., Asia)	30N 100E	94	Cauca, Rio (riv., S.Am.)	8N 75W	90
Branco, Rio (riv., S.Am.)	3N 62W	90	Caucasus Mountains	42N 40E	92
Brasilia, Brazil (city, nat. cap.)	16S 48W	91	Cayenne, French Guiana (city, nat. cap.)	5N 52W	91
Bratislava, Slovakia (city, nat. cap.)	48N 17E	93	Ceara (st., Brazil)	4S 40W	91
Brazil (country)	10S 52W	91	Celebes (island)	0 120E	94
Brazilian Highlands	18S 45W	90	Celebes Sea	2N 120E	94
Brazzaville, Congo (city, nat. cap.)	4S 15E	97	Central African Republic (country)	5N 20E	97
Brisbane, Queensland (city, st. cap., Aust.)	27S 153E	99	Ceram (island)	3S 129E	99
			Chaco (st., Argentina)	25S 60W	91

Name/Description	Latitude & Longitude	Page	Name/Description	Latitude & Longitude	Page
Chad *(country)*	15N 20E	97	Cook Strait	42S 175E	98
Chad, Lake	12N 12E	97	Copenhagen, Denmark *(city, nat. cap.)*	56N 12E	93
Changchun, China *(city)*	44N 125E	95	Copiapo, Chile *(city)*	27S 70W	91
Chari *(riv., Africa)*	11N 16E	96	Copiapo , Mt. 19,947	26S 70W	90
Charleston, SC *(city)*	33N 80W	89	Coquimbo, Chile *(city)*	30S 70W	91
Charleston, West Virginia *(city, st. cap., US)*	38N 82W	89	Coral Sea	15S 155E	98
Charlotte, NC *(city)*	35N 81W	89	Cordilleran Highlands	45N 118W	88
Charlotte Waters, Aust. *(city)*	26S 135E	99	Cordoba *(st., Argentina)*	32S 67W	91
Charlottetown, P.E.I. *(city, prov. cap., Can.)*	46N 63W	89	Cordoba, Cordoba *(city, st. cap., Argen.)*	32S 64W	91
Chelyabinsk, Russia *(city)*	55N 61E	93	Corrientes *(st., Argentina)*	27S 60W	91
Chengdu, China *(city)*	30N 104E	95	Corrientes, Corrientes *(city, st. cap., Argen.)*	27S 59W	91
Chesapeake Bay	36N 74W	88	Corsica *(island)*	42N 9E	93
Chetumal, Quintana Roo *(city, st. cap., Mex.)*	19N 88W	89	Cosmoledo Islands	9S 48E	96
Cheyenne, Wyoming *(city, st. cap., US)*	41N 105W	89	Costa Rica *(country)*	15N 84W	89
Chiapas *(st., Mex.)*	17N 92W	89	Cote d'Ivoire *(country)*	7N 86W	97
Chicago, IL *(city)*	42N 87W	89	Cotopaxi, Mt. 19,347	1S 78W	90
Chiclayo, Peru *(city)*	7S 80W	91	Crete *(island)*	36N 25W	92
Chidley, Cape	60N 65W	88	Croatia *(country)*	46N 20W	93
Chihuahua *(st., Mex.)*	30N 110W	89	Cuango *(riv., Africa)*	10S 16E	96
Chihuahua, Chihuahua *(city, st. cap., Mex.)*	29N 106W	89	Cuba *(country)*	22N 78W	89
Chile *(country)*	32S 75W	91	Cuiaba, Mato Grosso *(city, st. cap., Braz.)*	16S 56W	91
Chiloe *(island)*	43S 74W	90	Cuidad Victoria, Tamaulipas *(city, st. cap., Mex.)*	24N 99W	89
Chilpancingo, Guerrero *(city, st. cap., Mex.)*	19N 99W	89	Culiacan, Sinaloa *(city, st. cap., Mex.)*	25N 107W	89
Chimborazo, Mt. 20,702	2S 79W	90	Curitiba, Parana *(city, st. cap., Braz.)*	26S 49W	91
China *(country)*	38N 105E	95	Cusco, Peru *(city)*	14S 72W	91
Chisinau, Moldova *(city, nat. cap.)*	47N 29E	93	Cyprus *(island)*	36N 34E	92
Chongqing, China *(city)*	30N 107E	95	Czech Republic *(country)*	50N 16E	93
Christchurch, New Zealand *(city)*	43S 173E	99	d'Ambre, Cape	12S 50E	97
Chubut *(st., Argentina)*	44S 70W	91	Dakar, Senegal *(city, nat. cap.)*	15N 17W	97
Chubut, Rio *(riv., S.Am.)*	44S 71W	90	Dakhla, Western Sahara *(city)*	24N 16W	97
Cincinnati, OH *(city)*	39N 84W	89	Dallas, TX *(city)*	33N 97W	89
Cleveland *(city)*	41N 82W	89	Dalrymple , Mt. 4190	22S 148E	98
Coahuila *(st., Mex.)*	30N 105W	89	Daly *(riv., Australasia)*	14S 132E	98
Coast Mountains *(Can.)*	55N 130W	88	Damascus, Syria *(city, nat. cap.)*	34N 36E	93
Coast Ranges *(US)*	40N 120W	88	Danube *(riv., Europe)*	44N 24E	92
Coco Island	8N 88W	88	Dar es Salaam, Tanzania *(city, nat. cap.)*	7S 39E	97
Cod, Cape	42N 70W	88	Darien, Gulf of	9N 77W	90
Colima *(st., Mex.)*	18N 104W	89	Darling *(riv., Australasia)*	35S 144E	98
Colima, Colima *(city, st. cap., Mex.)*	19N 104W	89	Darling Range	33S 116W	98
Colombia *(country)*	4N 73W	91	Darwin, Northern Terr. *(city, st. cap., Aust.)*	12S 131E	99
Colombo, Sri Lanka *(city, nat. cap.)*	7N 80E	95	Davis Strait	57N 59W	88
Colorado *(riv., N.Am.)*	36N 110W	88	Deccan Plateau	20N 80E	94
Colorado *(st., US)*	38N 104W	89	DeGrey *(riv., Australasia)*	22S 120E	98
Colorado, Rio *(riv., S.Am.)*	38S 70W	90	Delaware *(st., US)*	38N 75W	89
Colorado (Texas) *(riv., N.Am.)*	30N 100W	88	Delaware *(riv., N.Am.)*	38N 77W	88
Columbia *(riv., N.Am.)*	45N 120W	89	Delhi, India *(city)*	30N 78E	97
Columbia, South Carolina *(city, st. cap., US)*	34N 81W	89	Denmark *(country)*	55N 10E	93
Columbus, Ohio *(city, st. cap., US)*	40N 83W	89	Denmark Strait	67N 27W	92
Comodoro Rivadavia, Argentina *(city)*	68S 70W	91	D'Entrecasteaux Islands	10S 153E	98
Comoros *(country)*	12S 44E	97	Denver, Colorado *(city, st. cap., US)*	40N 105W	89
Conakry, Guinea *(city, nat. cap.)*	9N 14W	93	Derby, Australia *(city)*	17S 124E	99
Concord, New Hampshire *(city, st. cap., US)*	43N 71W	89	Des Moines *(riv., N.Am.)*	43N 95W	88
Congo *(country)*	3S 15E	97	Des Moines, Iowa *(city, st. cap., US)*	42N 92W	89
Congo *(riv., Africa)*	3N 22E	96	Desolacion Island	54S 73W	90
Congo Basin	4N 22E	96	Detroit, MI *(city)*	42N 83W	89
Congo, Democratic Republic of *(country)*	5S 15E	97	Dhaka, Bangladesh *(city, nat. cap.)*	24N 90E	95
Connecticut *(st., US)*	43N 76W	89	Dinaric Alps	44N 20E	92
Connecticut *(riv., N.Am.)*	43N 76W	88	Djibouti *(country)*	12N 43E	97
Cook, Mt. 12,316	44S 170E	98	Djibouti, Djibouti *(city, nat. cap.)*	12N 43E	97

Name/Description	Latitude & Longitude	Page	Name/Description	Latitude & Longitude	Page
Dnepr (riv., Europe)	50N 34E	92	Finisterre, Cape	44N 10W	92
Dnipropetrovsk, Ukraine (city)	48N 35E	93	Finland (country)	62N 28E	93
Dodoma, Tanzania (city)	6S 36E	97	Finland, Gulf of	60N 20E	92
Dominican Republic (country)	20N 70W	89	Firth of Forth	56N 3W	92
Don (riv., Europe)	53N 39E	92	Fitzroy (riv., Australasia)	17S 125E	98
Donetsk, Ukraine (city)	48N 38E	93	Flinders Range	31S 139E	98
Dover, Delaware (city, st. cap., US)	39N 75W	89	Flores (island)	8S 121E	98
Dover, Strait of	52N 0	92	Florianopolis, Sta. Catarina (city, st. cap., Braz.)	27S 48W	91
Drakensberg	30S 30E	96	Florida (st., US)	28N 83W	89
Dublin, Ireland (city, nat. cap.)	53N 6W	93	Florida, Strait of	28N 80W	88
Duluth, MN (city)	47N 92W	89	Fly (riv., Australasia)	8S 143E	98
Dunedin, New Zealand (city)	46S 171E	99	Formosa (st., Argentina)	23S 60W	91
Durango (st., Mex.)	25N 108W	89	Formosa, Formosa (city, st. cap., Argen.)	27S 58W	91
Durango, Durango (city, st. cap., Mex.)	24N 105W	89	Fort Worth, TX (city)	33N 97W	89
Durban, South Africa (city)	30S 31E	97	Fortaleza, Ceara (city, st. cap., Braz.)	4S 39W	91
Dushanbe, Tajikistan (city, nat. cap.)	39N 69E	95	France (country)	46N 4E	93
Dvina (riv., Europe)	64N 42E	92	Frankfort, Kentucky (city, st. cap., US)	38N 85W	89
Dzhugdzhur Khrebet	58N 138E	94	Frankfurt, Germany (city)	50N 9E	93
East Cape (NZ)	37S 180E	98	Fraser (riv., N.Am.)	52N 122W	88
East China Sea	30N 128E	94	Fredericton, N.B. (city, prov. cap., Can.)	46N 67W	89
Eastern Ghats	15N 80E	94	Fremantle, Australia (city)	33S 116E	99
Ecuador (country)	3S 78W	91	Freetown, Sierra Leone (city, nat. cap.)	8N 13W	97
Edmonton, Alberta (city, prov. cap., Can.)	54N 114W	89	French Guiana (country)	4N 52W	91
Edward, Lake	0 30E	96	Fria, Cape	18S 12E	96
Egypt (country)	23N 30E	97	Fuzhou, China (city)	26N 119E	95
El Aaiun, Western Sahara (city)	27N 13W	97	Gabes, Gulf of	33N 12E	96
El Djouf	25N 15W	96	Gabes, Tunisia (city)	34N 10E	97
El Paso, TX (city)	32N 106W	89	Gabon (country)	2S 12E	97
El Salvador (country)	15N 90W	89	Gaborone, Botswana (city, nat. cap.)	25S 25E	97
Elbe (riv., Europe)	54N 10E	92	Gairdiner, Lake	32S 136E	98
Elburz Mountains	28N 60E	94	Galveston, TX (city)	29N 95W	89
Elbruz, Mt. 18,510	43N 42E	94	Gambia (country)	13N 15W	97
Elgon, Mt. 14,178	1N 34E	96	Gambia (riv., Africa)	13N 15W	96
English Channel	50N 0	92	Ganges (riv., Asia)	27N 85E	94
Entre Rios (st., Argentina)	32S 60W	91	Gascoyne (riv., Australasia)	25S 115E	98
Equatorial Guinea (country)	3N 10E	97	Gaspé Peninsula	50N 70W	88
Erg Iguidi	26N 6W	96	Gdansk, Poland (city)	54N 19E	93
Erie (lake, N.Am.)	42N 85W	88	Geelong, Aust. (city)	38S 144E	99
Eritrea (country)	16N 38E	97	Gees Gwardafuy (island)	15N 50E	96
Erzegebirge Mountains	50N 14E	92	Genoa, Gulf of	44N 10E	92
Espinhaco Mountains	15S 42W	90	Geographe Bay	35S 115E	98
Espiritu Santo (island)	15S 168E	99	Georgetown, Guyana (city, nat. cap.)	8N 58W	91
Espiritu Santo (st., Brazil)	20S 42W	91	Georgia (country)	42N 44E	93
Essen, Germany (city)	52N 8E	93	Georgia (st., US)	30N 82W	89
Estonia (country)	60N 26E	93	Germany (country)	50N 12E	93
Ethiopia (country)	8N 40E	97	Ghana (country)	8N 3W	97
Ethiopian Plateau	8N 40E	96	Gibraltar, Strait of	37N 6W	92
Euphrates (riv., Asia)	28N 50E	94	Gibson Desert	24S 124E	98
Everard, Lake	32S 135E	98	Gilbert (riv., Australasia)	8S 142E	98
Everard Ranges	28S 135E	98	Giluwe, Mt. 14,330	5S 144E	98
Everest, Mt. 29,028	28N 84E	94	Glasgow, Scotland (city)	56N 6W	93
Eyre, Lake	29S 136E	98	Gobi Desert	48N 105E	94
Faeroe Islands	62N 11W	92	Godavari (riv., Asia)	18N 82E	94
Fairbanks, AK (city)	63N 146W	89	Godwin-Austen (K2), Mt. 28,250	30N 70E	94
Falkland Islands (Islas Malvinas)	52S 60W	90	Goiania, Goias (city, st. cap., Braz.)	17S 49W	91
Farewell, Cape (NZ)	40S 170E	98	Goias (st., Brazil)	15S 50W	91
Fargo, ND (city)	47N 97W	89	Gongga Shan 24,790	26N 102E	94
Farquhar, Cape	24S 114E	98	Good Hope, Cape of	33S 18E	96
Fiji (country)	17S 178E	99	Goteborg, Sweden (city)	58N 12E	93

Name/Description	Latitude & Longitude	Page	Name/Description	Latitude & Longitude	Page
Gotland *(island)*	57N 20E	92	Hawaii *(st., US)*	21N 156W	88 inset
Grampian Mountains	57N 4W	92	Hebrides *(island)*	58N 8W	92
Gran Chaco	23S 70N	90	Helena, Montana *(city, st. cap., US)*	47N 112W	89
Grand Erg Occidental	29N 0	96	Helsinki, Finland *(city, nat. cap.)*	60N 25E	93
Grand Teton 13, 770	45N 112W	88	Herat, Afghanistan *(city)*	34N 62E	95
Great Artesian Basin	25S 145E	98	Hermosillo, Sonora *(city, st. cap., Mex.)*	29N 111W	89
Great Australian Bight	33S 130E	98	Hidalgo *(st., Mex.)*	20N 98W	89
Great Barrier Reef	15S 145E	98	Himalayas	26N 80E	94
Great Basin	39N 117W	88	Hindu Kush	30N 70E	94
Great Bear Lake *(lake, N.Am.)*	67N 120W	88	Ho Chi Minh City, Vietnam *(city)*	11N 107E	95
Great Dividing Range	20S 145E	98	Hobart, Tasmania *(city, st. cap., Aust.)*	43S 147E	99
Great Indian Desert	25N 72E	94	Hokkaido *(island)*	43N 142E	94
Great Namaland	25S 16E	96	Honduras *(country)*	16N 87W	89
Great Plains	40N 105W	88	Honduras, Gulf of	15N 88W	88
Great Salt Lake *(lake, N.Am.)*	40N 113W	88	Honiara, Solomon Islands *(city, nat. cap.)*	9S 160E	99
Great Sandy Desert	23S 125E	98	Honolulu, Hawaii *(city, st. cap., US)*	21N 158W	89 inset
Great Slave Lake *(lake, N.Am.)*	62N 110W	88	Honshu *(island)*	38N 140E	94
Great Victoria Desert	30S 125E	98	Hormuz, Strait of	25N 58E	94
Greater Khingan Range	50N 120E	94	Horn, Cape	55S 70W	90
Greece *(country)*	39N 21E	93	Houston, TX *(city)*	30N 95W	89
Greenland (Denmark) *(country)*	78N 40W	89	Howe, Cape	37S 150E	98
Gregory Range	18S 145E	98	Huambo, Angola *(city)*	13S 16E	97
Grey Range	26S 145E	98	Huang *(riv., Asia)*	30N 105E	94
Guadalajara, Jalisco *(city, st. cap., Mex.)*	21N 103W	89	Huascaran, Mt. 22,133	8N 79W	90
Guadalcanal *(island)*	9S 160E	99	Hudson *(riv., N.Am.)*	42N 76W	89
Guadeloupe *(island)*	29N 120W	88	Hudson Bay	60N 90W	88
Guanajuato *(st., Mex.)*	22N 100W	89	Hudson Strait	63N 70W	88
Guanajuato, Guanajuato *(city, st. cap., Mex.)*	21N 101W	89	Hue, Vietnam *(city)*	15N 110E	95
Guangzhou, China *(city)*	23N 113E	95	Hughes, Aust. *(city)*	30S 130E	99
Guapore, Rio *(riv., S.Am.)*	15S 63W	90	Hungary *(country)*	48N 20E	93
Guatemala *(country)*	14N 90W	89	Huron *(lake, N.Am.)*	45N 85W	88
Guatemala, Guatemala *(city, nat. cap.)*	15N 91W	89	Hyderabad, India *(city)*	17N 79E	95
Guayaquil, Ecuador *(city)*	2S 80W	91	Ibadan, Nigeria *(city)*	7N 4E	97
Guayaquil, Gulf of	3S 83W	90	Iceland *(country)*	64N 20W	93
Guerrero *(st., Mex.)*	18N 102W	89	Idaho *(st., US)*	43N 113W	89
Guianas Highlands	5N 60W	90	Iguassu Falls	25S 55W	90
Guinea *(country)*	10N 10W	97	Illimani, Mt. 20,741	16S 67W	90
Guinea, Gulf of	3N 0	96	Illinois *(riv., N.Am.)*	40N 90W	88
Guinea-Bissau *(country)*	12N 15W	97	Illinois *(st., US)*	44N 90W	89
Guyana *(country)*	6N 57W	91	India *(country)*	23N 80E	95
Gydan Range	62N 155E	94	Indiana *(st., US)*	46N 88W	89
Haiti *(country)*	18N 72W	89	Indianapolis, Indiana *(city, st. cap., US)*	40N 86W	89
Hakodate, Japan *(city)*	42N 140E	95	Indigirka *(riv., Asia)*	70N 145E	94
Halifax Bay	18S 146E	98	Indonesia *(country)*	2S 120E	95
Halifax, Nova Scotia *(city, prov. cap., Can.)*	45N 64W	89	Indus *(riv., Asia)*	25N 70E	94
Halmahera *(island)*	1N 128E	94 inset	Ionian Sea	38N 19E	92
Hamburg, Germany *(city)*	54N 10E	93	Iowa *(st., US)*	43N 95W	89
Hammersley Range	23S 116W	98	Iquitos, Peru *(city)*	4S 74W	91
Hann, Mt. 2,800	15S 127E	98	Iran *(country)*	30N 55E	95
Hanoi, Vietnam *(city, nat. cap.)*	21N 106E	95	Iraq *(country)*	30N 50E	95
Hanover Island	52S 74W	90	Ireland *(country)*	54N 8W	93
Harare, Zimbabwe *(city, nat. cap.)*	18S 31E	97	Irish Sea	54N 5W	93
Harbin, China *(city)*	46N 126E	95	Irkutsk, Russia *(city)*	52N 104E	95
Harer, Ethiopia *(city)*	10N 42E	97	Irrawaddy *(riv., Asia)*	25N 95E	94
Hargeysa, Somalia *(city)*	9N 44E	97	Irtysh *(riv., Asia)*	50N 70E	94
Harrisburg, Pennsylvania *(city, st. cap., US)*	40N 77W	89	Ishim *(riv., Asia)*	48N 70E	94
Hartford, Connecticut *(city, st. cap., US)*	42N 73W	89	Isla de los Estados *(island)*	55S 60W	90
Hatteras, Cape	32N 73W	88	Islamabad, Pakistan *(city, nat. cap.)*	34N 73E	95
Havana, Cuba *(city, nat. cap.)*	23N 82W	89	Isles of Scilly	50N 8W	92

Name/Description	Latitude & Longitude	Page	Name/Description	Latitude & Longitude	Page
Israel (country)	31N 36E	93	Kigali, Rwanda (city, nat. cap.)	2S 30E	97
Istanbul, Turkey (city)	41N 29E	93	Kilimanjaro, Mt. 19,340	4N 35E	96
Italy (country)	42N 12E	93	Kimberly, South Africa (city)	29S 25E	97
Jabal Marrah, 10,131	10N 23E	96	King Leopold Ranges	16S 125E	98
Jackson, Mississippi (city, st. cap., US)	32N 84W	89	Kingston, Jamaica (city, nat. cap.)	18N 77W	89
Jacksonville, FL (city)	30N 82W	89	Kinshasa, Congo Republic (city, nat. cap.)	4S 15E	97
Jakarta, Indonesia (city, nat. cap.)	6S 107E	95 inset	Kirghiz Steppe	40N 65E	94
Jalisco (st., Mex.)	20N 105W	89	Kisangani, Congo Republic (city)	1N 25E	97
Jamaica (country)	18N 78W	89	Kitayushu, Japan (city)	34N 130E	95
James Bay	54N 81W	88	Klyuchevskaya, Mt. 15,584	56N 160E	94
Japan (country)	35N 138E	95	Kobe, Japan (city)	34N 135E	95
Japan, Sea of	40N 135E	94	Kodiak Island	58N 152W	88 inset
Japura, Rio (riv., S.Am.)	3S 65W	90	Kolyma (riv., Asia)	70N 160E	94
Java (island)	6N 110E	94 inset	Kommunizma, Mt. 24,590	40N 70E	94
Jaya Peak 16,503	4S 136W	98	Komsomolsk, Russia (city)	51N 137E	95
Jayapura, New Guinea (Indon.) (city)	3S 141E	95 inset	Korea, North (country)	40N 128E	95
Jebel Toubkal 13,665	31N 8W	96	Korea, South (country)	3S 130W	95
Jefferson City, Missouri (city, st. cap., US)	39N 92W	89	Korea Strait	32N 130W	94
Jerusalem, Israel (city, nat. cap.)	32N 35E	93	Kosciusko, Mt. 7,310	36S 148E	98
Joao Pessoa, Paraiba (city, st. cap., Braz.)	7S 35W	91	Krasnoyarsk, Russia (city)	56N 93E	95
Johannesburg, South Africa (city)	26S 27E	97	Krishna (riv., Asia)	15N 76E	94
Jordan (country)	32N 36E	93	Kuala Lumpur, Malaysia (city, nat. cap.)	3N 107E	95
Juan Fernandez (island)	33S 80W	90	Kunlun Shan	36N 90E	94
Jubba (riv., Africa)	3N 43E	96	Kunming, China (city)	25N 103E	95
Jujuy (st., Argentina)	23S 67W	91	Kuril Islands	46N 147E	94
Jujuy, Jujuy (city, st. cap., Argen.)	23S 66W	91	Kutch, Gulf of	23N 70E	94
Juneau, Alaska (city, st. cap., US)	58N 134W	89	Kuwait (country)	29N 48E	93
Jura Mountains	46N 5E	92	Kuwait, Kuwait (city, nat. cap.)	29N 48E	93
Jurua, Rio (riv., S.Am.)	6S 70W	90	Kyoto, Japan (city)	35N 136E	95
Kabul, Afghanistan (city, nat. cap.)	35N 69E	95	Kyrgyzstan (country)	40N 75E	95
Kalahari Desert	25S 20E	96	Kyushu (island)	30N 130W	94
Kalgourie-Boulder, Australia (city)	31S 121E	99	La Pampa (st., Argentina)	36S 70W	91
Kaliningrad, Russia (city)	55N 21E	93	La Paz, Baja California Sur (city, st. cap., Mex.)	24N 110W	89
Kamchatka Range	55N 159E	94	La Paz, Bolivia (city, nat. cap.)	17S 68W	91
Kampala, Uganda (city, nat. cap.)	0 33E	97	La Plata, Argentina (city)	35S 58W	91
Kanchenjunga, Mt. 28,208	30N 83E	94	Laptev Sea	73N 120E	94
Kano, Nigeria (city)	12N 9E	97	La Rioja (st., Argentina)	30S 70W	91
Kanpur, India (city)	27N 80E	95	La Rioja, La Rioja (city, st. cap., Argen.)	29S 67W	91
Kansas (st., US)	40N 98W	89	Labrador Peninsula	52N 60W	91
Kansas City, MO (city)	39N 95W	89	Lachlan (riv., Australasia)	34S 145E	98
Kara Sea	69N 65E	94	Ladoga, Lake	61N 31E	92
Karachi, Pakistan (city)	25N 66E	95	Lagos, Nigeria (city, nat. cap.)	7N 3E	97
Karakorum Range	32N 78E	94	Lahore, Pakistan (city)	34N 74E	95
Karakum Desert	42N 52E	92	Lake of the Woods	50N 92W	88
Kasai (riv., Africa)	5S 18E	96	Lands End	50N 5W	92
Kashi, China (city)	39N 76E	95	Lansing, Michigan (city, st. cap., US)	43N 85W	89
Katherine, Aust. (city)	14S 132E	99	Lanzhou, China (city)	36N 104E	95
Kathmandu, Nepal (city, nat. cap.)	28N 85E	95	Laos (country)	20N 105E	95
Katowice, Poland (city)	50N 19E	93	Las Vegas, NV (city)	36N 115W	89
Kattegat, Strait of	57N 11E	92	Latvia (country)	56N 24E	93
Kazakhstan (country)	50N 70E	95	Laurentian Highlands	48N 72W	88
Kentucky (st., US)	37N 88W	89	Lebanon (country)	34N 35E	93
Kenya (country)	0 35E	97	Leeds, UK (city)	54N 2W	93
Kenya, Mt. 17,058	0 37E	96	Le Havre, France (city)	50N 0	93
Khabarovsk, Russia (city)	48N 135E	95	Lena (riv., Asia)	70N 125E	94
Khambhat, Gulf of	20N 73E	94	Lesotho (country)	30S 27E	97
Kharkiv, Ukraine (city)	50N 36E	93	Leveque, Cape	16S 123E	98
Khartoum, Sudan (city, nat. cap.)	16N 33E	97	Leyte (island)	12N 130E	94
Kiev, Ukraine (city, nat. cap.)	50N 31E	93	Lhasa, Tibet (China) (city)	30N 91E	95

Name/Description	Latitude & Longitude	Page	Name/Description	Latitude & Longitude	Page
Liberia (country)	6N 10W	97	Mandalay, Myamar (city)	22N 96E	95
Libreville, Gabon (city, nat. cap.)	0 9E	97	Manila, Philippines (city, nat. cap.)	115N 121E	95
Libya (country)	27N 17E	97	Manitoba (prov., Can.)	52N 93W	89
Libyan Desert	27N 25E	96	Mannar, Gulf of	9N 79E	94
Lille, France (city)	51N 3E	93	Maoke Mountains	5S 138E	98
Lilongwe, Malawi (city, nat. cap.)	14S 33E	97	Maputo, Mozambique (city, nat. cap.)	26S 33E	97
Lima, Peru (city, nat. cap.)	12S 77W	91	Maracaibo, Lake	10N 72W	91
Limpopo (riv., Africa)	22S 30E	96	Maracaibo, Venezuela (city)	11N 72W	91
Lincoln, Nebraska (city, st. cap., US)	41N 97W	89	Maracapa, Amapa (city, st. cap., Braz.)	0 51W	91
Lisbon, Portugal (city, nat. cap.)	39N 9W	93	Maranhao (st., Brazil)	4S 45W	91
Lithuania (country)	56N 24E	93	Maranon, Rio (riv., S.Am.)	5S 75W	90
Little Rock, Arkansas (city, st. cap., US)	35N 92W	89	Marseille, France (city)	43N 5E	93
Liverpool, UK (city)	53N 3W	93	Maryland (st., US)	37N 76W	89
Ljubljana, Slovenia (city, nat. cap.)	46N 14E	93	Masai Steppe	5S 35E	96
Llanos	33N 103W	90	Maseru, Lesotho (city, nat. cap.)	29S 27E	97
Logan, Mt. 18,551	62N 139W	88	Mashad, Iran (city)	36N 59E	95
Logone (riv., Africa)	10N 14E	96	Massachusetts (st., US)	42N 70W	89
Lome, Togo (city, nat. cap.)	6N 1E	97	Massif Central	45N 3E	92
London, United Kingdom (city, nat. cap.)	51N 0	93	Mato Grosso	16S 52W	90
Londonderry, Cape	14S 125E	98	Mato Grosso (st., Brazil)	15S 55W	91
Lopez, Cape	1S 8E	96	Mato Grosso do Sul (st., Brazil)	20S 55W	91
Los Angeles, CA (city)	34N 118W	89	Mauritania (country)	20N 10W	97
Los Chonos Archipelago	45S 74W	90	Mbandaka, Congo Republic (city)	0 18E	97
Louisiana (st., US)	30N 90W	89	McKinley, Mt. 20,320	62N 150W	88 inset
Lower Hutt, New Zealand (city)	45S 175E	99	Medellin, Colombia (city)	6N 76W	91
Luanda, Angola (city, nat. cap.)	9S 13E	97	Mediterranean Sea	36N 16E	92
Lubumbashi, Congo Republic (city)	12S 28E	97	Mekong (riv., Asia)	15N 108E	94
Lusaka, Zambia (city, nat. cap.)	15S 28E	97	Melbourne, Victoria (city, st. cap., Aust.)	38S 145E	99
Luxembourg (country)	50N 6E	93	Melville, Cape	15S 145E	98
Luxembourg, Luxembourg (city, nat. cap.)	50N 6E	93	Memphis, TN (city)	35N 90W	89
Luzon (island)	17N 121E	94	Mendoza (st., Argentina)	35S 70W	91
Luzon Strait	20N 121E	94	Mendoza, Mendoza (city, st. cap., Argen.)	33S 69W	91
Lyon, France (city)	46N 5E	93	Merida, Yucatan (city, st. cap. Mex.)	21N 90W	89
Lyon, Gulf of	42N 4E	92	Merauke, New Guinea (Indon.) (city)	9S 140E	99
Maccio, Alagoas (city, st. cap., Braz.)	10S 36W	91	Mexicali, Baja California (city, st. cap., Mex.)	32N 115W	89
Macdonnell Ranges	23S 135E	98	Mexico (country)	30N 110W	89
Macedonia (country)	41N 21E	93	Mexico (st., Mex.)	18N 100W	89
Mackenzie (riv., N.Am.)	68N 130W	88	Mexico City, Mexico (city, nat. cap.)	19N 99W	89
Macquarie (riv., Australasia)	33S 146E	98	Mexico, Gulf of	26N 90W	88
Madagascar (country)	20S 46E	97	Miami, FL (city)	26N 80W	89
Madeira, Rio (riv., S.Am.)	5S 60W	90	Michigan (st., US)	45N 82W	89
Madison, Wisconsin (city, st. cap., US)	43N 89W	89	Michigan (lake, N.Am.)	45N 90W	88
Madras, India (city)	13N 80E	95	Michoacan (st., Mex.)	17N 107W	89
Madrid, Spain (city, nat. cap.)	40N 4W	93	Milan, Italy (city)	45N 9E	93
Magdalena, Rio (riv., S.Am.)	8N 74W	90	Milwaukee, WI (city)	43N 88W	89
Magellan, Strait of	54S 68W	90	Minas Gerais (st., Brazil)	17S 45W	91
Maine (st., US)	46N 70W	89	Mindoro (island)	13N 120E	95
Malabo, Equatorial Guinea (city, nat. cap.)	4N 9E	97	Minneapolis, MN (city)	45N 93W	89
Malacca, Strait of	3N 100E	95	Minnesota (st., US)	45N 90W	89
Malawi (country)	13S 35E	97	Minsk, Belarus (city, nat. cap.)	54N 28E	93
Malaysia (country)	3N 110E	95	Misiones (st., Argentina)	25S 55W	91
Malekula (island)	16S 166E	98	Mississippi (riv., N.Am.)	28N 90W	88
Mali (country)	17N 5W	97	Mississippi (st., US)	30N 90W	89
Malpelo Island	8N 84W	88	Missouri (riv., N.Am.)	41N 96W	88
Malta (island)	36N 16E	92	Missouri (st., US)	35N 92W	89
Mamore, Rio (riv., S.Am.)	15S 65W	90	Misti, Mt. 19,101	15S 73W	90
Managua, Nicaragua (city, nat. cap.)	12N 86W	89	Mitchell (riv., Australasia)	16S 143E	98
Manaus, Amazonas (city, st. cap., Braz.)	3S 60W	91	Mobile, AL (city)	31N 88W	89
Manchester, UK (city)	53N 2W	93	Moçambique, Mozambique (city)	15S 40E	97

Name/Description	Latitude & Longitude	Page	Name/Description	Latitude & Longitude	Page
Mogadishu, Somalia (city, nat. cap.)	2N 45E	97	New Hanover (island)	3S 153E	98
Moldova (country)	49N 28E	93	New Hebrides (island)	15S 165E	98
Mombasa, Kenya (city)	4S 40E	97	New Ireland (island)	4S 154E	98
Monaco, Monaco (city)	44N 8E	93	New Jersey (st., US)	40N 75W	89
Mongolia (country)	45N 100E	95	New Mexico (st., US)	30N 108W	89
Monrovia, Liberia (city, nat. cap.)	6N 11W	97	New Orleans, LA (city)	30N 90W	89
Montana (st., US)	50N 110W	89	New Siberian Islands	74N 140E	94
Monterrey, Nuevo Leon (city, st. cap., Mex.)	26N 100W	89	New South Wales (st., Aust.)	35S 145E	99
Montevideo, Uruguay (city, nat. cap.)	35S 56W	91	Newcastle, Aust. (city)	33S 152E	99
Montgomery, Alabama (city, st. cap., US)	32N 86W	89	New York (city)	41N 74W	89
Montpelier, Vermont (city, st. cap., US)	44N 73W	89	New York (st., US)	45N 75W	89
Montreal, Canada (city)	45N 74W	89	New Zealand (country)	40S 170E	99
Morelin, Michoacan (city, st. cap., Mex.)	20N 100W	89	Newcastle, UK (city)	55N 2W	93
Morocco (country)	34N 10W	97	Newfoundland (prov., Can.)	53N 60W	89
Moroni, Comoros (city, nat. cap.)	12S 42E	97	Nicaragua (country)	10N 90W	89
Moscow, Russia (city, nat. cap.)	56N 38E	93	Niamey, Niger (city, nat. cap.)	14N 2E	97
Mountain Nile (riv., Africa)	5N 30E	96	Nicobar Islands	5N 93E	94
Mozambique (country)	19N 35E	97	Niger (country)	10N 8E	97
Mozambique Channel	19N 42E	96	Niger (riv., Africa)	12N 0	96
Munich, Germany (city)	48N 12E	93	Nigeria (country)	8N 5E	97
Murchison (riv., Australasia)	26S 115E	98	Nile (riv., Africa)	25N 31E	96
Murmansk, Russia (city)	69N 33E	93	Nipigon (lake, N.Am.)	50N 87W	88
Murray (riv., Australasia)	36S 143E	98	Nizhny-Novgorod, Russia (city)	56N 44E	93
Murrumbidgee (riv., Australasia)	35S 146E	98	Norfolk, VA (city)	37N 76W	89
Muscat, Oman (city, nat. cap.)	23N 58E	95	North Cape (NZ)	36N 174W	98
Musgrave Ranges	28S 135E	98	North Carolina (st., US)	30N 78W	89
Myanmar (Burma) (country)	20N 95E	95	North Channel	56N 5W	92
Nairobi, Kenya (city, nat. cap.)	1S 37E	97	North Dakota (st., US)	49N 100W	89
Namibe, Angola (city)	16S 13E	97	North Island (NZ)	37S 175W	98
Namibia (country)	20S 16E	97	North Saskatchewan (riv., N.Am.)	55N 110W	88
Namoi (riv., Australasia)	31S 150E	98	North Sea	56N 3E	92
Nan Ling Mountains	25N 110E	94	North West Cape	22S 115W	98
Nanda Devi, Mt. 25,645	30N 80E	94	Northern Territory (st., Aust.)	20S 134W	98
Nanjing, China (city)	32N 119E	95	Northwest Territories (prov., Can.)	65N 125W	89
Nansei Shoto (island)	27N 125E	94	Norway (country)	62N 8E	93
Naples, Italy (city)	41N 14E	93	Nouakchott, Mauritania (city, nat. cap.)	18N 16W	97
Nashville, Tennessee (city, st. cap., US)	36N 87W	89	Noumea, New Caledonia (city)	22S 167E	99
Nasser, Lake	22N 32E	96	Nova Scotia (prov., Can.)	46N 67W	89
Natal, Rio Grande do Norte (city, st. cap., Braz.)	6S 5W	91	Novaya Zemlya (island)	72N 55E	94
Naturaliste, Cape	35S 115E	98	Novosibirsk, Russia (city)	55N 83E	95
Nayarit (st., Mex.)	22N 106W	89	Nubian Desert	20N 30E	96
N'Djamena, Chad (city, nat. cap.)	12N 15E	97	Nuevo Leon (st., Mex.)	25N 100W	89
Nebraska (st., US)	42N 100W	89	Nullarbor Plain	34S 125W	98
Negro, Rio (Argentina) (riv., S.Am.)	40S 70W	90	Nyasa, Lake	10S 35E	96
Negro, Rio (Brazil) (riv., S.Am.)	0 65W	90	Oakland, CA (city)	38N 122W	89
Negros (island)	10N 125E	94	Oaxaca (st., Mex.)	17N 97W	89
Nelson (riv., N.Am.)	56N 90W	88	Oaxaca, Oaxaca (city, st. cap., Mex.)	17N 97W	89
Nepal (country)	29N 85E	95	Ob (riv., Asia)	60N 78E	94
Netherlands (country)	54N 6E	93	Ohio (riv., N.Am.)	38N 85W	88
Neuquen (st., Argentina)	38S 68W	91	Ohio (st., US)	42N 85W	89
Neuquen, Neuquen (city, st. cap., Argen.)	39S 68W	91	Okavongo (riv., Africa)	18S 18E	96
Nevada (st., US)	37N 117W	89	Okavango Swamp	21S 23E	96
New Britain (island)	5S 152E	98	Okeechobee (lake, N.Am.)	28N 82W	88
New Brunswick (prov., Can.)	47N 67W	89	Okhotsk, Russia (city)	59N 140E	95
New Caledonia (island)	21S 165E	98	Okhotsk, Sea of	57N 150E	94
New Delhi, India (city, nat. cap.)	29N 77E	95	Oklahoma (st., US)	36N 95W	89
New Georgia (island)	8S 157E	98	Oklahoma City, Oklahoma (city, st. cap., US)	35N 98W	89
New Guinea (island)	5S 142E	98	Oland (island)	57N 17E	92
New Hampshire (st., US)	45N 70W	89	Olympia, Washington (city, st. cap., US)	47N 123W	90

Name/Description	Latitude & Longitude	Page	Name/Description	Latitude & Longitude	Page
Omaha, NE (city)	41N 96W	89	Piaui (st., Brazil)	7S 44W	91
Oman (country)	20N 55E	95	Piaui Range	10S 45W	90
Oman, Gulf of	23N 55E	94	Pic Touside 10,712	20N 12E	96
Omdurman, Sudan (city)	16N 32E	97	Pierre, South Dakota (city, st. cap., US)	44N 100W	89
Omsk, Russia (city)	55N 73E	95	Pietermaritzburg, South Africa (city)	30S 30E	97
Onega, Lake	62N 35E	92	Pike's Peak 14,110	36N 110W	88
Ontario (lake, N.Am.)	45N 77W	88	Pilcomayo, Rio (riv., S.Am.)	23S 60W	90
Ontario (prov., Can.)	50N 90W	89	Pittsburgh, PA (city)	40N 80W	89
Oodnadatta, Aust. (city)	28S 135E	99	Plateau of Iran	26N 60E	94
Oran, Algeria (city)	36N 1W	97	Plateau of Tibet	26N 85E	94
Oregon (st., US)	46N 120W	89	Platte (riv., N.Am.)	41N 105W	88
Orinoco, Rio (riv., S.Am.)	8N 65W	90	Po (riv., Europe)	45N 12E	92
Orizaba Peak 18,406	19N 97W	88	Point Barrow	70N 156W	88 inset
Orkney Islands	60N 0	92	Poland (country)	54N 20E	93
Osaka, Japan (city)	35N 135E	95	Poopo, Lake	16S 67W	90
Oslo, Norway (city, nat. cap.)	60N 11W	93	Popocatepetl 17,887	17N 100W	88
Ossa, Mt. 5.305 (Tasm.)	43S 145E	98	Port Elizabeth, South Africa (city)	34S 26E	97
Ottawa, Canada (city, nat. cap.)	45N 76W	89	Port Lincoln, Aust. (city)	35S 135E	99
Otway, Cape	40S 142W	98	Port Moresby, Papua N. G. (city, nat. cap.)	10S 147E	99
Ougadougou, Burkina Faso (city, nat. cap.)	12N 2W	97	Port Vila, Vanatu (city, nat. cap.)	17S 169E	99
Owen Stanley Range	9S 148E	98	Port-au-Prince, Haiti (city, nat. cap.)	19N 72W	89
Pachuca, Hidalgo (city, st. cap. Mex.)	20N 99W	89	Portland, OR (city)	46N 123W	89
Pacific Ocean	20N 115W	88	Porto Alegre, R. Gr. do Sul (city, st. cap., Braz.)	30S 51W	91
Pakistan (country)	25N 72E	95	Porto Novo, Benin (city, nat. cap.)	7N 3E	97
Palawan (island)	10N 119E	94	Porto Velho, Rondonia (city, st. cap., Braz.)	9S 64W	91
Palmas, Cape	8N 8W	96	Portugal (country)	38N 8W	93
Palmas, Tocantins (city, st. cap., Braz.)	10S 49W	91	Potomac (riv., N.Am.)	35N 75W	88
Pamirs	32N 70E	94	Potosi, Bolivia (city)	20S 66W	91
Pampas	36S 73W	90	Prague, Czech Republic (city, nat. cap.)	50N 14E	93
Panama (country)	10N 80W	90	Pretoria, South Africa (city, nat. cap.)	26S 28E	97
Panama, Gulf of	10N 80W	89	Pribilof Islands	56N 170W	88 inset
Panama, Panama (city, nat. cap.)	9N 80W	89	Prince Edward Island (prov., Can.)	50N 67W	89
Papua, Gulf of	8S 144E	98	Pripyat Marshes	54N 24E	92
Papua New Guinea (country)	6S 144E	98	Providence, Rhode Island (city, st. cap., US)	42N 71W	89
Para (st., Brazil)	4S 54W	91	Puebla (st., Mex.)	18N 96W	89
Paraguay (country)	23S 60W	91	Puebla, Puebla (city, st. cap., Mex.)	19N 98W	89
Paraguay, Rio (riv., S.Am.)	17S 60W	90	Puerto Monte, Chile (city)	42S 74W	91
Paraiba (st., Brazil)	6S 35W	91	Purus, Rio (riv., S.Am.)	5S 68W	90
Paramaribo, Suriname (city, nat. cap.)	5N 55W	91	Putumayo, Rio (riv., S.Am.)	3S 74W	90
Parana (st., Brazil)	25S 55W	91	Pyongyang, Korea, North (city, nat. cap.)	39N 126E	95
Parana, Entre Rios (city, st. cap., Argen.)	32S 60W	91	Pyrenees Mountains	43N 2E	92
Parana, Rio (riv., S.Am.)	20S 50W	90	Qingdao, China (city)	36N 120E	95
Paris, France (city, nat. cap.)	49N 2E	93	Quebec (prov., Can.)	52N 70W	89
Pasadas, Misiones (city, st. cap., Argen.)	27S 56W	91	Quebec, Quebec (city, prov. cap., Can.)	47N 71W	89
Patagonia	43S 70W	90	Queen Charlotte Islands	50N 130W	88
Paulo Afonso Falls	10S 40W	90	Queen Elizabeth Islands	75N 110W	88
Peace (riv., N.Am.)	55N 120W	88	Queensland (st., Aust.)	24S 145E	99
Pennsylvania (st., US)	43N 80W	89	Queraturo (st., Mex.)	22N 96W	89
Pernambuco (st., Brazil)	7S 36W	91	Queraturo, Queraturo (city, st. cap., Mex.)	21N 100W	89
Persian Gulf	28N 50E	94	Quintana Roo (st., Mex.)	18N 88W	89
Perth, W. Australia (city, st. cap., Aust.)	32S 116E	99	Quito, Ecuador (city, nat. cap.)	0 79W	91
Peru (country)	10S 75W	91	Rabat, Morocco (city, nat. cap.)	34N 7W	97
Peshawar, Pakistan (city)	34N 72E	95	Race, Cape	46N 52W	88
Philadelphia, PA (city)	40N 75W	89	Rainier, Mt. 14,410	48N 120W	88
Philippine Sea	15N 125E	94	Raleigh, North Carolina (city, st. cap., US)	36N 79W	89
Philippines (country)	15N 120E	95	Rangoon, Myanmar (Burma) (city, nat. cap.)	17N 96E	95
Phnom Penh, Cambodia (city, nat. cap.)	12N 105E	95	Rapid City, SD (city)	44N 103W	89
Phoenix, Arizona (city, st. cap., US)	33N 112W	89	Rawalpindi, India (city)	34N 73E	95
Phou Bia 9,249	24N 102E	94	Rawson, Chubuy (city, st. cap., Argen.)	43S 65W	91

Name/Description	Latitude & Longitude	Page	Name/Description	Latitude & Longitude	Page
Recife, Pernambuco (city, st. cap., Braz.)	8S 35W	91	Salta, Salta (city, st. cap., Argen.)	25S 65W	91
Red (of the North) (riv., N.Am.)	50N 98W	91	Saltillo, Coahuila (city, st. cap., Mex.)	26N 101W	89
Red (riv., N.Am.)	42N 96W	91	Salvador, Bahia (city, st. cap., Braz.)	13S 38W	91
Red Sea	20N 35E	96	Salween (riv., Asia)	18N 98E	94
Regina, Canada (city)	51N 104W	89	Samar (island)	12N 124E	94
Reindeer (lake, N.Am.)	57N 100W	88	Samara, Russia (city)	53N 50E	93
Repulse Bay	22S 147E	98	Samarkand, Uzbekistan (city)	40N 67E	93
Resistencia, Chaco (city, st. cap., Argen.)	27S 59W	91	San Antonio, TX (city)	29N 98W	89
Revillagigedo Island	18N 110W	88	San Cristobal (island)	12S 162E	98
Reykjavik, Iceland (city, nat. cap.)	64N 22W	93	San Diego, CA (city)	33N 117W	89
Rhine (riv., Europe)	50N 10E	92	San Francisco, CA (city)	38N 122W	89
Rhode Island (st., US)	42N 70W	89	San Francisco, Rio (riv., S.Am.)	10S 40W	90
Rhone (riv., Europe)	42N 8E	92	San Joaquin (riv., N.Am.)	37N 121W	88
Richmond, Virginia (city, st. cap., US)	38N 77W	89	San Jorge, Gulf of	45S 68W	90
Riga, Gulf of	58N 24E	92	San Jose, Costa Rica (city, nat. cap.)	10N 84W	89
Riga, Latvia (city, nat. cap.)	57N 24E	93	San Juan (st., Argentina)	30S 70W	91
Rio Branco, Acre (city, st. cap., Braz.)	10S 68W	91	San Juan, San Juan (city, st. cap., Argen.)	18N 66W	89
Rio de Janeiro (st., Brazil)	22S 45W	91	San Lucas, Cape	23N 110W	88
Rio de Janeiro, R. de Jan. (city, st. cap., Braz.)	23S 43W	91	San Luis Potosi (st., Mex.)	22N 101W	89
Rio de la Plata	35S 55W	90	San Luis Potosi, S. Luis P. (city, st. cap., Mex.)	22N 101W	89
Rio Gallegos, Santa Cruz (city, st. cap., Argen.)	52S 68W	91	San Matias, Gulf of	43S 65W	90
Rio Grande (riv., N.Am.)	30N 100W	88	San Salvador, El Salvador (city, nat. cap.)	14N 89W	89
Rio Grande do Norte (st., Brazil)	5S 35W	91	Sanaa, Yemen (city)	16N 44E	97
Rio Grande do Sul (st., Brazil)	30S 55W	91	Santa Catarina (st., Brazil)	28S 50W	91
Rio Negro (st., Argentina)	40S 70W	91	Santa Cruz (st., Argentina)	50S 70W	91
Riyadh, Saudi Arabia (city, nat. cap.)	25N 47E	93	Santa Cruz Islands	8S 168E	98
Roanoke (riv., N.Am.)	34N 75W	88	Santa Fe (st., Argentina)	30S 62W	91
Roberts, Mt. 4,495	28S 154E	98	Santa Fe de Bogota, Colombia (city, nat. cap.)	5N 74W	91
Rockhampton, Aust. (city)	23S 150E	99	Santa Fe, New Mexico (city, st. cap., US)	35N 106W	89
Rocky Mountains	50N 108W	88	Santa Rosa, La Pampa (city, st. cap., Argen.)	37S 64W	91
Roebuck Bay	18S 125E	98	Santiago, Chile (city, nat. cap.)	33S 71W	91
Romania (country)	46N 24E	93	Santiago del Estero (st., Argentina)	25S 65W	91
Rome, Italy (city, nat. cap.)	42N 13E	93	Santiago, Sant. del Estero (city, st. cap., Argen.)	28S 64W	91
Rondonia (st., Brazil)	12S 65W	91	Santo Domingo, Dominican Rep. (city, nat. cap.)	18N 70W	89
Roosevelt, Rio (riv., S.Am.)	10S 60W	90	Santos, Brazil (city)	24S 46W	91
Roper (riv., Australasia)	15S 135W	98	Sao Luis, Maranhao (city, st. cap., Braz.)	3S 43W	91
Roraima (st., Brazil)	2N 62W	91	Sao Paulo (st., Brazil)	22S 50W	91
Ros Dashen Terrara 15,158	12N 40E	96	Sao Paulo, Sao Paulo (city, st. cap., Braz.)	24S 47W	91
Rosario, Santa Fe (city, st. cap., Argen.)	33S 61W	91	Sarajevo, Bosnia and Herz. (city, nat. cap.)	43N 18E	93
Rostov, Russia (city)	47N 40E	93	Sardinia (island)	40N 10E	92
Rotterdam, Netherlands (city)	52N 4E	93	Sarmiento, Mt. 8,100	55S 72W	90
Ruapehu, Mt. 9,177	39S 176W	98	Saskatchewan (riv., N.Am.)	52N 108W	88
Rub al Khali	20N 50E	94	Saudi Arabia (country)	25N 50E	95
Rudolph, Lake	3N 34E	96	Savannah (riv., N.Am.)	33N 82W	88
Russia (country)	58N 56E	93	Savannah, GA (city)	32N 81W	89
Ruvuma (riv., Africa)	12S 38E	96	Sayan Range	45N 90E	94
Ruwenzori Mountains	0 30E	96	Seattle, WA (city)	48N 122W	89
Rwanda (country)	3S 30E	97	Seine (riv., Europe)	49N 3E	92
Rybinsk, Lake	58N 38E	92	Senegal (country)	15N 15W	97
S. Saskatchewan (riv., N.Am.)	50N 110W	88	Senegal (riv., Africa)	15N 15W	96
Sable, Cape	45N 70W	88	Seoul, Korea, South (city, nat. cap.)	38N 127E	95
Sacramento (riv., N.Am.)	40N 122W	88	Sepik (riv., Australasia)	4S 142E	98
Sacramento, California (city, st. cap., US)	39 121W	89	Sergipe (st., Brazil)	12S 36W	91
Sahara	18N 10E	96	Sev Dvina (riv., Asia)	60N 50E	94
Sakhalin Island	50N 143E	94	Severnaya Zemlya (island)	80N 88E	94
Salado, Rio (riv., S.Am.)	35S 70W	90	Shanghai, China (city)	31N 121E	95
Salem, Oregon (city, st. cap., US)	45N 123W	89	Shasta, Mt. 14,162	42N 120W	88
Salt Lake City, Utah (city, st. cap., US)	41N 112W	89	Shenyang, China (city)	42N 123E	95
Salta (st., Argentina)	25S 70W	91	Shetland Islands	60N 5W	92

Name/Description	Latitude & Longitude	Page	Name/Description	Latitude & Longitude	Page
Shikoku (island)	34N 130E	94	Sudan (country)	10N 30E	97
Shiraz, Iran (city)	30N 52E	95	Sulaiman Range	28N 70E	94
Sicily (island)	38N 14E	93	Sulu Islands	8N 120E	95
Sierra Leone (country)	6N 14W	97	Sulu Sea	10N 120E	95
Sierra Madre Occidental	27N 108W	88	Sumatra (island)	0 100E	94 inset
Sierra Madre Oriental	27N 100W	88	Sumba (island)	10S 120E	98
Sierra Nevada	38N 120W	88	Sumbawa (island)	8S 116E	98
Sikhote Alin	45N 135E	94	Sunda Islands	12S 118E	98
Simpson Desert	25S 136E	98	Superior (lake, N.Am.)	50N 90W	88
Sinai Peninsula	28N 33E	96	Surabaya, Java (Indonesia) (city)	7S 113E	95 inset
Sinaloa (st., Mex.)	25N 110W	89	Suriname (country)	5N 55W	91
Singapore (city, nat. cap.)	1N 104E	95	Svalbard Islands	75N 20E	94
Sitka Island	57N 125W	88	Swan (riv., Australasia)	34S 115E	98
Skagerrak, Strait of	58N 8E	92	Sweden (country)	62N 16E	93
Skopje, Macedonia (city, nat. cap.)	42N 21E	93	Sydney, N.S.Wales (city, st. cap., Aust.)	34S 151E	99
Slovakia (country)	50N 20E	93	Syr Darya (riv., Asia)	36N 65E	94
Slovenia (country)	47N 14E	93	Syria (country)	37N 36E	93
Snake (riv., N.Am.)	45N 110W	88	Tabasco (st., Mex.)	16N 90W	89
Snowy Mountains	37S 148E	98	Tabriz, Iran (city)	38N 46E	95
Sofia, Bulgaria (city, nat. cap.)	43N 23E	90	Tahat, Mt. 9,541	23N 8E	96
Solimoes, Rio (riv., S.Am.)	3S 65W	90	Taipei, Taiwan (city, nat. cap.)	25N 121E	95
Solomon Islands (country)	7S 160E	98	Taiwan (country)	25N 122E	95
Somalia (country)	5N 45E	97	Taiwan Strait	25N 120E	94
Sonora (st., Mex.)	30N 110W	89	Tajikistan (country)	35N 75E	95
South Africa (country)	30S 25E	97	Takla Makan	37N 90E	94
South Australia (st., Aust.)	30S 125E	99	Tallahassee, Florida (city, st. cap., US)	30N 84W	89
South Cape, New Guinea	8S 150E	98	Tallinn, Estonia (city, nat. cap.)	59N 25E	93
South Carolina (st., US)	33N 79W	89	Tamaulipas (st., Mex.)	25N 95W	89
South China Sea	15N 115E	98	Tampico, Mexico (city)	22N 98W	89
South Dakota (st., US)	45N 100W	89	Tanganyika, Lake	5S 30E	96
South Georgia (island)	55S 40W	90	Tanzania (country)	8S 35E	97
South Island (NZ)	45S 170E	98	Tapajos, Rio (riv., S.Am.)	5S 55W	90
Southampton Island	68N 86W	88	Tarim Basin	37N 85E	94
Southern Alps (NZ)	45S 170E	98	Tashkent, Uzbekistan (city, nat. cap.)	41N 69E	95
Southwest Cape (NZ)	47S 167E	98	Tasman Sea	38S 160E	98
Spain (country)	38N 4W	93	Tasmania (st., Aust.).	42S 145E	99
Spokane, WA (city)	48N 117W	89	Tatar Strait	50N 142E	94
Springfield, Illinois (city, st. cap., US)	40N 90W	89	Tbilisi, Georgia (city, nat. cap.)	42N 45E	93
Sri Lanka (country)	8N 80E	95	Teguicigalpa, Honduras (city, nat. cap.)	14N 87W	89
Srinagar, India (city)	34N 75E	95	Tehran, Iran (city, nat. cap.)	36N 51E	95
St. Elias, Mt. 18,008	61N 139W	88	Tel Aviv, Israel (city)	32N 35E	93
St. George's Channel	53N 5W	92	Tennant Creek, Aust. (city)	19S 134E	99
St. Helena (island)	16S 5W	97	Tennessee (st., US)	37N 88W	89
St. John's, Nwfndlnd (city, prov. cap., Can.)	48N 53W	89	Tennessee (riv., N.Am.)	32N 88W	88
St. Louis, MO (city)	39N 90W	89	Tepic, Nayarit (city, st. cap., Mex.)	22N 105W	89
St. Lawrence (island)	65N 170W	88 inset	Teresina, Piaui (city, st. cap., Braz.)	5S 43W	91
St. Lawrence (riv., N.Am.)	50N 65W	88	Texas (st., US)	30N 95W	89
St. Lawrence, Gulf of	50N 65W	88	Thailand (country)	15N 105E	95
St. Marie, Cape	25S 45E	97	Thailand, Gulf of	10N 105E	94
St. Paul, Minnesota (city, st. cap., US)	45N 93W	89	Thames (riv., Europe)	52N 4W	92
St. Petersburg, Russia (city)	60N 30E	93	The Hague, Netherlands (city, nat. cap.)	52N 4E	93
St. Vincente, Cape of	37N 10W	92	The Round Mountain 5,300	29S 152E	98
Stanovoy Range	55N 125E	94	Thimphu, Bhutan (city, nat. cap.)	28N 90E	95
Stavanger, Norway (city)	59N 6E	93	Tianjin, China (city)	39N 117E	95
Steep Point	25S 115E	98	Tibest Massif	20N 20E	96
Stockholm, Sweden (city, nat. cap.)	59N 18E	93	Tien Shan	40N 80E	94
Stuart Range	32S 135E	98	Tierra del Fuego	54S 68W	90
Stuttgart, Germany (city)	49N 9E	93	Tierra del Fuego (st., Argentina)	54S 68W	91
Sucre, Bolivia (city)	19S 65W	91	Tigris (riv., Asia)	37N 40E	92

Name/Description	Latitude & Longitude	Page	Name/Description	Latitude & Longitude	Page
Timor *(island)*	7S 126E	94	Uzbekistan *(country)*	42N 58E	93
Timor Sea	11S 125E	99	Vaal *(riv., Africa)*	27S 27E	96
Tirane, Albania *(city, nat. cap.)*	41N 20E	93	Valdivia, Chile *(city)*	40S 73W	91
Titicaca, Lake	15S 70W	90	Valencia, Spain *(city)*	39N 0	93
Tlaxcala *(st., Mex.)*	20N 96W	89	Valencia, Venezuela *(city)*	10N 68W	91
Tlaxcala, Tlaxcala *(city, st. cap., Mex.)*	19N 98W	89	Valparaiso, Chile *(city)*	33S 72W	91
Toamasino, Madagascar *(city)*	18S 49E	97	van Diemen, Cape	11S 130E	98
Tocantins *(st., Brazil)*	12S 50W	91	van Rees Mountains	4S 140E	98
Tocantins, Rio *(riv., S.Am.)*	5S 50W	90	Vanatu *(country)*	15S 167E	98
Togo *(country)*	8N 1E	97	Vancouver, Canada *(city)*	49N 123W	89
Tokyo, Japan *(city, nat. cap.)*	36N 140E	95	Vancouver Island	50N 130W	88
Toliara, Madagascar *(city)*	23S 44E	97	Vanern, Lake	60N 12E	92
Tolima, Mt. 17,110	5N 75W	90	Vattern, Lake	56N 12E	92
Toluca, Mexico *(city, st. cap., Mex.)*	19N 100W	89	Venezuela *(country)*	5N 65W	91
Tombouctou, Mali *(city)*	24N 3W	97	Venezuela, Gulf of	12N 72W	90
Tomsk, Russia *(city)*	56N 85E	95	Venice, Italy *(city)*	45N 12E	93
Tonkin, Gulf of	20N 108E	94	Vera Cruz *(st., Mex.)*	20N 97W	89
Topeka, Kansas *(city, st. cap., US)*	39N 96W	89	Vera Cruz, Mexico *(city)*	19N 96W	89
Toronto, Ontario *(city, prov. cap., Can.)*	44N 79W	89	Verkhoyanskiy Range	65N 130E	94
Toros Mountains	37N 45E	94	Vermont *(st., US)*	45N 73W	89
Torrens, Lake	33S 136W	98	Vert, Cape	15N 17W	96
Torres Strait	10S 142E	98	Vestfjord	68N 14E	92
Townsville, Aust. *(city)*	19S 146E	99	Viangchan, Laos *(city, nat. cap.)*	18N 103E	95
Transylvanian Alps	46N 20E	92	Victoria *(riv., Australasia)*	15S 130E	98
Trenton, New Jersey *(city, st. cap., US)*	40N 75W	89	Victoria *(st., Aust.)*	37S 145W	99
Tricara Peak 15,584	4S 137E	98	Victoria, B.C. *(city, prov. cap., Can.)*	48N 123W	89
Trinidad and Tobago *(island)*	9N 60W	90	Victoria, Lake	3S 35E	96
Tripoli, Libya *(city, nat. cap.)*	33N 13E	97	Victoria, Mt. 13,238	9S 137E	98
Trujillo, Peru *(city)*	8S 79W	91	Victoria Riv. Downs, Aust. *(city)*	17S 131E	99
Tucson, AZ *(city)*	32N 111W	89	Viedma, Rio Negro *(city, st. cap., Argen.)*	41S 63W	91
Tucuman *(st., Argentina)*	25S 65W	91	Vienna, Austria *(city)*	48N 16E	93
Tucuman, Tucuman *(city, st. cap., Argen.)*	27S 65W	91	Vietnam *(country)*	10N 110E	95
Tunis, Tunisia *(city, nat. cap.)*	37N 10E	97	Villahermosa, Tabasco *(city, st. cap., Mex.)*	18N 93W	89
Tunisia *(country)*	34N 9E	97	Vilnius, Lithuania *(city, nat. cap.)*	55N 25E	93
Turin, Italy *(city)*	45N 8E	93	Virginia *(st., US)*	35N 78W	89
Turkey *(country)*	39N 32E	93	Viscount Melville Sound	72N 110W	88
Turkmenistan *(country)*	39N 56E	93	Vitoria, Espiritu Santo *(city, st. cap., Braz.)*	20S 40W	91
Turku, Finland *(city)*	60N 22E	93	Vladivostock, Russia *(city)*	43N 132E	95
Tuxtla Gutierrez, Chiapas *(city, st. cap., Mex.)*	17N 93W	89	Volga *(riv., Europe)*	46N 46E	92
Tyrrhenian Sea	40N 12E	92	Volgograd, Russia *(city)*	54N 44E	93
Ubangi *(riv., Africa)*	0 20E	96	Volta *(riv., Africa)*	10N 15E	96
Ucayali, Rio *(riv., S.Am.)*	7S 75W	90	Volta, Lake	8N 2W	96
Uele *(riv., Africa)*	3N 25E	96	Vosges Mountains	48N 7E	92
Uganda *(country)*	3N 30E	97	Wabash *(riv., N.Am.)*	43N 90W	88
Ujungpandang, Celebes (Indon.) *(city)*	5S 119E	95 inset	Walvis Bay, Namibia *(city)*	23S 14E	97
Ukraine *(country)*	53N 32E	93	Warsaw, Poland *(city, nat. cap.)*	52N 21E	93
Ulan Bator, Mongolia *(city, nat. cap.)*	47N 107E	95	Washington *(st., US)*	48N 122W	89
Uliastay, Mongolia *(city)*	48N 97E	95	Washington, D.C., United St.s *(city, nat. cap.)*	39N 77W	89
Ungava Peninsula	60N 72W	88	Wellington Island	48S 74W	90
United Arab Emirates *(country)*	25N 55E	95	Wellington, New Zealand *(city, nat. cap.)*	41S 175E	99
United Kingdom *(country)*	54N 4W	93	Weser *(riv., Europe)*	54N 8E	92
United States *(country)*	40N 100W	89	West Cape Howe	36S 115E	98
Uppsala, Sweden *(city)*	60N 18E	93	West Indies	18N 75W	88
Ural *(riv., Asia)*	45N 55E	94	West Siberian Lowland	60N 80E	94
Ural Mountains	50N 60E	94	West Virginia *(st., US)*	38N 80W	89
Uruguay *(country)*	37S 67W	91	Western Australia *(st., Aust.)*	25S 122W	99
Uruguay, Rio *(riv., S.Am.)*	30S 57W	90	Western Ghats	15N 72E	94
Urumqui, China *(city)*	44N 88E	95	Western Sahara *(country)*	25N 13W	97
Utah *(st., US)*	38N 110W	89	White Nile *(riv., Africa)*	13N 30E	96

Name/Description	Latitude & Longitude	Page	Name/Description	Latitude & Longitude	Page
White Sea	64N 36E	92	Yellowknife, N.W.T. (city, prov. cap., Can.)	62N 115W	89
Whitney, Mt. 14,494	33N 118W	88	Yellowstone (riv., N.Am.)	46N 110W	88
Wichita, KS (city)	38N 97W	89	Yemen (country)	15N 50E	95
Wilhelm, Mt. 14,793	4S 145E	98	Yenisey (riv., Asia)	68N 85E	94
Windhoek, Namibia (city, nat. cap.)	22S 17E	97	Yerevan, Armenia (city, nat. cap.)	40N 44E	93
Winnipeg (lake, N.Am.)	50N 100W	88	Yokohama, Japan (city)	36N 140E	95
Winnipeg, Manitoba (city, prov. cap., Can.)	53N 98W	89	York, Cape	75N 65W	88
Wisconsin (st., US)	50N 90W	89	Yucatan (st., Mex.)	20N 88W	89
Wollongong, Aust. (city)	34S 151E	99	Yucatan Channel	22N 88W	88
Woodroffe, Mt. 4,724	26S 133W	98	Yucatan Peninsula	20N 88W	88
Woomera, Aust. (city)	32S 137E	99	Yugoslavia (country)	44N 20E	93
Wrangell (island)	72N 180E	94	Yukon (riv., N.Am.)	63N 150W	88 inset
Wuhan, China (city)	30N 114E	95	Zacatecas (st., Mex.)	23N 103W	89
Wyndham, Australia (city)	16S 129E	99	Zacatecas, Zacatecas (city, st. cap., Mex.)	23N 103W	89
Wyoming (st., US)	45N 110W	89	Zagreb, Croatia (city, nat. cap.)	46N 16E	93
Xalapa, Vera Cruz (city, st. cap., Mex.)	20N 97W	89	Zagros Mountains	27N 52E	94
Xingu, Rio (riv., S.Am.)	5S 54W	90	Zambezi (riv., Africa)	18S 30E	96
Yablonovyy Range	50N 100E	94	Zambia (country)	15S 25E	97
Yakutsk, Russia (city)	62N 130E	95	Zanzibar (island)	5S 39E	96
Yamoussoukio, Cote d'Ivoire (city)	7N 4W	97	Zemlya Frantsa Josifa (island)	80N 40E	94
Yangtze (Chang Jiang) (riv., Asia)	30N 108W	94	Ziel, Mt. 4,955	23S 134E	98
Yaounde, Cameroon (city, nat. cap.)	4N 12E	97	Zimbabwe (country)	20S 30E	97
Yekaterinburg, Russia (city)	57N 61E	93			

Sources

BP Statistical Review of World Energy 1998, http://www.bp.com/bpstats.

Crabb, C. (1993, January). Soiling the planet. *Discover, 14* (1), 74–75. [For information regarding Map 60 on page 83 of this book]

DeBlij, H. J., & Muller, P. (1998). *Geography: Realms, regions and concepts* (8th ed.). New York: John Wiley & Sons.

Domke, K. (1988). *War and the changing global system.* New Haven, CT: Yale University Press.

Goode's world atlas. (1995, 19th ed.). New York: Rand McNally.

Gunnemark, Erik V., *Countries, peoples and their languages.* Gothenburg, Sweden: The Geolinguistic Handbook (n.d., early 1990s).

Hammond atlas of the world. (1993). Maplewood, NJ: Hammond.

Information please almanac, atlas, and yearbook 1997. (1997). Boston & New York: Houghton Mifflin.

Information Resources Centre, Canadian Forces College; http://www. cfcsc.dnd.ca/ links/wars/index.html.

Johnson, D. (1977). *Population, society, and desertification.* New York: United Nations Conference on Desertification, United Nations Environment Programme.

Köppen, W., & Geiger, R. (1954). *Klima der erde* [Climate of the earth]. Darmstadt, Germany: Justus Perthes.

Lindeman, M. (1990). *The United States and the Soviet Union: Choices for the 21st century.* Guilford, CT: Dushkin Publishing Group.

Murphy, R. E. (1968). Landforms of the world [Map supplement No. 9]. *Annals of the Association of American Geographers, 58* (1), 198–200.

National Oceanic and Atmospheric Administration. (1990–1992). Unpublished data. Washington, DC: NOAA.

NY Times; http://archives.nytimes.com/archives/.

Population Reference Bureau. (1998). *1998 world population data sheet.* New York: Population Reference Bureau.

Rourke, J. T. (1997). *International politics on the world stage* (6th ed.). Guilford, CT: Dushkin/McGraw-Hill.

Spector, L. S., & Smith, J. R. (1990). *Nuclear ambitions: The spread of nuclear weapons.* Boulder, CO: Westview Press.

Time atlas of world history, London, 1978.

United Nations Population Fund. (1997). *The state of the world's population.* New York: United Nations Population Fund.

The universal almanac 1999. (1999). Kansas City, MO: Andrews & McNeel.

Uranium Institute 1997; http://www.uilondon.org/safetab.htm.

U.S. Arms Control and Disarmament Agency. (1993). *World military expenditures and arms transfers.* Washington, DC: U.S. Government Printing Office.

U.S. Census Bureau. (1998). *World population growth.* Washington, DC: U.S. Government Printing Office.

U.S. Committee for Refugees. (1999). *1999 world refugee survey.* Washington, DC: U.S. Committee for Refugees; www.refugees.org/world/statistics/ wrs98_tableindex.htm.

U.S. Department of State. (1998). *Statesman's year-book, 1997–98.* Washington, DC: U.S. Government Printing Office.

U.S. Forest Service. (1989). *Ecoregions of the continents.* Washington, DC: U.S. Government Printing Office.

The world almanac and book of facts 1999. (1999). Mahwah, NJ: World Almanac Books.

World Bank, *World development indicators 1999,* 1999. World Bank, Washington DC; http://www.worldbank.org/data/.

The world factbook; http://www.odci.gov/cia/publications/factbook/.

World Health Organization. (1998). *World health statistics annual.* Geneva: World Health Organization.

World Resources Institute. *World resources 1998–1999,* 1998, New York; http://www.wri.org.